Atari Portfolio/ DIP Pocket PC Companion

Peter Baron

SIGMA PRESS – Wilmslow, United Kingdom

First published in 1990 by

Sigma Press, 1 South Oak Lane, Wilmslow, Cheshire SK9 6AR, England.

British Library Cataloguing in Publication Data

A CIP catalogue record for this book is available from the British Library.

ISBN: 1-85058-164-9

Typesetting and design by

Sigma Hi-Tech Services Ltd

Printed and bound by

Manchester Free Press, Paragon Mill, Jersey Street, Manchester M4 6FP.

Distributed by

John Wiley & Sons Ltd., Baffins Lane, Chichester, West Sussex, England.

Preface

There is no need to make a case for the existence of a portable computer. The fact that people on the move find IBM compatible machines useful has already been demonstrated by the numerous lap top machines currently on sale. But perhaps it would be better to think of these portable computers as luggable. They do tend to be too large and weighty for comfort, so the search has continued for something lighter in weight and easier to use.

Distributed Information Processing (DIP) have taken a step further in this search by developing the Portfolio, the world's first pocket sized personal computer. Hopefully, this lightweight machine heralds a period when computer technology will be even more accessible to ordinary people in everyday occupations. But how will it be used?

An idealist may wish that this sort of development would have profound significance in terms of personal freedom and democracy, though the increasing use of computers, principally mainframes, as technological and social tools seems, instead, to have provided the establishment at large with a more effective means of exerting power over the population.

But, leaving aside notions of liberty, fraternity and equality, the DIP Pocket P.C. and its brother the Portfolio, do qualify for the role of a truly personal computer, even the one in your pocket.

Such a machine can be of advantage in both company and personal terms. Those who need to give clients an individual service can do so in face to face situations, yet have all the data conveniently to hand. Highly personal quotations can be given in a standardised format, using basic company data, and resulting deals, reports and contracts can be fed back to a central administrative facility via telephone lines. Standardisation of this kind leads to greater consistency, efficiency and presumably, an eventual saving in costs.

In this book I have attempted to provide users with a detailed guide to the Portfolio and its built in software. In addition there is a section which gives some indication of the sort of additional software which is being developed. It has taken some time to get all the information together and I hope that you find it of use. I shall be very happy to receive any constructive suggestions which readers may care to make.

Lastly, I would like to express gratitude to my wife Jean, for her tolerance and very considerable help, and to DIP for their co-operation and assistance in supplying me with a great deal of information which has been used in the preparation of this manuscript.

Peter Baron

Contents

FREE SOFTWARE OFFER

DIP are offering purchasers of this book a comprehensive software package for the DIP Pocket PC/Atari Portfolio.

With the *File Manager* program, you need never see the DOS prompt again. This software has been designed to make your life easier, by providing you with a simpler way to run applications and use your files, directories and disks. Also included in the FREE software pack is an easy to use *Tutorial and Welcome* program which introduces some of the features of the product.

DIP, the suppliers of this software, are also the designers of the Pocket PC technology and granted a license to Atari to market the product as the Portfolio.

Please note that the software is supplied on a standard IBM-PC floppy disk so you will need to transfer the files to the DIP Pocket PC/Atari Portfolio using an optional Parallel peripheral or the PC Card Drive product.

To apply for the FREE software package please send in your name, address, phone number and answers to the questions below. You can either photocopy the form or write the information on a postcard. Please post to the FREEPOST address below: (There is no need to attach a stamp if posted within the UK).

Sigma Press Software Offer
Distributed Information Processing Ltd
FREEPOST
Surrey Research Park
Guildford
Surrey GU2 5BR

Name: _____

Address: _____

_____Postcode_____

Home Tel: _____ Work Tel: _____

Please answer all of the questions 1 to 4 below:
1) Product(s)_____
    Please enter all the Pocket PC/Portfolio products which you have bought.

2) Did you buy the product for business ___ or personal ___ use? Please tick.
3) What do you mainly use the Pocket PC for? _____

4) In which format do you want your FREE IBM-PC floppy disk:
    5.25 inch___ or 3.5 inch ___ (please tick)

DIP has a policy of continuous product development, therefore small specification changes may not be
reflected in the above offer. This offer is valid until December 1992.

1

Opening your Portfolio

Although the Portfolio is marketed by Atari, it was designed by Distributed Information Processing Limited (DIP) in Guildford, U.K. The machine is also sold in Britain as the DIP Pocket PC.

The Portfolio is a pocket sized computer which has a high degree of compatibility and functional similarity with the standard IBM type desk top PC, yet it weighs only 450 grams. Identification with the desktop PC is achieved by using a PC compatible Basic Input Output System (BIOS) and an MS-DOS compatible disk operating system.

Built in applications software which the Portfolio runs from its read only memory (ROM), is supplied as a standard feature. This software includes an address book, a diary and time manager, a calculator, word processor and Lotus 1-2-3 compatible worksheet.

On the right side of the case there is an expansion bus connector for various peripherals, such as the optional serial and parallel interfaces. On the left is a drive slot to accommodate credit card sized memory cards which this computer uses for permanent data storage, instead of floppy disks employed by IBM type PCs. A RAM disk memory partition is also provided.

All the Portfolio's components have a low power consumption and this, together with an autopowerdown mechanism, means that the small AA size batteries which it uses have a fairly long life. Ultimately, battery longevity depends, of course, upon the length of time for which the machine is used each day.

The screen is a super twist liquid crystal display (LCD) measuring approximately 11.5 cm x 4.0 cm. This accommodates the normal 40 column x 8 line display and also acts as a window on the larger 80 x 25 standard PC screen used by many external programs.

A QWERTY style keyboard, which provides positive keypress feedback to the user, is built in and the plastic case containing the components can be folded up in a clam like fashion, so that the keyboard and LCD screen face each other.

Starting Up

It is very simple to start using a Portfolio, but just as well to go through the necessary preliminaries in an orderly fashion, so that the machine is working in the way you want it to from the beginning.

Inserting the batteries

Unpack the Portfolio and, leaving it closed, turn it so that the base with battery access cover is facing up. Insert the three AA size batteries by slipping them in one after the other, making sure that the negative ends go first. The third battery is pressed down, with the pull tape under it, and contact is made by the positive end as indicated by the diagram on the bottom of the battery compartment. Finally slide the cover back on the base and turn the computer over. The lid with the Atari Portfolio logo should now be facing up. Undo the catch and open the lid. The screen and keyboard should face you and are now ready for use.

Choosing a language

When the batteries are inserted for the first time, the Portfolio is automatically switched on and the screen will show the DIP copyright sign. When a key is pressed, the screen will ask you to choose a language. Keyboards are provided in English QWERTY, French AZERTY and German QWERTZ styles. Press [E] for English, [F] for French or [D] for German, which selects both the language and the keyboard layout, the physical appearance being appropriate to the country in which the macine is marketed.

```
Copyright (c) 1989 DIP
Distributed Information Processing Ltd
Surrey Research Park, Guildford, England
All rights reserved
Tous droits réservés
Alle Rechte vorbehalten

BIOS: 1.030    Operating system: 1.030
```

The DIP Copyright sign-on

```
Keyboard - Clavier - Tastatur

Type      "E" for  English   (QWERTY)
Taper     "F" pour Français  (AZERTY)
Drücken   "D" für  Deutsch   (QWERTZ)
```

Screen request for keyboard selection

Setting date and time

Next you should type in the current date setting in the form mm-dd-yy, where mm is the month, dd the day and yy the year. When you have done this press [Enter], which is the large ↵ shaped key on the right. Note that this key is referred to as RETURN or [RTN] in the Owner's manual. The terms ENTER and RETURN mean the same thing, but ENTER is the term usually used when reference to IBM PCs is made.

The time is input in the format of the 24 hour clock, as hh:mm:ss:xx, where hh is hours, mm minutes, ss seconds and xx is hundredths of a second. It is only necessary to type in the hours and the minutes and then press [Enter].

After these little tasks have been completed, the Portfolio's clock will keep track of the time and date for you. If the Country code is set in the CONFIG.SYS file, the date will be altered to the familiar British style. A basic CONFIG.SYS file is detailed further on in this chapter and more information about it is given in Chapter 2.

When the time has been set the screen will show the message:

```
DIP Operating System 2.11 v0.000
Copyright (c) 1989 DIP
```

and the operating system prompt:

```
C>
```

RAM disk

As mentioned above, data is stored on an internal RAM disk, which is used by the built in Applications software. The RAM disk can be set to various sizes, but, for the time being, we will assume that you want maximum capacity. Since it is vital to have a means to store data, set the size now.

The default value is 25% of the total RAM (memory) capacity, that is 128/4 = 32K, but you can have as much as 66K.

To set the RAM disk to 66K type:

```
FDISK 66[Enter]
```

Further information on this command is given in Chapter 2.

The RAM disk is called drive C: and the operating system prompt (C>) shown above includes the drive name.

Switching off

The Portfolio has a standby mode, which reduces power consumption, yet still allows the machine to retain data and remain capable of sounding alarms. To switch to standby press

```
[Fn]+[O]
```

at any time, and release the O before the Fn,

or from the DOS screen type

```
off[Enter]
```

The screen will go blank and the Portfolio will go into its standby mode. Pressing any key will cause it to become active again. The DOS screen is displayed when no software is in use.

Arranging the date sequence

Various date formats can be set on PC type computers. In Britain we use the dd/mm/yy system. If you want your Portfolio to conform to this and also wish to set the buffers and files defaults as recommended, type in the following CONFIG.SYS file at the C> prompt on the DOS screen, exactly as shown.

```
COPY CON CONFIG.SYS[Enter]
FILES=20[Enter]
BUFFERS=32[Enter]
COUNTRY=044[Enter]
[Ctrl]+[Z][Enter]
```

After you have typed the first line, the Portfolio will show:

```
CON to C:\CONFIG.SYS
```

Just carry on. When the last line has been typed, the screen will show

```
1 File copied
```

The CONFIG.SYS file has now been created. To bring it into action type

`[Ctrl]+[Alt]+[Del]`

These keys, when pressed together, cause the Portfolio to go through its warm boot procedure. See Chapter 2 for further details.

Another important start up file, which you might like to use, is called AUTOEXEC.BAT. More information is given about this and related matters in Chapter 2.

Keyboard

Most of the usual computer keys can be easily located on the keyboard, which has the general layout found on many desktop PCs. When pressed, the shift keys give uppercase letters and the various symbols printed in black above the unshifted keys.

The Portfolio's keyboard

Keyboard conventions used in this book

[ ] Anything enclosed in square brackets indicates a key on the keyboard.

[ ]+[ ] Where two such keys are linked by a plus, you should press them together.

[ ] [ ] When two or more keys are shown together, but are not linked, they should be pressed in sequence.

[Enter] In this book the term [Enter] is used to show the large ⏎ shaped key on the right of the keyboard. This is also known as the Return key (carriage return), or just Return in the Portfolio Owner's Manual, but it is usually called Enter on IBM PCs.

Enter is pressed at the end of DOS commands, Address Book lines, Diary entries and Editor paragraphs. This key also acts as an = sign when the Calculator is being used and is pressed to confirm an entry into a Worksheet cell.

[Fn] The Function key, printed in blue, is used in conjunction with the number keys to obtain the same effect as the function keys on a PC. In other words, if you wanted F1, you would press the [Fn] and [1] keys, together or one after the other. The other keys which are printed in blue can also be used in conjunction with the Fn key. For instance, to send the cursor Home, you would press [Fn] and [Home] together.

The Function key is also used within the Applications software. The functions which are common to all the components of the Applications software are listed later in this chapter and those which are more specific are given in the sections which cover individual applications.

The Atari key,)|(,when pressed, brings up menus and starts the built in applications software. If you wanted to see the main applications software menu, you would press)|(and [Z] together. The names of the applications are printed in pink below the keys with the which the Atari key can be used.

[Lock] serves as an upper case lock for capitals, as a number lock for the numeric key pad and as a scroll lock.

Key press	Effect
[Lock]	Displays date, time and any locks in effect
[Lock]+[Fn]	Scroll lock. Prevents cursor keys from scrolling the screen
[Lock]+[Shift]	Shift lock. Only capital letters can be typed.
[Lock]+ [)|(]	Number lock. The keys with red figures only respond with numbers when pressed. The cursor is changed to _ .
[Lock] +[Esc]	Clears all locks

The **Cursor keys** are the keys marked ←↑↓→ and located in the lower right corner of the keyboard. Basically, they serve to move the flashing cursor round the screen.

[Esc] The full name for this key is Escape and this is a reasonable description of its function. It is used to escape from the current activity and to back out from applications menus. You can sometimes avoid carrying out a command by pressing Escape when you have made a mistake.

The **Backspace** key is the one with a left pointing arrow at the top right corner of the keyboard. It can be used to erase text to the left of it when Insert is switched on. If overtype is in operation, the Backspace key will act like a left cursor key..

[Ctrl] The Control key is used in conjunction with other keys to control certain processes. For instance, pressing [Ctrl]+[C] will stop a batch file from running. Chapters 2 and 7 give further information on the use of [Ctrl], and its use in text editing within the Applications software is described later in this chapter.

[Alt] The Alternate key. On the Portfolio, this key provides a means for entering non keyboard characters. Chapter 6 details these.

Screen contrast is adjusted by pressing the [J|\] and the up or down cursor keys.

Key press	*Effect*
[J|\]+[↑]	Increase contrast
[J|\]+[↓]	Decrease contrast

Numeric keypad. The keys marked with red numbers form a numeric keypad within the keyboard. When [J|\]+[Lock] are pressed, or when the Applications Calculator is used, the cursor changes to _ and the keys marked with red numbers and symbols will only respond according to the red markings. The keypad can be switched off by pressing [J|\]+[Lock] again.

Portfolio PC Key Equivalents

Although the Portfolio's keyboard is similar in layout to that of a desktop PC it has fewer keys. Therefore some of the keys which are present on the PC keyboard are obtained on the Portfolio by key combinations. The following table shows what keys to press.

Desktop PC Key	*Keys to Press on Portfolio*
[Home]	[Fn]+[Home]
[PgUp]	[Fn]+[PgUp]
[PgDn]	[Fn]+[PgDn]
[End]	[Fn]+[End]
[Ctrl]+[Break]	[Fn]+[B] or [Ctrl]+[Fn]+[S]
[Caps Lock]	[Shift]+[Lock] or [Fn]+[C]
[Num Lock]	[J|\]+[Lock] or [Fn]+[N]
[Scroll Lock]	[Fn]+[Lock] or [Fn]+[S]
[Insert]	[Fn]+[Ins]
[Ctrl Numlock]	[Fn]+[Q] or [Ctrl]+[Fn]+[N]
[Print Screen]	[Fn]+[P] or [Ctrl]+[Fn]+[P]
[£]	[Alt]+[{]
[~]	[Alt]+[}]
[`]	[Alt]+[']

Battery replacement

Sooner or later the batteries on your Portfolio will run out. When this occurs, the screen will show a Low Battery message. The computer will switch off automatically and you should replace the batteries as soon as possible. The designers say that data should be retained on the RAM disk for several days, but it is better not to take chances. If the Portfolio does not switch itself to standby when the low battery message has been shown, press [Fn+O] before you do the change over. Removing batteries when the Portfolio is not switched to standby can cause loss of data in some of the earlier versions.

Because the batteries can run down very quickly, it is wise to always carry a spare set. Changing the batteries is simply a matter of undoing the battery compartment cover, removing the old batteries, slipping the new ones in (making sure the polarity is correct) and then replacing the cover. When the batteries have been replaced the Portfolio will be in its active mode.

Error messages

From time to time the Portfolio will show an error message on its screen. The messages vary and depend on what the computer is doing at the time. When you see an error message, take note of what it says and then press [Esc] to resume your activity, if that is possible. In some cases you may be forced to take some alternative action, but the cause is frequently an unintended or inappropriately typed instruction.

Details of the error messages are given in Appendix B.

The built in Applications software

The built in software is an invaluable asset which enables the Portfolio's user to perform most of the bread and butter tasks that would be undertaken on a personal computer. On other machines which are not sold with 'bundled software' a full set of applications programs could cost several hundred pounds. Furthermore, since the Portfolio's applications software is stored on ROM (Read Only Memory) it cannot be accidentally erased and is instantly available for use.

What there is

When you press [J|\]+[Z], the main Applications software menu is shown on the screen.

```
(c) DIP 1989 0.392
Address Book
Calculator
Diary
Editor
Setup
Worksheet
```

The Main Applications software menu

It contains a list of the various components of the built in software provided with the Portfolio. These are briefly described below.

Address Book

The Address Book works as a card index system, so that names, addresses and telephone numbers can be filed ready for instant access. A Portfolio can dial the telephone numbers for you, when it has access to suitable System X exchanges. Names are automatically arranged in alphabetical order and it is also possible to select subsets from the main group and save these as separate files. Since the Address Book operates as a card system, it is not confined to names and addresses.

Calculator

A versatile calculator with five memories is also available for performing rapid calculations in scientific, engineering, fixed decimal and general formats. An editable record of the entries is kept during the number processing, so that the effect of variations can be considered without the need to enter all the figures every time. Although figures entered in the calculator can be sent to a printer they cannot be stored on a disk and cannot be transferred to other applications.

Diary

Apart from its obvious function, the Diary also acts as a time manager because it incorporates a calendar and a system of visual and audio alarms. By moving through the calendar, items which have previously been entered in the Diary can be viewed as desired and alarms set on them. When you enter the Diary, its calendar shows the current day and the appointments can be viewed just by pressing [Enter]. The list of appointments is presented in such a way that you can scroll through it and edit as necessary.

Editor

The Editor is a comprehensive text processor which is easy to use. While it is capable of producing fairly sophisticated documents, it is simple enough for routine use as a memorandum. It offers the usual search and replace functions, as well as, wordwrap, simple formatting and the ability to transmit printer codes.

Worksheet

A very powerful and versatile tool for mathematical operations is provided in the form of the Worksheet, which is a Lotus 1-2-3 compatible spreadsheet able to read version 1 and 2.01 files. It can accommodate 255 rows by 127 columns of data and contains a variety of built in functions which act in the same way as complex formulae. Both simple and complex mathematical formulae may also be entered.

Setup

Setup is not an item of Applications software. It provides a means by which the user can set many of the Portfolio's basic functions.These influence the way that data is shown, the Clipboard, language, keyboard, printer, serial port and file transfer.

Clipboard

The Clipboard is not an item on the main Applications menu, but can used by pressing [Fn][3]. It serves to transfer data from place to place within, or between, applications.

How to use the menu system

All the items of the built in software are accessible through a hierarchical menu system. This means that it all starts with a main menu and this leads on to subsidiary menus as you select the various items.

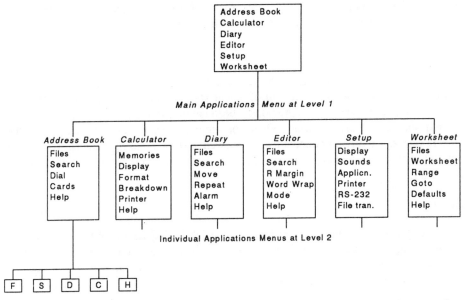

A hierarchical menu: each option on a menu leads to a further menu. Each press of a key moves one level down. Each press of [Esc] moves one level up.

It might sound complicated, but once you have the idea, the menu system is very simple to operate. Try it with the main menu. If it is already on the screen ignore the next line.

Press [⏎|\]+[Z] to obtain the main Applications menu

Each item on this menu can be obtained either by positioning the cursor on the initial letter and pressing [Enter], or by pressing the relevant letter key on the keyboard.

Press [E] and the Editor screen will be shown.

Once in, how do you get out? That is what the escape key is used for. Press [Esc] and you will move back to the main Applications menu. As a general rule pressing the [Esc] key will move you back upwards through the menu hierarchy.

From the main Applications menu press [E] again and return to the Editor. For the time being just glance at the screen layout to observe that it has a frame, date and time at lower left and drive and file names in the upper left.

Next, press the [◢ | ◣] key and the next level of menu will appear on the screen.

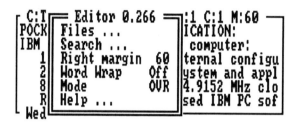

The main Editor menu

You may select any item on this menu by the same means as before. Either press the key representing the initial letter of the desired item, or position the cursor on the item and press [Enter]. If you press [F], you get the Files menu and from that you can press [S] for Save as . . . (where . . . indicates that there are further choices).

A dialogue box

At this level you reach the actual operation of saving a file, and the screen has presented what is known as a dialogue box. The default information in the box can be altered, or removed by use of the delete or backspace keys, and a completely new entry placed there. Movement of the cursor along the text in the box can be effected by means of the right or left cursor keys. The important point to note is that the information placed in the box will allow the software to proceed. Entry of information into a dialogue box is terminated by pressing [Enter]. If no new information is put in the box and [Enter] is pressed, the default information in the box will be the basis on which the software proceeds.

After you have examined the dialogue box, back out by repeatedly pressing [Esc], until you return to the main Applications menu. You can back out of this into the DOS screen, also by using [Esc].

General features of the Applications software

Although the elements of the Applications software perform different functions, each has certain features in common with the others. From the user's point of view this has the advantage of making the operation of the software rather easier than it might otherwise be. The rest of this chapter will deal with these common features.

The screen layout

All the Applications programs show a frame around the screen. This frame is distinct from the windows which contain the menus. At the top left of the frame the drive, directory and file name are shown. At the top right of the frame various information, specific to the application being run, appears. Also in this position, some applications show the ? character when an alteration has been made to the existing file. The lower left of the screen frame includes the day, date and time, while on the right of this are indicators of the current keyboard status.

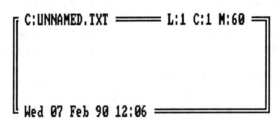

The general layout, demonstrated by the Editor screen

Keyboard status indicators

Indicator	Meaning
CAPS	Capital lock is on
NUM	Number lock is on
INS	New data will be inserted between that already there, at the position of the cursor
SCR	Scroll lock is on

In all the applications, the screen frame and its information can be switched on or off by pressing [Fn]+[5]. When the screen frame is off another two lines of data can be viewed on the screen.

Function keys

At the top of the keyboard, above the number keys, there are ten function key symbols, numbered F1 - F10. The number keys actually double up as function keys when [Fn] is pressed. Therefore, to use a function key, just press [Fn]+ a number key. The two keys can be pressed in sequence or together.

Some of the function keys are application specific, but the others perform the same function in each of the applications.

Function keys and their effects

Function key	Keys to press	Effect
F1	[Fn][1]	Shows the main menu for the current application
F2	[Fn][2]	Shows the general help information
F3	[Fn][3]	Enables the Clipboard to be used
F4	[Fn][4]	Reclaims the most recently deleted information and inserts it at the current cursor position
F5	[Fn][5]	Toggles the screen frame on or off
F6	[Fn][6]	Not used
F7	[Fn][7]	All these keys are application specific
F8	[Fn][8]	,,
F9	[Fn][9]	,,
F10	[Fn][0]	,,

The [J|\] key performs the same function as [Fn]+[1]

As previously mentioned, various PC equivalent keys can be obtained by using the Fn key in combination with other keys.

Control keys

The [Ctrl] key is also used in combination with other keys to perform certain functions. Some of these combinations are specific to particular applications and are detailed in the chapters dealing with them, others, like the function keys above, perform the same task in each application where they can be used.

General text editing functions

Keys to press	Effect
[Ctrl]+[A]	Place cursor at beginning of current file
[Ctrl]+[B]	Delete left to start of current line
[Ctrl]+[E]	Delete right to end of current line
[Ctrl]+[L]	Delete whole of current line
[Ctrl]+[U]	Return cursor to previous position
[Ctrl]+[W]	Delete word to right of cursor position
[Ctrl]+[Z]	Take cursor to end of current file
[Ctrl]+[BS]	Delete word to left of cursor position
[Ctrl]+[→]	Move cursor one word right
[Ctrl]+[←]	Move cursor one word left
[Fn][↑]	Move cursor to start of current line
[Fn][↓]	Move cursor to end of current line

File handling

The information which you enter into the Address Book, Diary, Editor or Worksheet, can be saved for future use. This is done by storing the data in discrete units called files on the RAM disk C:, or on memory cards inserted in drive A: . Each of the applications which uses files provides a menu by which the various commands can be given. Files belonging to a particular application are distinguished by means of a unique ending to the file name.

All the applications will call the file UNNAMED, unless you enter another. This is a default file name.

Application	File name ending	Full default file name
Address Book	.ADR	UNNAMED.ADR
Diary	.DRY	UNNAMED.DRY
Editor	.TXT	UNNAMED.TXT
Worksheet	.WKS	UNNAMED.WKS

The files are stored on the disks in larger units, called directories. When you first start the Portfolio it has two directories, C:\ which is known as the root directory and C:\SYSTEM which is called the SYSTEM subdirectory. More information is given on directories in Chapter 2, but note that C: is the drive designator and \ is the name of the root directory, while SYSTEM is that of the SYSTEM subdirectory.

There is no need to worry about the complexities of this situation at present because the menu system will place your files in the appropriate directory automatically. Detailed information on filing for particular applications is given in the relevant chapters. This brief account is provided by way of an introduction.

Using the Files menu system

Basic File commands

All the applications which use files utilise certain basic menu commands, as explained below. To obtain the Files menu for any application, load the application and then, when the application's screen is shown, press [⁄]|[][F].

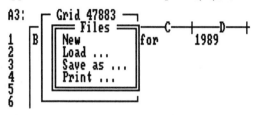

The Files menu offered by the Worksheet

New

This option is used to clear the existing data from the Portfolio's screen, so that something new can be started. To operate the New command, when the Files menu is shown on the screen, press [N], or [Enter] when the cursor is positioned on New. The screen will then clear and the file name in the top left of the frame will revert to UNNAMED.XXX . The XXX is, of course, the file ending specific to that particular application program. Eventually you will want to move to another task and at this time the you should allocate a file name to the new data which you have entered, and save it with the File Save. as.. command. If you do not do so, the Portfolio's safeguard system will operate.

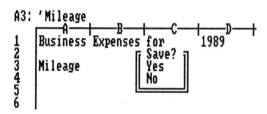

The exit application Save ? box

At the last press of [Esc] before you leave the application, the screen will ask whether or not you want to save the data. If you answer No, it will be lost. If Yes, it will be saved under the name UNNAMED.XXX. This is a sort of last resort situation though, because if you have other data previously saved in the UNNAMED file it will be lost and replaced by the most recent information saved to that file. It is common practice among PC users to have a file called TEMP which holds data until one can decide what to do with it. Perhaps the Portfolio's UNNAMED files should be regarded in the same sort of way - not to be used except as a last resort. You can always give the UNNAMED file another name. If you want to know how to do this refer to the REName command, which is explained in Chapter 2. When the UNNAMED file is renamed the same data remains in the file and the system will generate another UNNAMED file when required and save fresh data into it, without deleting the data in the file which you have renamed.

Load

When a file is loaded, the data in it is placed in whatever application you are running. Use of the Load command allows you to recover data which has been saved previously. You can then continue work on that data. To use the Load command, press [L] or, when the cursor is positioned on Load, [Enter]. At this point an option box will be presented on the screen. The option box will contain a default name and if you press [Enter] that file will be loaded.

If you want to see what files are already in the current directory, type [*][Enter] .All the files for the current application which are in the current directory will then be listed. To load one of these, position the cursor on it and press [Enter]. If the list of files is so long that they cannot all fit in the box, you can scroll it up and down with the appropriate cursor keys. You can also type a file name into the Load box. To do this, just type in any file name which exists in the current directory and then press [Enter]. There is no need to add the file name extension, the computer does that for you.

Save as...

Save as... is the reverse of load. By using this option data is placed in a file on the disk, so that it can recovered and used in the future.

You must give the new data a file name. Instead of giving your files a motley assortment of names, do try and develop a system which relates a file name to its contents. You may use up to eight characters for a file name, which limits the scope for variety, but allows such possibilities as BLO-L1 , where BLO represents the first three characters of a name, L stands for letter and 1 is a sequence number. The date when the file is saved is automatically entered by the Portfolio, though it can only be seen when you use the DIRectory command, explained in Chapter 2.

To use the Save as... command, press [S] when the menu Files menu is showing, or [Enter] when the cursor is positioned on Save as... Next, the Save box will shown on the screen and you can type your new name into it. The save will take place when you press [Enter]. If you would like to see what files are already on your disk, type [*][Enter] into the dialogue box and the file list will be shown. You can get back to the dialogue box by pressing [Esc]. As with Load, when the dialogue box is first shown it will contain a default name. If you press [Enter] at this stage, your new data will be saved under this default name, and it will replace anything in the file which already has that name. Also, if you duplicate a file name inadvertently, the new data will replace all the data formerly in that file and it will be lost. You can protect files against overwriting in this way by using the utility program called ATTRIB which is mentioned in Chapter 11.

Print

Print is used to output the data in the current application to a printer which is connected via the Portfolio's serial or parallel interface. This allows you to get what is known as hard copy. In other words, a tangible record on paper. The printing process is covered by Chapter 10 and some information is also given in the chapters which are devoted to particular applications programs.

Other File commands

In addition to the File commands so far described, there are two others. Merge is used by the Address Book, Diary and Editor, and Write Selected, which is only used by the Address Book.

The Address Book menu

Merge

By using the Merge command it is possible to merge one file with another, so as to form a single larger, more comprehensive file. For instance, if you had a list of addresses of government departments and also had a file with large company addresses you could merge the two for easier access. Also, it is possible to import address files from a desktop PC and you could merge one or more of these with your existing data. Diary appointments and text documents can also be merged.

Before Merge is used, you should have loaded one of the files to be merged into the application being used. To use Merge, obtain the Files menu for the current application and then press [M]. A name box will then be shown on the screen and you should enter the name of the file which is to be merged with the one which has already been loaded. If you cannot remember the name, type [*][Enter] and the file list will appear at the top left of the screen. You can then select the file by placing the cursor on it and pressing [Enter].

When the two files have been merged, you must use Save as... and save the new file under a unique name, otherwise the merged data will be lost. The original files which were merged will stay on the disk in their original form whether or not you save the merged data to a new file.

Write Selected

This option only appears in the Address Book Files menu. It is used to save addresses which have been culled from a larger list by use of the Select command on the Cards menu. These addresses can be kept in a special file and retrieved later. Full details are given in Chapter 3.

Always safeguard your data

The information you put in the Portfolio will gradually accumulate and may represent a great deal of work. Unfortunately, computers have a habit of losing data! This could occur because a component breaks down, or in some cases a loss of power is enough to cause a RAM disk to fail. In any case you must take steps to save your information.

In the case of the Portfolio you could do this in two ways.

1. Transfer the files to a desktop PC by means of the optional parallel interface and then save the files to a floppy disk. Do not trust the PC's hard disk, because it too will break down sooner or later.

2. Save the files to a memory card in the Portfolio's drive A:

This is called backing up the data. When it has been done, you will have duplicated your valuable files, by having the working version on the Portfolio's RAM disk C: and the backed up version on a memory card or PC disk. Every so often, it will be necessary to update these files by backing them up again.

2

Starting and Using the Portfolio's Disk Operating System

What the Operating System does and where it is

An operating system is a collection of computer programs, usually supplied with the computer. These serve to provide the basic control functions which supervise the running of other computer programs. The disk operating system, called DOS, is built into the Portfolio. Among other things, it facilitates access to stored files and programs. The total effect of the operating system is to give you complete control of the various pieces of electronic hardware, together with whatever program software is linked with them. Use of the system should, therefore, enable you to decide what your Portfolio does and how it does it.

A basic task of an operating system is to permit the use of task-specific or applications programs. The Portfolio has a set of applications programs built into it.

DOS also allows direct interaction to occur between the user and the machine, so that you can give certain instructions to achieve specific effects. These DOS instructions take the form of exact 'commands' which can be typed on the keyboard. A frequently used example is 'DIR', an abbreviation of DIRECTORY, which instructs DOS to list the contents of a 'disk drive'. When this command is used, the Portfolio screen will display the 'files' contained in a particular directory.

Anybody new to computers should realise that the instructions given to DOS must be exact. You can usually get away with typing commands in lower case, but introducing an illegitimate space, or omitting one that should be there, could well result in the on screen message Bad command or program not found. This is one of the 'Error Messages' included in Appendix B.

Many people make only minimum direct use of the operating system because they are chiefly concerned with performing tasks which utilise wordprocessors and spreadsheet programs that communicate directly with DOS. Even so, an understanding of the way DOS works allows one to organise and manipulate the contents of the computer in accordance with personal preference and efficiency.

Details of the DOS commands are given later in the chapter.

The Portfolio's operating system is similar, in use, to those employed to control IBM and compatible personal computers. The disk operating system is compatible with a version of MS-DOS (Microsoft Disk Operating System). MS-DOS is like the PC-DOS that is used on true IBM PCs. Although the version of MS-DOS, with which the Portfolio is compatible, may not be the most recent, (version 4.1 is current) it is an industry standard with which the majority of external software can be run.

You can find out what version of DIP DOS is running on the Portfolio by typing VER when you see the prompt >. The Portfolio used for this book runs:

```
DIP Operating System 2.11 v1.030
```

Starting the System

Basic hardware cold start

When you first receive a new Portfolio, it is necessary to load the three AA size cells into the battery slot located on the rear of the base. Close the lid of the machine and turn it over. Remove the battery compartment cover by sliding in the direction indicated and slip the three batteries in, located as shown by the diagram on the base of the compartment.

Once the batteries have been loaded, the Portfolio is automatically switched on and the screen shows an initial copyright message. After this it is necessary to go through the procedures for setting the keyboard, date and time. It is also necessary to configure the RAM disk.

The routine described above is the basic cold start. Each time you renew the batteries the Portfolio goes through a similar reset process, but on these occasions it will usually only display the operating system message:

```
DIP Operating System 2.11 vX.XXX
```

Following this you may need to reset the date and time.

Although the Portfolio normally displays a Low Battery message as an early warning, Alkaline and rechargeable batteries can run down very quickly and you may even miss the low battery message. The power in these batteries can fall below the required level in a matter of minutes, a much shorter period of time than indicated in the handbook.

Normally, the Portfolio will switch itself off, or you type off at the > prompt, or [Fn]+[O], but if the batteries fail while the computer is being used and you do not manage to switch the screen display off, you may lose your RAM disk data during the battery change. If this happens, contact your dealer, who should be able to provide a 'fix'.

Warm start or reset

Using [Ctrl]+[Alt]+[Del]

Sometimes a computer will hang in the middle of a program. That is, it will not respond to keyboard commands. Under these circumstances, it is usual to attempt a warm reset or 'boot'. To do this, press [Ctrl]+[Alt]+[Del]. You will then be given the option to reset the date and time, but no data stored on the RAM disk should be lost and the blockage in memory should be cleared.

Booting and rebooting

The term 'bootstrapping' -booting for short - is used to describe the routine used to start up the computer after a cold start or warm reset. Unlike desktop PCs whose DOS is usually loaded from a disk, the Portfolio's bootstrap program, together with its DOS, is stored on a chip built into the computer and this means that once the batteries are in it can be started very quickly by the press of a key.

Drives

The information which you put into the computer is stored in files which are kept on 'drives'. The term drive is derived from the mechanically driven disk drives used with other types of computers. Such disk drives use small plastic disks, coated with a magnetic medium on which information is stored. This information can also be erased. The Portfolio's drives perform the same functions, but work in different ways.

Drive names

Drives are named as letters of the alphabet, followed by a colon. The Portfolio has drives A: and C: built in.

The current drive is also the default drive.

RAM Drive

The RAM drive is an area of the Portfolio's random access memory which is set aside for use as an electronic disk for the storage of files. The Portfolio's RAM drive is designated C: The size of drive C: is set by using the FDISK command, but this erases all data on the RAM drive.

Memory Card Drives

Drive A: is the Portfolio's memory card drive. Solid state memory cards with a preset storage capacity of up to 128K (roughly equivalent to 128,000 characters) can be plugged into the slot on the left side of your machine. The cards must be formatted before use, and the information is loaded from and written to them by using the LOAD and SAVE commands. Information is not lost when a memory card is removed and they are, therefore, useful for storing valuable data which is not required immediately, but which needs to be kept for a lengthy period.

Other drives

Data can be transferred to and from a desktop PC by using the optional parallel or serial interfaces available for the Portfolio. Data transferred from the Portfolio can then be saved from the PC to its own conventional disk drives.

Additional card drives, which can be linked directly to a PC, are available as optional extras from Atari and DIP

Changing drives

When cold booted, for example, after the batteries have been removed, the Portfolio defaults to drive C: . The default drive can be changed, simply by typing in the name of another drive, followed by a colon, then [Enter] after the prompt sign >.

To change from drive C to drive A type A: [Enter] after the C> shown on the screen; the change is confirmed by the screen showing A>

Files and File names

Files are stored on 'disks' and are used by the computer as a means of organising and storing the information which it must keep. The Portfolio's memory cards are the users equivalent of disks on the IBM and other personal computers. But the maximum storage capacity of a memory card is only 128K, instead of the minimum 360K available on PC disks. There are different types of files, some of which are used for data, while others can be used to store programs of various kinds. All of them must be named in accordance with DOS rules.

Backing Up Data

Whenever you put valuable information into a computer, including the Portfolio, you should back it up. This means that you should always have two copies of your data in case one is inadvertently lost.

The Portfolio uses batteries which regularly run down. When they do it is possible for the data on the RAM disk to be lost. Therefore, you should always SAVE your valuable data to a memory card, or transfer it to a desktop PC and save it to the PCs floppy disk; NOT to its hard disk.

File names

The basic rules for file naming are simple. A file name consists of two parts, the main filename, which may be up to eight characters long, followed by a full stop, and the extension which can consist of up to three characters. The example below shows a typical file name.

JONES.TXT

All normal alphanumeric keyboard characters are valid and the system makes no distinction between upper and lower case. Spaces cannot be embedded in a filename.

Valid keyboard characters

ABCDEFGHIJKLMNOPQRSTUVWXYZ 0123456789!@$#%^&()'~{}`-_

The following characters must *not* be used:

\ * ?

The backslash \ has a special significance for DOS because is is used with directory names, and the asterisk * and question mark ? are used as wildcards.

Restrictions

There are a few restrictions on filenames (not extensions) which DOS reserves for itself, otherwise you can call a file by virtually any name you wish. The names given below are reserved by DOS because they are already being used. When an attempt is made to save a file with any of these names it will be ignored by the applications software, although it is permissible to use them as file name extensions.

Restricted File Names:

AUX CON COM CLOCK$ LPT NUL PRN

Also avoid giving files any of the following file name extensions unless you understand exactly what you are doing. They are used for program files, and no error message will be shown on the screen. Once you have gained some experience, you might want to alter your CONFIG.SYS file and to build .BAT files to perform special tasks.

Extension	Meaning
.EXE	Executable. DOS runs this program when the name is typed
.COM	Command. DOS also will run this program when its name is typed
.SYS	System. A file used only by DOS
.BAT	Batch. A text file which contains a series of DOS commands which are run when the file name is typed.
.BAS	Basic. Contains a program written in BASIC. The BASIC language needs to be present in order to run it.

Portfolio Applications default names

It is a good idea to develop a system of working and to make your filenames as descriptive of the file's contents as possible. In the interests of efficiency and to avoid confusion it is also wise to remember that the Portfolio's application software uses special extensions for its files.

Remember that the default file name of the Portfolio's Applications is UNNAMED, followed by the appropriate extension.

Portfolio Application Software Extension Names

Application	Default File name	File Extension Name
Editor	UNNAMED	.TXT
Worksheet	UNNAMED	.WKS
Address Book	UNNAMED	.ADR
Diary	UNNAMED	.DRY

When using any of these applications, you should enter up to eight characters for the first part of the name of the file containing new or altered data which you want to save separately from any default files that might have been loaded. The Portfolio will automatically add the extension when it saves the file.

Wildcards

As mentioned previously, two of the characters which cannot be used as part of a specific file or directory name are:

* and ?

They are special symbols that may be used to substitute for any of the other legitimate keyboard characters.

? Can be used to substitute for any legitimate single filename character, so J??? would match

JOHN JACK JIM or JOSH

But it is often much more convenient to use * to substitute for as many character spaces (up to the permitted 8) as you like in a name. For example, J*, would match all the names given above and more besides.

A frequent and useful method of applying the * wildcard is to substitute it for the filename extension. For example, if you wanted to copy all the files called UNNAMED to another directory, you would type COPY UNNAMED.* C:\NEW-DIR, where NEWDIR is the name of the directory where the files are to be copied to on the C: drive.

Configuring the system with CONFIG.SYS

This is an important file, read automatically by DOS when the system boots. By using it, various parameters can be set according to the user's requirements. For instance, the date format, which varies from country to country, may be set within CONFIG.SYS, and this dictates the way in which the dates are shown in the Diary and other applications. If you want to examine an existing CONFIG.SYS file, just load it into the Editor, or use TYPE CONFIG.SYS [Enter] from the DOS screen.

Commands which can be used within CONFIG.SYS

BREAK on/off BREAK is set to off initially. In this condition, the Portfolio will stop its current activity only when input is from the keyboard. Switching BREAK to on will allow it also to terminate during some disk operations.

BUFFERS=nn Buffers are RAM divisions which the Portfolio uses to store data read from disks. The amount of space used can be varied by the user up to a maximum of 64. 32 is the recommended size.

COUNTRY=nnn This command is used with a three figure code to set the date format. Permitted countries and their codes are shown in the following list.

Country	nnn	Date format
Australia	061	dd/mm/yy
Belgium	032	dd/mm/yy
Denmark	045	dd/mm/yy
Finland	358	dd/mm/yy
France	033	dd/mm/yy
Germany	049	dd/mm/yy
Italy	039	dd/mm/yy
Netherlands	031	dd/mm/yy
Norway	047	dd/mm/yy
Spain	034	dd/mm/yy
Sweden	046	yy/mm/dd
Switzerland	041	dd/mm/yy
UK	044	dd/mm/yy
USA	001	mm/dd/yy

DEVICE=[name] Sets a device driver specified in [name]. No files of this sort are supplied with the Portfolio, though devices such as MOUSE.SYS and ANSI.SYS, are commonly used with desktop PCs.

FILES=nn Sets the number of internal files which can be open at one time. Both the maximum and recommended values are 20.

Sample CONFIG.SYS file

To save this to disk, from the DOS screen type COPY CON CONFIG.SYS[Enter]. The Portfolio will respond with CON to C:\CONFIG.SYS. Then type the following, pressing [Enter] at the end of each line:

```
Files=20
Buffers=32
Country=044
[Ctrl]+[Z]
```

CONFIG.SYS will be read by DOS when it is restarted, for example with [Ctrl]+[Alt]+[Del].

Directories

DOS places files in directories which are an important further aid to the organisation of data. The system has a root directory which may be divided into several subdirectories, and these may again be divided.

Directory Structure

The DOS directory structure is hierarchical. In other words, there is a single root directory, shown as \, and below this succeeding levels of subdirectories. The structure can resemble a pyramid sales organisation, or an ancestral tree which shows offspring going back through parents, grandparents, great-grandparents and so on. The root directory is the parent of them all.

Level	*Appearance on the DOS Screen*
Root	\
Subdirectory to 3 levels	NAME1\NAME2\NAME3

When you boot the Portfolio it starts in the root directory of drive C:, which is described by the single backslash character \, demonstrated when you type CD at the prompt > . You have no influence over this, but can make, change, delete or rename any directories beyond this level. If you do not make any subdirectories every file saved will be placed in the root directory and, since there can be up 112 of them, this might make it difficult to see a group of files which all relate to a specific subject.

Therefore, the creation of subdirectories allows a user to group files together according to his own system of organisation. As with files, directories can be given any suitable name up to eight characters in length. Directory names do not have an extension. Each disk on each drive has its own root directory.

DOS Commands

As indicated earlier in this chapter, DOS is controlled by a set of commands which are available to the Portfolio user. If you type HELP when the > prompt is showing, the computer will respond by displaying a list of these commands, classified according to their use.

```
FILE  DIR  DISK    ETC...     BATCH
copy  cd   chkdsk  app off    @ do echo
del   md   fdisk   break      errorlevel
dir   rd   format  cls date   exist for
ren   path label   prompt     goto if in
type       verify  run set    not pause
           vol      time ver  rem shift
```

The Portfolio's DOS Help screen

Summary List of DOS Commands

Category	*Command*	*Meaning*
FILE		
	COPY	Copy file(s)
	DEL	Delete a file(s)
	DIR	List the files in a directory
	REN	Rename a file
	TYPE	Display the contents of a text file, usually on the screen
DIRECTORY		
	CD	Change to another directory
	MD	Create a new directory
	RD	Remove an empty directory from the disk
	PATH	Set or show the route for DOS to search for a program
DISK		
	CHKDSK	Check the status of a disk or memory card
	FDISDK	Reset the size of the RAM disk C:
	FORMAT	Format a memory card
	LABEL	Modify or make a disk volume label
	VERIFY	When on, checks data data written to a disk
	VOL	Shows volume name assigned to a disk

Category ETC...	*Command*	*Meaning*
	APP	Runs Portfolio applications software
	BREAK	Toggles break key ([Fn]+[B]) on or off
	CLS	Clear the screen
	DATE	Display and set date
	HELP	Displays DOS commands on the Portfolio's screen
	OFF	Switches Portfolio to standby mode
	PROMPT	Change the prompt
	RUN	Used ONLY with a memory card to run DOS software
	SET	Set or display the DOS environment settings
	TIME	Display and set the time
	VER	Shows DOS version number
BATCH		
	@	Prevents screen echo. Particularly valuable with ECHO
	DO	Used only with FOR
	ECHO	Switches screen echo of batch file commands on or off
	ERRORLEVEL	Used only with IF
	EXIST	Used only with IF
	FOR	With IN and DO provides a repeating structure
	GOTO	Causes jump to a label in a batch file
	IF	Conditional structure command
	IN	Part of the FOR command
	NOT	Part of the IF command
	PAUSE	Causes a batch file to suspend batch file execution
	REM	Allows insertion of a remark in a batch file
	SHIFT	Extends the availability of batch file parameters

DOS Command Syntax

The commands which are employed to control DOS must be typed in a particular form, described as the syntax. Syntax is, in practice, a set of rules which govern the structure of the DOS statements. In the event of an infringement, the infamous message SYNTAX ERROR will be delivered to the Portfolio's screen !

The DOS command is first typed at the > prompt. It may then be followed by other arguments or switches. The complete command, with arguments or switches is called the DOS command line.

The conventions for describing the arguments and switches are as follows. Only the contents, not the brackets, are typed in with the command.

[d]   drive. Usually used in the form A:

[dir]   directory

[fname]   a full file name. That is a file name with its extension, as in JONES.TXT

[path]   drive and directory. If no drive is included, the default drive is assumed. Similarly, if no directory is given the current directory is used

(/w)   an optional parameter or switch

...   ellipses., these indicate that further parameters can be included, following on from those shown

[(/p)(/a)]   square brackets indicate a range of options. Only one at a time may be used.

[n]   a number, used as specified.

When DOS commands are described in this chapter, the syntax is given on the same line as the heading.

Control Characters and Function Keys

A copy of all DOS commands are stored in the Portfolio's memory. If the same command has to be entered again, using a function key or control character may enable it to be used without retyping the word in full. Note that the function keys are redefined by the Portfolio when used with the applications software.

[Fn][1]

Copies a single character from memory to the command line. Each succeeding press of [F1] will copy another character to the command line.

[Fn][2]x

Copies characters from the memory to the command line, up to the one specified as x.

[Fn][3]

After [Fn][1] or [Fn][2], copies all remaining characters from the memory to the command line.

[Fn][4]x

Omits all characters up to that specified by x.

[Fn][5]

When a new command line is typed in, pressing [Fn][5] before you press [Enter] will cause it to be transferred to the memory template without being executed.

[Fn][6]

Places a Control Z in the memory template. Control Z ([Ctrl]+[Z]) is the character which signifies End Of File. Used in creating files with COPY CON, like CONFIG.SYS and AUTOEXEC.BAT

[DEL]

If used when copying from the memory to the screen, omits the next character.

[ESC]

Inactivates the current command line.

[INS]

Allows other characters to be typed into the memory template.

[CTRL]+[C]

Aborts the current process, for example, any .BAT file which is running, and returns to the screen prompt.

[CTRL]+[P]

Press this once and all output from DOS to the Portfolio's screen will be sent to any printer which is connected via the appropriate interface and cable. Make sure that the Portfolio's Setup option has been properly configured. Pressing [CTRL]+[P] again will switch the DOS output back to screen only.

For example, entering:

```
[CTRL]+[P] DIR[Enter][CTRL]+[P]
```

will cause DOS output to go to the printer, a listing of the current directory to be output and consequently printed and will then switch output back to the screen only.

[CTRL]+[S]

Can be very useful when you are, for instance, listing a long directory to the screen, or a text file with the [TYPE] command. Pressing [CTRL]+[S] causes output to the screen to pause at that point. Pressing any key will cause the output to be started again.

DOS File Commands

Copy   COPY [path][fname] [path][fname]

This is a powerful command which can be used to copy files from one directory to another, or from drive to drive. It can also be employed to copy input from a device like a modem to a file, or from a file to a modem or a printer.

Copying files

In its simplest form the command can be used within the same directory. For instance, if you wanted to copy a file called JONES.TXT you could do so, provided you altered the name:

```
COPY JONES.TXT JONES2.TXT
```

The original file is not damaged or erased, and a duplicate of it will be put into the file JONES2.TXT. The same name cannot be used to copy a file (to itself!) in the same directory, but it is possible to use the same name in another directory. If DOS was set in the TEMP subdirectory, with subdirectories INV and COR at the next level, entering:

```
COPY INV\JONES.TXT COR\JONES.TXT
```

would copy the JONES.TXT file from the subdirectory INV\ to the subdirectory COR\ and the file could have the same name in each of these subdirectories. When a file has been successfully copied DOS will show the message

```
C:\TEMP\INV\JONES.TXT to C:\TEMP\COR\JONES.TXT
                1 File copied
```

When copying to another drive or directory, in order to avoid mistakes I think it is best to enter the full drive and directory names of the destination. If you were in the subdirectory INV on drive C: the JONES.TXT file could be copied to the root directory in drive A: by entering:

```
COPY JONES.TXT A:\
```

DOS assumes that if the drive name and directory are not specified they are those from which you are currently working, i.e. those to which the system would default. In this case, no destination file name has been given and it therefore assumes that the file name will be the same. If you copy multiple files by using the wildcard *, as in:

```
COPY *.* A:\
```

All the files copied will have the same name on the new drive as on the old one.

Though abbreviations are possible, as indicated above, the COPY command is basically used in the form:

```
COPY [pathname of source file] [pathname of target file] [Enter]
```

and it is essential to keep the spaces between COPY, the pathname specification of the file's origin and that of its destination. If a file with the same name exists in the destination directory it will be overwritten and erased. It is therefore wise to give each file and directory in your Portfolio a unique name.

If you inadvertently try to copy a file back to the same directory with the same name, the message

```
Must specify source and target files
                0 Files copied
```

will appear on the screen.

Copying Files to Devices

The COPY command can be used to send files to a variety of destinations involving 'devices'.

Device Name	Function	Input or Output
AUX	Auxiliary (Default communications port, i.e. COM1)	Both
CON	Console (Keyboard only for input and display only for output)	Both
PRN	The default parallel printer (LPT1)	Output

The serial communications port is named COM1. This is used with the serial interface for serial printers and modems.

The parallel printer outlet used with the parallel interface is called LPT1. Contrary to usual practice, the file transfer software, supplied with the Portfolio's optional parallel interface, uses this port for two way traffic.

COPY CON is often used to create batch files. Thus,

```
COPY CON PRINT.BAT
```

could be used to create the file PRINT.BAT, and the command would be followed by lines of text containing DOS commands, names, variables and the like, followed by Control Z, which is the end of file indicator. This topic is dealt with in greater detail in the section on batch files.

```
COPY CON PRN
```

Copies everything typed on the keyboard to the printer.

When external devices are used with the Portfolio, they must be connected via the appropriate Portfolio interfaces and must be switched on. Before employing any DOS external device commands you MUST read the advice and warnings given in the instructions about the use of the interfaces with some of the Portfolio's software.

Joining Files

On computers running MS-DOS a second form of the COPY command can be used to copy and join files together, but this is not available on the Portfolio's D.I.P DOS 2.11. An alternative for joining ASCII files, such as those with the .TXT, .ADR, .BAT, .WKS, and .DRY is to use an output command like TYPE to append one file to another. For example to append the file PART2.ADR to an already existing file called PART1.ADR in the same directory, you can use the TYPE command as follows

```
TYPE PART2.ADR >> PART1.ADR[Enter]
```

It is also possible to join files, or parts of them, by means of the Portfolio's Editor in connection with the Editor's File Menu Merge option, and the Clipboard.

DEL   **DEL [path][fname]**

In order to maintain the organisation of the Portfolio DOS it is necessary to erase old or obsolete files from time to time by using the command DEL. Be warned that it is easy to make mistakes and that slap happy use of this command can result in the loss of valuable data, or even whole directories of data.

To delete an unprotected file called JACK.TXT from the current directory, all you need to do is to enter:

```
DEL JACK.TXT
```

If the file is on another drive or in another directory, you can enter as much of the pathname as necessary. For instance if JACK.TXT was in the root directory on drive

A: you would enter:

```
DEL A:\JACK.TXT
```

and if it was in another subdirectory, next level down from root and called LETTERS on your current drive:

```
DEL \LETTERS\JACK.TXT
```

Deleting more than one file at a time

Several methods can be used to delete more than one file at a time.

Deleting the contents of a directory

Entering:

```
DEL A:\LETTERS
```

would be followed by a warning on the screen

```
Are you sure Y/N ?
```

If you replied Y to this question, all files in the LETTERS directory of drive A:\ would be deleted! Similarly, if there was a directory called JACK below the LETTERS directory (A:\LETTERS\JACK) and you entered:

```
DEL JACK
```

from the LETTERS directory, a reply of Y to the question 'Are you sure Y/N ?' would result in the deletion of all files in the JACK subdirectory.

It is also possible to use wild cards with the delete command. I have found * to be the most valuable. The * can usefully take the place of either the file name or the extension. Entering:

```
DEL *.*
```

from the current directory will delete all the files in that directory, though the caution 'Are you sure Y/N ?' must be answered before this will happen.

Deleting categories of files

If you enter:

```
DEL JACK.*
```

all the versions of the JACK file will be deleted.

And entering:

DEL *.TXT

will result in all the files with a TXT extension being deleted from the current directory.

Directory   **DIR [path](/P)(/W)**

To see a list of files in the root directory on the current disk, type DIR[Enter] at the > prompt.

```
permdata dat     730  13-11-01  12:18
diary    dry     313  26-12-89  11:13
undelete dat    1974  11-01-90  17:23
unnamed  adr       0  27-12-89  18:24
pb       adr     381   9-01-90  10:37
russians txt     687   1-01-90  12:18
formula  txt      47  30-12-89  15:54
clipbord dat      93   1-01-90  15:42
```

A directory list showing file size and the dates and times of origin

Used in this way, the directory list shows the filenames, their extensions, the size of the file in bytes, and the date and time of creation. The number of files listed, and the amount of free space on the current drive are shown at the bottom. Normally, the list scrolls up on the screen, but can be stopped by pressing [Ctrl]+[S].

Wildcards can be used. For instance, if you type *.TXT, all the files in the current directory which have a .TXT ending will be shown, but no others.

When you type DIR[Enter], you will also see any subdirectories. They are listed by name, followed by <DIR>. To get a listing of subdirectories without files, type DIR *.[Enter]

There are two switches which can be used to control the directory command. Either, or both, can be entered after DIR.

/P Files are displayed in the same way as for DIR, but they are listed on the screen one page at a time. Up to seven file names at a time are shown on the screen. Press any key to show the next seven, and so on until all the files have been displayed.

/W This switch causes files to be listed in wide mode. Only file names and extensions are shown, but they are displayed across the whole width of the screen so that more names can be seen.

```
Volume in drive c is pedro
Directory of c:\SYSTEM

.            ..             permdata dat
diary    dry undelete dat unnamed adr
pb       adr russians txt formula txt
clipbord dat unnamed  txt puss2   txt
```

The directory as presented when the /w switch is used

REN   **REN [oldfname]   [newfname]**

Sometimes it is desirable to change the original name given to a file, perhaps to make it more informative. To do this, enter:

```
REN [oldfilename] [newfilename]
```

REN is the command, the old file name is followed by the new file name, spaces being entered between each block of characters. If no drive or directory specified DOS presumes that they are those which are current, i.e. the default drive and directory.

If you wanted to rename a file called JAMES.TXT in subdirectory INV on drive A: to JAMES.LET the command would be entered as:

```
REN A:INV\JAMES.TXT JAMES.LET
```

Wildcards can be used. If you wanted to rename all the files with the extension .TXT to .LET, you could enter:

```
REN *.TXT *.LET
```

If you attempt to rename a file to the name of a file which is present in the current directory, this message will be displayed:

```
Target file exists
```

TYPE   **TYPE [fname] (/p)**

In its simplest form this command causes the contents of an ASCII text file to be displayed on the screen. To show a file called UNNAMED.TXT, you would enter:

```
TYPE UNNAMED.TXT
```

Often the text is too lengthy to fit on the screen all at once. It can be prevented from scrolling too rapidly by pressing [Ctrl]+[S], and started again by pressing any other key. Better still, use the /p switch, which scrolls the text on to the Portfolio's screen a page at a time, with the message Strike a key when ready ...

As already indicated, TYPE is an output command and the data may therefore be redirected. If you press [Ctrl]+[P] before you enter the TYPE command the contents of the text file can be sent directly to your printer, when connected to the appropriate interface. Also, the use of the operator > will cause output to be sent to the file or device named. Entering:

```
TYPE UNNAMED.TXT > PRN
```

would also cause the Editor file UNNAMED.TXT to be sent to the default printer via the parallel interface.

Using TYPE with files which are not composed of ASCII characters will probably result in the Portfolio's screen showing a mass of indecipherable symbols!

Directory Commands

Make Directory   MD [directory]

The Make Directory command is used to create a new subdirectory. This command is entered on the keyboard as MKDIR, or MD . If you typed

```
MD LETTERS [Enter]
```

a new subdirectory called LETTERS would be created on the current disk, but in order to work in it you would have to use CD LETTERS to change from the current directory into LETTERS.

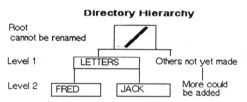

The relationship of ROOT (\), LETTERS, FRED and JACK subdirectories

If the root directory is thought of as the top level, and the subdirectory as a lower level, it is possible to continue the process of making further subdirectories to lower and lower levels. For example, if you are in the C:\LETTERS subdirectory, you might want to establish a subsubdirectory for all the correspondence sent to a customer called Jack. In this case you could enter MD JACK. If you had another customer called Fred, you could also make another subsubdirectory for him called Fred by entering MD FRED from the the C:\LETTERS subdirectory.

When naming a directory, remember that a maximum of eight characters may be used; anything longer will be truncated to fit.

Change Directory   **CD [path]**

It is always wise to see which directory you are currently in before trying to change.
Therefore, check by typing cd [Enter]. If you are in the root directory of drive C, the
screen will show:

```
C:\
```

If this is not shown on the Portfolio's screen type CD\ to get into the root directory.

In the rest of the description of the CD command, it will help if you refer again to the
directories made by using MD. The following subdirectory structures are used:

```
C:\LETTERS\JACK
C:\LETTERS\FRED
```

From the root, to change into the new subdirectory, type CD LETTERS [Enter]. If
you check the directory by entering CD[Enter] again, the screen will show
C:\LETTERS, or if you type DIR[Enter]

```
Volume in drive C: has no label
Directory of C:\LETTERS
```

followed by any files which might be in the subdirectory. Note that there are always
two files present, even in an empty directory. These are shown as:

```
.            <DIR>
..           <DIR>
```

To get into the FRED subdirectory while in C:\LETTERS you simply type
CD FRED[Enter]. After doing this, if CD[Enter] is typed, the directory would be
shown as C:\LETTERS\FRED .

How do you get into the JACK subsubdirectory? The move can be done simply by
typing CD \LETTERS\JACK [Enter]. Typing CD..\JACK will also work because
CD.. has the effect of taking the user down one step in the directory sequence, while
\JACK means go to the JACK subdirectory. It is also possible to return to the root
directory, by typing CD\, and start again with CD\LETTERS\JACK .

Remove Directory   **RD [directory]**

This command is used to get rid of unwanted directories from the Portfolio system.
The command Rmdir, or RD, is followed by the name of the subdirectory you want
to remove. The Root directory cannot be removed and, as a safety precaution, no
directory which contains files can be erased unless the files are deleted or transferred
first. If you attempt to remove a subdirectory containing files, the message 'Directory
not found or not empty' is shown. Furthermore, you cannot remove the subdirectory
which you have currently selected; in other words, the one you are in at the time.

Once the directory is empty, it can be removed by typing RD followed by the full directory description, or if you are in the parent directory, just the name of the subdirectory you want to remove.

Taking the example above, if you were in the C:\LETTERS directory and wanted to remove the FRED subdirectory, you would only type RD FRED, but if you were in the root directory it would be necessary to type RD LETTERS\FRED .

Path   **PATH [Pathname](;Pathname)...**

DOS usually looks for a command file in the current directory. PATH tells DOS where else to search for .COM, .EXE or .BAT files. When no path has been set, typing PATH on the Portfolio will cause the screen to show PATH= . If a PATH has been set the screen will show the PATH, which might look like:

```
PATH=C:\;C:SYSTEM
```

This particular PATH instructs DOS to look through the root directory C:\ for a file and then to look through the C:\SYSTEM subdirectory. If the drive name is omitted DOS will look through directories on the current drive.

More than one directory can be included, but where this is done the full description, including drive name, should be given. Different directories are separated by a semicolon (;) .

If DOS finds two executable files with the same name it uses the priority:

```
.COM
.EXE
.BAT
```

Disk Commands

Chkdsk   **CHKDSK [d](/p)**

This command checks the disk specified for errors and displays information about directories, files, total capacity, free memory and disk space.

```
 62720 bytes total disk capacity
   768 bytes in 2 directories
 23296 bytes in 19 user files
 38400 bytes available on disk
126976 bytes total memory
 32608 bytes free
```

The Portfolio screen showing the results of CHKDSK on drive C:

Fdisk   **FDISK [n]**

Do not use this command until you have read through the information below. FDISK will erase all the data on the RAM disk C: When the command is entered, a warning is shown on the screen, and at this stage you can abort the action, by pressing [Esc].

*** All files on c: will be lost ***

Fdisk is used to set the size of the Portfolio's internal RAM drive C: and it re-boots the system. All the files stored on the RAM disk will be deleted.

To reset the RAM disk size type FDISK followed by any number between 8 and 66K. Then press [Enter].

Format   **FORMAT [d](/v)**

Format is used specifically to format or reformat a memory card, so that it can receive data saved to it from the Portfolio in the form of files. A memory card cannot be used to store files until it has been formatted. The FORMAT process deletes all existing files and directories. Drive names may be A:, or B: if an external drive has been fitted. If you enter the command:

```
FORMAT A:
```

the message:

```
Insert new disk in drive A
Strike a key when ready ...
```

is displayed and when a key is pressed the card in drive A will be formatted and the message

```
Formatting ...
```

will be shown on the screen.

One optional switch can be used with format and it is entered after the command and drive name.

The /v option, entered as Format A:/v[Enter] will allow the addition of a volume name to a newly formatted memory card and thus enable you to give it a unique label. This is quite a useful procedure for distinguishing between cards which contain duplicate copies, or slightly different versions of similar files.

Label   **LABEL [d](label)**

If you format a memory card, but do not give it a volume name at that time, the name can be given later by using Label.

Typing only LABEL [Enter] will produce a screen message as follows:

```
Volume in drive [n] is (name)
if the disk already has a volume name
Volume label ?
```

If the disk does not have a label, only the second line is shown. You can then enter a name and press [Enter]. If only [Enter] is pressed, this message is shown:

```
Delete current label (Y/N)?
```

Verify   **VERIFY [(off) (on)]**

When switched on, this command verifies all data written to a disk. Typing VERIFY [Enter] enables you to check the command's present state and the screen will respond with:

```
VERIFY is off
```

or

```
VERIFY is on
```

You can then switch it on or off by typing VERIFY on or VERIFY off.

Vol   **VOL [d]**

Shows the volume name for the drive given. If no drive is given, the volume name of the default drive is shown.

Miscellaneous DOS Commands

These are shown under ETC... on the HELP screen

App   **APP [(/A)(/C)(/D)(/E)(/S)(/W)]**

When typed from the DOS screen without any of the switches APP takes you directly to the main Applications menu. If typed with one of the switches, the Portfolio will immediately present an appropriate applications program:

Switch	Application
APP /A	Address Book
APP /C	Calculator
APP /D	Diary
APP /E	Editor
APP /S	Setup
APP /W	Worksheet

Break   **BREAK [(on) (off)]**

Break checks the condition of the Break key, which can be on or off.

If you type BREAK[Enter] it will respond by showing either

BREAK is off

or

BREAK is on

The Break key on the Portfolio is [Fn][B].

Pressing the Break key when it is off will cancel the current activity during output to the screen or input from the keyboard.

Pressing Break when it is switched on will make the current activity terminate in the same way as above, but also during some disk operations.

CLS   **CLS**

Clears the screen. With a screenful of text, type CLS [Enter] and it clears to leave a blank screen. The cursor is positioned at the top left of the screen. If the display is the 80 x 25 screen, the cursor will be returned to Home at line 1, column 1.

Date   **DATE[mm/dd/yy]**

Allows you to set or reset the date of the Portfolio's internal clock/calendar. Note that the order of [mm/dd/yy] varies according to the setting of COUNTRY. This is important for the applications software, if you decide to display the current date with the prompt, and for getting the current date stamps on the files you save to disk.

To reset the date type DATE at the DOS prompt, you can type DATE(DD/mm/yy). If you type DATE by itself, the Portfolio will show the existing date:

```
Date: Tue  1-01-1980
New date (dd-mm-yy):
```

The screen response to typing DATE

To set a new date, type the new date in the required form and then press [Enter]. If you simply press [Enter] the date will remain as it is.

Off   **OFF**

Typing [off] [Enter] at the > prompt switches the Portfolio to standby mode. The off state can also be achieved by pressing [Fn]+[O]. To switch the Portfolio back to an active state, press any key.

Prompt   **PROMPT [text]**

When you switch on the Portfolio for the first time, the prompt following the drive name which appears on the screen is simply > . In this form it gives no information, but this situation can be changed.

For example, if you wanted the current path to be shown with the prompt, this could be arranged by entering at the sign > PROMPT pg . The $ sign tells the Portfolio that the character following is a special symbol. In this case the p represents path and the g is the code for >. Therefore, if you were in the JACK subdirectory and had made this prompt alteration you would see the following on the screen:

```
C:\LETTERS\JACK>
```

This way, you always know where you are in the DOS directory structure.

There are a number of other special symbols which you can use with the prompt command:

Symbol	Prompt shows
d	current date
t	current time
p	current directory on the current drive
v	DOS version number
n	current drive
g	the > character
l	the < character
b	the l character
_	carriage return & line feed
s	leading space character
h	backspace character
e	escape character

Time and date could easily be added to the information already displayed. In this case you would enter

```
prompt $p$g$_Time = $t$_Date = $d
```

to get, for example:

```
C:\LETTERS\JACK>
Time = 10:47:14.57
Date = Wed 31-05-1993
```

Prompt will accept any text string which is typed after it.

Run   **RUN [d][fname]**

Run is only used to run Portfolio software from a memory card. Only use Run when directed to do so by a Portfolio software manual.

Set   **SET [string1]=[string2]**

If you type SET [Enter] alone, the Portfolio will respond by showing you the parameters which have been set.

COMSPEC=\COMMAND.COM
PATH=C:\;C:\SYSTEM
PROMPT=$g

Path, Comspec and Prompt parameters shown in response to SET

Path shows any path which has been set Comspec shows which command processor is being used Prompt will show any user alteration to Prompt

The Path and Prompt displays may be those set from within the autoexec.bat file.

If the variable %fname% was included in a batch file SET could be used to set the name as required. To do this you would type the name required after the variable name, as follows:

```
SET fname=invoices
```

To test this, type:

```
COPY CON TESTSET.BAT @ECHO The file name is %fname%
[Ctrl][Z]
```

A batch file called TESTSET.BAT will be saved to the current drive and directory. Then type in the SET phrase given above. Then see what file name is given when you run the batch file by typing TESTSET.

Time   **TIME[hh:mm:ss:hundredths]**

This command is used in a similar way to DATE to set the Portfolio's internal clock. If only the command is typed, the screen will show the current time and request an entry.

Time: 20:49:32.00
New time:

The screen response to typing TIME

Type in the time in the format given above and press [Enter]. Alternatively, type the command, followed by the time. There is no need to enter all the parameters. For instance, if you only want to set the hours and minutes, that is all you need to enter.

VER **VER**

This command returns the current version of DOS.

```
DIP Operating System 2.11  v1.030
Copyright (c) DIP 1989
```

The screen response to VER

Batch Files

Batch files enable you to tell the computer to perform a number of tasks by typing in a single command. They are potentially one of the most useful productivity tools available to a computer user. In essence, the batch file is a program which consists of a sequence of DOS commands, and it is run simply by typing in the name of the program, without the extension .BAT .

The hands on method is a great way to learn about batch files! Here is a very simple batch file which lists files in the current directory to the screen a few lines at a time.

From the DOS prompt > type:

```
copy con dirp.bat[Enter]
dir /p[Enter]
[Ctrl][Z][Enter]
```

When entered as instructed, a file called dirp.bat will be saved to your current directory. Press the [Ctrl] and [Z] keys together.

What does it all mean?

COPY CON, you will recall, is a use of the command COPY which allows the keyboard input to be sent to a file via the console device. In this case, the name of the file is 'dirp.bat'. Once the file has been created and saved, typing DIRP at the keyboard will cause the list of files in the current directory to be sent to the screen, one page at a time. In other words, the list will not scroll rapidly off the screen, but each screenful will remain in position until a key is pressed. [Ctrl][Z] is the standard character which signifies the end of a file (shows as ^Z on the screen) and it causes the newly created file to be saved to disk.

The DIRP file is a simple instance of the way in which batch files enable you to create your own commands and customise DOS.

AUTOEXEC.BAT

The AUTOEXEC.BAT is an important file because it allows you to automatically execute commands when you boot the Portfolio with [Ctrl]+[Alt]+[Del]. This means that you could automatically define the prompt and other environmental settings, like PATH, and run one or more programs without having to type the names on the keyboard.

Sample AUTOEXEC.BAT file

From the DOS screen in the C:\ directory type the following, and use [Enter] at the end of each line

```
COPY CON AUTOEXEC.BAT
```

The computer will respond with CON to C:\AUTOEXEC.BAT, then carry on with:

```
ECHO off
CLS
PATH=C:\;C:\SYSTEM
PROMPT $g$p$t
ECHO Hello I'm ready. Are you ?
[Ctrl]+[Z]
```

The file can be used for the first time by typing AUTOEXEC. Give it a try !

The general principles which apply to other batch files apply also to AUTO-EXEC.BAT and it can contain any of the batch file or other DOS commands-used with care.

Variables

A variable allows you to insert any name in a program, so that your batch file is not bound to use a particular name written into the program, but will use whatever you enter from the keyboard. This approach is useful in all sorts of situations, such as when it is necessary to input a file name.

In order to insert a variable in a batch file you use % followed by a number. Up to 10 variables can be used in one batch file, labelled 1%, 2%, 3%, 4%, 5%, 6%, 7%, 8%, and 9%. The 0% variable is used instead of the batch file name.

Environmental variables, such as %prompt% and %path% can also be included in batch files. If prompt or path have been set the parameters used will replace the environmental variable name in the batch file.

The example %fname%, given under SET, shows how you can create variables which can be included in batch files.

Batch file commands

All the DOS commands can be utilized in batch files, but those following are frequently employed and are listed under the Batch category of HELP.

Echo   **ECHO [(on) (off) (text)]**

If ECHO is on, the instructions carried out by a batch file are printed on the screen. Echo can be used in a batch file to send a message to the screen, or to switch this off.

ECHO Off   Switches output to the screen off. Also causes REM messages not to be displayed

ECHO On   switches output to the screen on

ECHO message   would print 'message' on the screen

It can also be entered at the command line prompt and is used as:

ECHO On   to turn output to the screen on

ECHO Off   to turn the screen output off

Typing ECHO [Enter] from the keyboard causes the screen to show an appropriate confirming message about the current state of the ECHO command, that is:

ECHO is on

or

ECHO is off

@ECHO works like ECHO but affects the command line as well, which is shown on the screen when the ECHO without @ is used. The ECHO line itself can, therefore, be prevented from appearing on the screen, during the execution of a batch file, by using @ECHO OFF in that batch file.

FOR   **FOR %%a in ([set]) do [command] %%a**

One of the advantages of using a computer is that, with the right programming, you can get it to do boring repetitive tasks. FOR is a DOS tool which allows looping to be done within batch files, but it is unfortunately not as powerful as the FOR command in BASIC because its looping ability is confined to one line.

The FOR [command] can be used in a batch file or from the keyboard. If used from the keyboard, any variable should be preceded by only one % sign. As in:

%F   from the keyboard

%%F   in a batch file

For instance, the FOR command could be used in a batch file to read text files generated by the Portfolio's Editor. In this case it would be entered as:

```
FOR %%F IN (*.TXT) DO TYPE/p %%F
```

Remember that * is a wildcard which can stand for a string of characters. Here, the asterisk stands for any file name. In the above example, the FOR command takes every file in the current directory with a .TXT extension and carries out the TYPE command which causes the output to be sent to the screen.

If entered from the keyboard, FOR would be used as follows:

```
FOR %F IN *.TXT DO TYPE/p %F
```

Interestingly, the wildcard * when used with TYPE from the keyboard will only read a single file.

As shown in the above lines, the FOR command consists of the following parts:

```
FOR
```

`%%` followed by any alphabetic, but not numeric, character. e.g. `%%P`

`IN`   followed by a series of characters separated by spaces and enclosed in parentheses; e.g. `IN (A B C D)`

DO   followed by another DOS command; e.g. `DO ECHO %%P;` or `DO TYPE %%F`

So the complete command would be

```
FOR %%<alphabetic character representing a variable name> IN
(Character Character) DO <DOS command> %%<alphabetic charac-
ter representing a variable name>
```

The loop runs from the beginning to the end of the line for as many times as there are characters, or strings, enclosed in parentheses, following IN. The characters following IN could be single, alphanumeric, or file or other names and the command following DO can be any legitimate DOS command. For instance, by slightly altering DEMSHIFT.BAT (included under the Shift command), you could display files on screen:

```
:BEGIN
ECHO OFF
FOR %%P IN (%0) DO TYPE %%P
SHIFT
PAUSE
GOTO BEGIN
```

If you enter and save this file, give it another name to prevent DOS from overwriting the DEMSHIFT.BAT file. You could call it TYPESHFT.BAT , for example.

It could then be used as TYPESHFT FILE1.TXT FILE2.TXT FILE3.TXT. On the first pass the program shows:

```
ECHO OFF
File not found
Strike a key when ready...
```

because it tries to read its own name, but when you press a key again it starts to read the text files whose names you have typed in after TYPESHFT. As previously, the file can be stopped at any pass by pressing [Ctrl]+[C] at the pause.

Note that in DEMSHIFT and TYPESHFT the variable %0 is treated by the FOR command as if it was a character and each file name typed at the keyboard with TYPESHFT is SHIFTed left through variable %0 until they have all been read.

GOTO   GOTO [label]

This command instructs the computer to jump to another part of the batch file. GOTO is used with a label, which must be prefixed by a colon where it occurs in the batch file. Thus, :END or :START .

The batch file below illustrates the use of GOTO:

```
COPYTXT.BAT
:BEGIN
PAUSE
Place disk to be copied in drive A and formatted target disk in drive B
COPY A:*.TXT B:
GOTO BEGIN
```

This batch file will copy all files with a .TXT extension from the disk in drive A to that in drive B. It will keep cycling, with a pause, until [Ctrl]+[C] is pressed, and then it will end. When this program is used, [Ctrl]+[C] should be pressed at the pause. In answer to Halt batch job (Y/N) ?, you answer Y to stop the program.

If /Exist/Errorlevel/Not   IF [condition] [command]

IF is used to set conditions for progression to some other part of the program. A batch file program can therefore be made to check a condition and act on a command only if that condition is fulfilled. If the condition is not fulfilled, the command is ignored and the computer continues on through the remaining sequence of commands in the program.

Strings

One use of IF is to compare two string values, which may be a set of alphabetic or numerical characters without commas or spaces, by means of the signs == . The form in which this is used is [string1] == [string2] .

For example the line

```
IF %1 == WKS GOTO CWKS
```

uses the variable %1 to compare whatever the user has entered with WKS. If the user had typed WKS, the batch file program would obey the command GOTO and jump to the label CWKS. Otherwise, it would continue to work its way sequentially through the list of commands.

This might be made use of in the following program segment which you could employ to sort spreadsheet and editor files which are in the same SYSTEM directory on your Portfolio, and at the same time back them up to a memory card in drive A. The card would have to be previously formatted and the destination directories on it created with the command MD.

To do this, you would change to drive A by typing A: after the prompt > , then use the command MD LETS[Enter] to create one directory and MD SS[Enter] to create the other.

```
SRTF.BATIF %1 == WKS GOTO CWKS
COPY C:\SYSTEM\*.TXT A:\LETS
GOTO END
:CWKS
COPY C:\SYSTEM\*.WKS A:\SS
:END
```

You would use this batch file either by typing its name SRTF [Enter] alone, or by typing SRTF WKS [Enter]. If you typed SRTF the program would skip the first line and continue to copy all your .TXT files from the system directory on drive C to a directory called LETS on drive A, then it would go to the label END and finish. If you typed SRTF WKS the batch program would jump to the label CWKS and copy only the files with a .WKS extension to the SS directory on drive A.

You would therefore have to run this batch file twice, once with the variable WKS after the file name and once without the variable, in order to sort your .TXT and .WKS files and transfer them to another disk on drive A. None of the other files on drive C: would be copied. By omitting the drive name A, and inserting the correct names, this batch file can be used to copy between directories on drive C.

Negative condition set with NOT

The condition set for IF can be reversed by using NOT. As an example, it could be added to give the SRTF batch file another dimension.

SRTF1.BAT

```
IF %1 == WKS GOTO CWKS
IF %1 == TXT GOTO TXT
IF NOT %1 == WKS GOTO AD
:TXT
COPY C:\SYSTEM\*.TXT A:\LETS
GOTO END
:CWKS
COPY C:\SYSTEM\*.WKS A:\SS
GOTO END
:AD
COPY C:\SYSTEM\*.ADR A:\ADRS
:END
```

Here, if the name of the batch file SRTF1 only is typed, it copies only the .ADR files from the system directory in drive C, because neither of the two conditions set in the first two lines of the program have been met. The computer therefore skips these two lines and acts on the third, which causes it to jump to the label :AD. It works through the next two and then reaches END.

If SRTF1 WKS is typed it copies only the .WKS files, because the variable %1 consists of the character string typed after SRTF1 and line 1 detects that this is equal to WKS. As instructed by line 1, the computer jumps to the label :CWKS, acts on the next line, and then goes to the label :END.

When you type SRTF1 TXT, the variable %1 is detected, by line two, as being equal to TXT and, accordingly, the .TXT files are copied before the computer jumps to the END label.

To do a complete transfer of the .TXT, .WKS and .ADR files to your memory card in drive A, you would need to run the program three times, using its name only, then again with the name followed by .TXT, then one more time with the name followed by .WKS. As previously, the destination directories would have to be created before you could run the program. You may find that the Portfolio is case sensitive, so type all your program instructions in upper case.

Use of EXIST

EXIST may also be used with the IF command in the forms of:

```
EXIST [filename]
```

```
NOT EXIST [filename]
```

The line:

```
IF NOT EXIST %1.* ECHO Cannot find file
```

could be used to test for the presence of a file when writing a batch file program.

ERRORLEVEL

External programs can be made to affect batch file execution when IF is used with ERRORLEVEL as part of the condition. When an external program terminates it can set the ERRORLEVEL to a number between 0 and 255, and this is held by DOS. Practical use of this is made when a line like:

```
IF ERRORLEVEL 1 GOTO [label]
```

is included in a batch file. The condition is said to be true if the previous program executed had an exit code equal to the number included. Therefore, if the ERRORLEVEL returned by DOS was 0, the GOTO instruction would not be acted upon.

An example of ERRORLEVEL use is given in a batch file included in the handbook which accompanies the Portfolio's parallel interface. Here the File Transfer program returns an ERRORLEVEL of 0 if transfer was completely successful, 1 if only some of the files were transferred and 2 if file transfer failed completely. The batch file goes to a :FAILED label and warning notice if ERRORLEVEL is 2 and to a :HALF label and incomplete notice if ERRORLEVEL 1 is returned.

Pause   **PAUSE [text]**

This command temporarily stops the batch file. Pause can be followed by a message which will be printed on the screen. If you entered the following line in a batch file:

```
PAUSE Place memory card in drive A
```

the program would be suspended when it reached the PAUSE command and the message Place memory card in drive A would be shown on the screen, together with Strike a key when ready .

REM   **REM [remark]**

REM enables the programmer to document batch files. In other words, you can put explanatory remarks in your batch file. The remarks do not appear when the program is run, but can be read when it is TYPED or printed.

So the following, when included in a batch file, would remain with the program, but would not be executed:

```
REM This command allows you to enter explanations.
```

Shift SHIFT

Batch files can normally accommodate up to 10 variables which are called:

```
%0 %1 %2 %3 %4 %5 %6 %7 %8 %9
```

%0 is used for the batch file name.

SHIFT makes it possible to use more than 10 variables by eliminating the contents of %0 and then moving each variable to the left for each use of the command.

Use COPY CON or the Editor to type in and save the following program which demonstrates the action of SHIFT:

```
DEMSHIFT.BAT

:BEGIN
ECHO OFF
FOR %%P IN (%0) DO ECHO %%P
SHIFT
PAUSE
GOTO BEGIN
```

If you type DEMSHIFT 1 2 3 4 5 6 7 8 9 [Enter], the .BAT file takes its own name and then the numbers which you have typed in, displaying each in turn. It follows the instructions in sequence and returns from GOTO to the label :BEGIN once for every press of a key. Each time it cycles, line two causes it to display the variable, assigned during that pass, to the 0 variable. Therefore, as the variables which you have typed in are shifted left, each passes through 0 and is displayed on the screen. The first item of data assigned to %0 is the file name, so on the first pass the screen displays:

```
ECHO OFF
DEMSHIFT
Strike a key when ready...
```

and on the next:

```
1
Strike a key when ready...
```

and so on:

```
2
Strike a key when ready...
```

```
3
Strike a key when ready...

4
Strike a key when ready...
```

until all the variables typed have been used up. The program can be stopped at any time by pressing [Ctrl]+[C] at the pause stage, and then answering Y when asked if the batch file job is to be terminated. Needless to say, the figures can be replaced by names or letters.

Output redirection

When you ask DOS to show the directory, by typing DIR, it creates an output which is sent to the screen of the Portfolio. There are other commands, like TYPE, which are also capable of producing a fair amount of information. The trouble with the Portfolio is that not much will fit on the screen at any single time, and when it has vanished one has a tendency to forget what had been there. An obvious way to overcome this kind of difficulty is to print the data on paper.

DOS Commands which produce output

All DOS commands producing any kind of output can be set to have the output redirected to a file or printer by using the > character. For example, to send the current directory to a parallel printer on the port LPT1: you would enter:

```
DIR > LPT1:
```

and, providing that the printer is switched on and the parallel interface is connected to the Portfolio, the information will appear on the paper.

If you wanted to send a text file through the optional serial interface to another computer, you could enter:

```
TYPE > COM1:
```

or from the directory to a text file named DIR.TXT:

```
DIR > DIR.TXT
```

Even HELP can be made to send the screen contents to a file. Typing:

```
HELP > HH.TXT [Enter]
```

will write the contents of the help screen to disk, and entering:

```
CHKDSK > CHECK.TXT
```

would send the results of a check on the current disk to a text file which could be loaded into the Editor and examined or altered.

Such commands would overwrite any present files with the same names, but by using

```
DIR >> DIR.TXT[Enter]
```

the information would be appended to an existing file of the same name.

Note that the parallel ports on an IBM type personal computer are designated LPT1:, LPT2:, and LPT3: and that the serial ports are called COM1: and COM2: .

Input Redirection

Information is most frequently sent to the computer by means of the keyboard, but it is also possible to use other types of input. Two common methods, which carry an option to extend beyond the simple transmission of data to the control of processes, are the batch file and remote input from a distant computer via a modem and telephone line.

3

The Address Book

Introduction

The Portfolio's Address Book is really an electronic card index. Each entry can be treated as a card in the index, but unlike the traditional system, individual cards need not be restricted to a specific size. This means that normal limitations on the number of lines which can be written on a paper card do not apply. In computer terminology each card is described as a record, and each card index system as a file. Of course, you can have more than one Address Book card index system, each with a different name. For instance, there could be one for personal friends, and others for business associates, customers, club members and so on.

Each card in an Address Book file can contain any number of lines and a variety of alternative telephone numbers which the Portfolio will dial automatically when you instruct it. Address Book files are automatically sorted using the first character of the first entry line of each card. The order in which characters are sorted is:

First: A - Z;

Next: 0 - 9;

Last: Other characters, according to their ASCII value

How to Use the Address Book

As with the other components of the Portfolio's Applications software, you can start the Address Book by any one of the following methods.

Method 1. Using the main Applications Menu:

From DOS press [J|lJ+[Z] [A]

Selects the main Applications Menu and then the Address Book Menu.

```
                    ┌ (c) DIP 1989 0.392 ┐
  C)Qecho o││ Address Book
  Bad comma││ Calculator
                   ││ Diary
  C)c:\syst││ Editor
                   ││ Setup
  C)c:\syst││ Worksheet
                    └                    ┘
```

The main Applications menu

Method 2. Bypassing the main Applications Menu:

From DOS press [J|lJ +[A]

Bypasses the Main menu and selects the Address Book screen.

Method 3. Typing a command from DOS:

Typing app/a [Enter] from DOS also takes you straight to the Address Book screen and bypasses all menus.

Data Entry

The Address Book has two types of displays; Page Mode and Line Mode. You may see either one of these displays, depending on whether or not the Address Book contains some data.

If the Address Book contains data, the first screen you see will be Line Mode, as shown below, and you obtain Page Mode by pressing [Enter]. Movement back to Page Mode is effected by pressing [Esc].

```
              <---Enter-------
    Page mode    .  Line mode
              ----------Esc-------->
```

Diagram of movement between the two modes

If the Address Book does not contain any data, the first screen presented is that of Page Mode

Line mode is useful for quickly viewing names and telephone numbers, without the addresses, and in Page Mode you can see the whole entry, including the address.

Initially, the default Address Book file, called UNNAMED.ADR, does not contain any data. You are confronted by a blank screen in Page Mode and can place your first entry in the Address Book without changing screens. Data can only be placed in the Address Book from Page Mode.

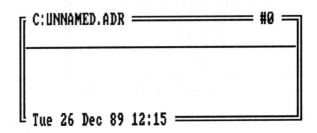

Blank Page Mode screen.

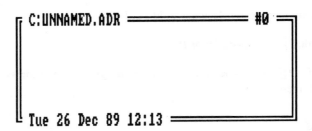

Blank Line Mode screen.

Both Page and Line Mode screens show the current drive and file name at the top left side. The number of records contained in this file are shown after the # on the top right and the day, date and time are shown in the bottom left of the screen.

Entering the First Record

To enter the first name and address, obtain Page Mode, then type in your entry, pressing [Enter] after each line. For example:

```
Joe Bloggs, W:(01) 298 8921, H:(0123) 2988921
Bloggs Bloomers Ltd.,
10, The Causeway,
London E22 5AA
```

```
┌ C:UNNAMED.ADR ══════════ #18 ┐
│ Joe Bloggs, W:(01) 298 8921, H:(0123 │
│                                       │
│ Bloggs Bloomers Ltd.,                 │
│ 10, The Causeway,                     │
│ London E22 5AA                        │
└ Tue 26 Dec 89 12:20 ═════════════════ ┘
```

Page Mode screen containing data.

Telephone Numbers

Telephone numbers should be positioned on the first line (above the bar) and separated from the name and each other by a comma. In this example, the W: is a label which stands for work while the H: means home. The Portfolio's autodialler accepts numbers in parentheses as dialling codes, commas as separators. A number not in parentheses will be treated as a local telephone number. Further details of the format for telephone numbers are given at the end of this chapter.

Editing the Entry

The following keys will delete characters which have been typed into the current or subsequent screens.

[Del]	Delete one character at a time to the right
[Ctrl]+[E]	Delete to the end of the line right of the cursor
[Ctrl]+[B]	Delete to the beginning of the line left of the cursor
[Ctrl]+[L]	Delete whole line
[Ctrl]+[W]	Delete one word to the right of the cursor
[Ctrl]+[Backspace]	Delete one word to the left of the cursor

Ending the entry

At the end of the entry press [Fn][↓] to end the current entry and move to a new blank entry page, or [Esc] to go back to Line Mode.

Movement Round the Screen.

Note that the text is scrollable, up and down, as well as right to left and visa versa. When you type beyond 40 characters, the screen automatically scrolls to a width of 255 and does not start the next line until you press [Enter]. If you are not entering data, the information on the screen may be scrolled up, down or sideways, using the cursor or Control keys.

Key	*Cursor Movement*
[↑]	Up one line
[↓]	Down one line
[Fn][↑]	Move up one screen
[Fn][↓]	Move down one screen
[←]	Left one character
[→]	Right one character
[Ctrl]+[→]	Right one word
[Ctrl]+[←]	Left one word
[Fn][←]	Go to beginning of line
[Fn][→]	Go to end of line
[Ctrl]+[A]	Go to beginning of current file
[Ctrl]+[Z]	Go to end of current file
[Ctrl]+[U]	Return to former cursor position.

Further Entries

If you have used [Esc] to return to Line Mode, press [Tab] to obtain another blank record card. If you have just finished filling in a record card in Page Mode, press [Fn][↓] to move to the new blank card. This is filled in the same way as the first.

When you have entered several addresses you can move from record to record, in Page Mode, by pressing [Fn][↓] to go forward and [Fn][↑] to go backwards.

Saving the Entries

When you have filled in all the cards you wish, the whole card index should be saved as a file. The data is automatically saved to UNNAMED.ADR when you press [Esc] to leave the Address Book and then [Enter] when the Save ? box is displayed with the block cursor on the Yes option.

Function keys

In the Address Book pressing [Fn] followed by a number key enables certain operations to be carried out immediately.

[Fn][1] or [/]\[\]	Display Address Book main menu
[Fn][2]	Get general help
[Fn][3]	Use the Clipboard
[Fn][4]	Recover previously deleted characters
[Fn][5]	Toggle screen frame on or off
[Fn][6] to [Fn][10]	Not available.

Main Address Book Menu

Various command options for processing data in the Address Book may be selected by using the command menus and function keys.

How to get the main Address Book menu on the screen

When the Portfolio is showing the Address Book screen press:

[Fn]+[1] *or*

[/][/]

The main Address Book command menu

The topics which follow are discussed in the sequence of their positions on the command menu and can be obtained either by placing the cursor on the appropriate initial letter of the item required and pressing [Enter], or simply by typing in the initial letter: e.g. typing [C] will bring up the the cards menu.

Files . . .

Pressing [F] from the main Address Book menu will cause the files menu to be shown on the screen. On it there are six options.

The Files menu

New

Pressing [N] will clear all data from the memory and start you off on a new, completely blank, file. You should therefore make sure that anything of value in the current file is saved before using this option. The Portfolio provides a safeguard, so that if anything has been added to a file since it was last saved you are given the chance to resave by entering [Y] or to discard by entering [N] in the selection box shown on the screen.

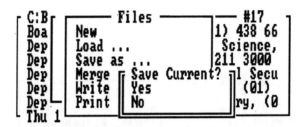

The Yes/No box

The new blank file name reverts to UNNAMED.ADR when [N] is selected.

Load . . .

Using [L] will cause an already existing file to be loaded into the Address Book. A dialogue box will be shown with the default file name.

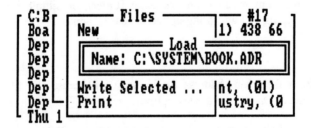

The Load dialogue box

You can load the default file by pressing [Enter], or enter a new file name, directory, and drive, or any one of these. Using the [Del] key will allow you to erase the existing information for appropriate editing.

If the file present in the Address Book when you attempt to load another has not been altered the new file will be loaded.

Accepting the default file name

If the file present in the Address Book when you attempt to load the default file has been altered and still has the default file name, the old file will be loaded without warning and any information entered into the existing file will be lost.

Using a new file name

If the current file has been altered and you enter a new file name in the dialogue box an option box is shown on the screen, so that you get the chance to save the current file before loading a new one. As with the New command, simply move the cursor to Yes to save or No to discard the current file and press [Enter]. Pressing [Esc] returns you to the Load menu.

If you are not sure of the files which are available for loading, they can be viewed on any drive in any directory:

Type [:][Enter] to view all files and subdirectories in the current directory.

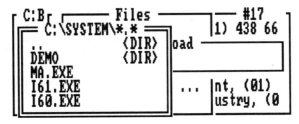

The directory and file list superimposed on the load dialogue box

Type [*][Enter] to view all Address files from the current directory.

If you want to change the drive and/or directory, type the path name into the dialogue box. If no file name is given, the wild card *.ADR is automatically entered and then all the address files in that directory will be shown. All files and directories will be shown if you type in the path name followed by *.* . If the file list is long, you can scroll up or down by using the cursor keys [↑] or [↓].

A file can then be loaded, simply by placing the cursor on the file name and pressing [Enter]. If you use *.*, please note that ASCII files other than address files can be loaded.

Save as . . .

A file can be saved under its existing name, or a new name with this command. Press [S] from the Files menu and the Save dialogue box will be shown on the screen.

If [Enter] is pressed the file will be saved under the default name without warning.

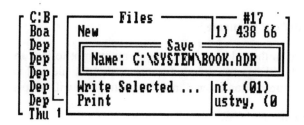

The Save as... dialogue box

You can alter the file name in the dialogue box by using the [Del] and cursor keys. If you try to save a file with a new name to one which already exists in the same directory, the Portfolio will ask if it should overwrite the existing file. If you answer yes, by pressing [Enter], the data in the file on the disk will be deleted. Otherwise move the cursor to No and press [Enter], or back out with [Esc].

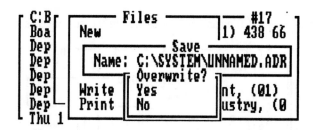

The overwrite dialogue box

Entering [*] in the dialogue box will allow you to view existing files, as you may with the Load command.

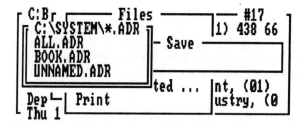

The Save dialogue box and listed files superimposed

Merge . . .

Pressing [M] from the Files menu will allow you to merge a file on disk with one which is already loaded. Any new addresses merged will be sorted into alphabetical order, with those which already exist.

When you select Merge, you may either enter a new name into the box, or enter * to view a list of available Address Book files. Files in other directories, or on memory cards, may be merged by entering the appropriate path name.

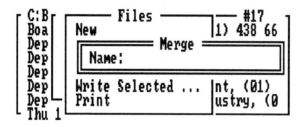

The Merge box awaiting entry

The current file name is not altered by the merging process, so you may wish to use a new name when you save the merged file.

Write Selected

If the Card:Select option has been used to compile a selected list of addresses, these can be saved to a new file, for future use, by using the Write Selected command. Press [W] from the Files menu and enter your new file name, and if necessary, path, into the box shown on the screen. If the current file name is used, all data in the current file will be replaced by the selection!

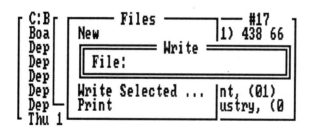

The Write Select box

As usual, a list of existing files can be viewed by entering [*][Enter], or simply pressing [Enter] when the blank box is shown.

Print

Pressing [P] prints the current Address Book file to a printer via the optional parallel or serial interfaces, if fitted. Even if an interface is not fitted the printing box will be shown on the screen.

The printing box

Character size, margins and page length are defined by using the Setup menu, so please refer to that chapter for further details.

The Address Book files are in ASCII format and can, therefore, be loaded into a PC word processor for printing. They could also be transferred to a PC database, file program or mail merge system. Chapter 10 shows the format of an Address Book file.

Search

To use the Search option press [Fn][1] and [S] when the Address Book command menu is displayed. These actions bring up a dialogue box which asks you to enter the data which you want to search for in the current Address Book file. From Line Mode press [Fn][1] and then [S].

When starting a search for names in the Address Book, it is good practice to use [Ctrl]+[A] to position the cursor on the first entry. Do this before the menu appears on the screen.

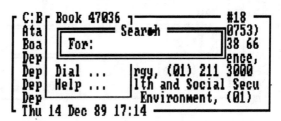

The Search dialogue box

Enter the characters you want to find. Next, press [↑] to search up through the list or [↓] to search down. After the search has been carried out and data found, the cursor will be left at the position in the list where the first piece of data has been found. To continue searching in the same direction for the same data, press [Ctrl]+[S]. When the dialogue box is showing, pressing [Enter] will cause the search for the data in the box to be continued in the same direction as previously.

If the data is not found, the Portfolio's screen will show the message 'String not found'.

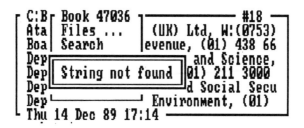

The String Not Found report

The 'String not found' message is also shown when the cursor is actually on the information which you have entered in the dialogue box. It is therefore worth reading the text on that line!

Any part of an entry may be specified, but it is also possible to enter a keyword with the data in the Address Book. For example all big spenders might be identified by adding a unique code '@BiS' on the name line. It is then possible to select all those people in this particular category by using the code and moving through the list by pressing Enter after each one is identified.

At a later time, you could save this list of names and addresses to a special file by using the Cards Select command in the Cards menu, as indicated below.

Cards . . .

The Cards Menu may be obtained from either Line or Page Mode by using [Fn][1] and then pressing the [C] key. Its purpose is to allow the entry of information on new cards, deletion of unwanted cards, selection of cards containing specific information and the temporary addition of a prefix to a telephone number already listed in the Address Book.

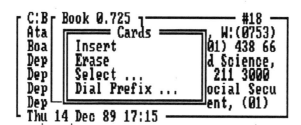

The Cards menu

Insert

Pressing [I] from the Cards Menu allows a card to be placed in the current Address Book file. When the blank Page Mode is shown on the screen, enter the new name and address and then press [Fn][↑] to return to the Line Mode. Remember that files are always sorted as they are loaded into the Address Book, so that the correct alphabetical positioning of the card is guaranteed.

Erase

Care is needed when using this option, in order to avoid unintentional erasures. Its purpose is to allow you to delete an entry from the current Address Book file. Ensure that the Address Book is in Line Mode when you select Erase. As soon as the [E] is pressed, the name under which the cursor is situated will be deleted. The whole of the entry on the current card will be removed. The cursor then moves down to the next name.

If you make a mistake and wish to recover the lost data from the current card, simply press [Fn][4] and its contents will reappear in Page Mode. [Esc] will get you back to Line Mode.

From Line Mode, it is also possible, and perhaps easier, to delete entries by simply pressing the [Del] key. Each time the [Del] key is pressed, the card belonging to the name on which the cursor is resting is deleted. The list then moves up to fill the blank space and the cursor rests on the initial letter of the entry which was underneath the one deleted. Lost data can still be recovered by pressing [Fn][4]. In fact, you can recover many successively deleted normal address entries this way.

Select ...

This command selects cards according to the information which you tell the system to search for. Press [S] from the Cards menu and a dialogue box will then be shown.

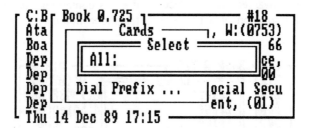

The Select dialogue box

For instance, if your address file lists people in various cities, entering 'London', will select only those cards containing this word, excluding the rest. If [Esc] is pressed, the London list will be lost and the screen shows the original list which will, of course, still include the London addresses. If, instead of [Esc], you press [Fn] [1] to get the Address Book menu, then [F] to get files and from this [W] for Write Selected, the London list can be saved as a separate file. For example, entering London in the Write Selected dialogue box, will result in the London addresses being saved to a London file.

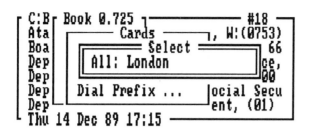

```
 ┌ C:B ┌ Book 0.725 ┐──────────── #18 ──┐
 │ Ata ┌──── Cards ─────┐, W:(0753)
 │ Boa │ ══════ Select ══════ │ 66
 │ Dep │ │ All: London │ │ce,
 │ Dep │ │ │00
 │ Dep │ Dial Prefix ... │ocial Secu
 │ Dep └────────────────────┘ent, (01)
 └ Thu 14 Dec 89 17:15 ───────────┘
```

The Select dialogue box with London entered

Select allows one to search for all available characters, so special telephone numbers can also be obtained. For example, to select all the people with London telephone numbers, enter (071 or 081) in the dialogue box.

Dial Prefix . . .

This command will place any number entered in the dialogue box ahead of a telephone number selected with the Dial option of the Address Book menu. Select [D] from the Cards menu, enter the number in the dialogue box and press [Enter]. The Portfolio then returns to the Address Book Line Mode and the prefixed number is shown in the top right corner of the screen after P: . For as long as the prefix remains, all numbers called with the Dial command will automatically have the additional prefix numerics placed in front.

To remove a prefix, obtain the Dial Prefix dialogue box and place the cursor at the beginning of any number previously entered. Then press [Del] until the numbers no longer appear in the box and finally, [Enter].

Dial

Note that the Portfolio's autodialler will at present only work with telephone exchanges which accept DTMF tone dialling. In the U.K., this means that you can only use it for dialling a number on one of the new System X exchanges. The installation of System X seems to be rather patchy throughout the country, but a list of local exchanges which have been updated can be obtained from your operator.

To automatically dial a telephone number from your address list, first place the mouthpiece of the telephone over the loudspeaker in the lid of the Portfolio. Next, obtain the Address Book menu by pressing [Fn][1] while the Line or Page Modes are displayed, enter [D] and the telephone number corresponding to the card displayed in Page Mode will be shown in a box on the screen. If you press [Enter], the number on which the cursor is situated will be tone dialled. When the tones have stopped, pick up your telephone and listen for a reply. When two numbers are shown, either one may be selected by moving the cursor.

The Dial box with two numbers

The dialogue box also shows an Edit option. If you select this, another number can be entered, and this is the one which the computer will dial. The new number is shown beneath the permanent number in the Edit box, but will not replace the one(s) shown in the permanent address file. Therefore, the Edit option provides an opportunity to call someone not included in current address file, or to ring a temporary number.

Format of telephone number entries

Parentheses indicate a code, e.g. (071) or (021) or (0544). You are not obliged to list a dialling code. For example, (071) 812 8900 might appear as 812 8900 in the address list of somebody living in London, where there is no need to dial the code before the number. Even if you do include a dialling code, the Dial menu will give you the chance to omit the code when dialling.

Commas are used to separate different telephone numbers. 8900, 8901 are ,therefore, alternative numbers.

A space, full stop or minus sign can be used to insert a pause in the dialling sequence. This is sometimes of value in international dialling. For example, if you were calling an exchange called Scottsdale in Arizona, U.S.A. the dialling codes could be entered as (010-1-602-998) followed by the four figure subscriber number. In your address list the whole number would appear as (010-1-602-998) 8913.

Square brackets indicate comments. If placed before the telephone number, the comment will not be included in the Dial box, but if placed after the telephone number it is. E.g. Maggie, [Not Fri or Sat] 071 369 6969 would be displayed as:

(071) 369 6969
369 6969

while Maggie, (071) 369 6969 [Not Fri or Sat] would show as

(0711) 369 6969 [Not Fri or Sat]
369 6969 [Not Fri or Sat]

A slash may be used to separate alternative numbers. If Maggie has more than one number, an economical entry in the address list would be:

```
Maggie, [Not Fri or Sat] (071) 369 6969/8
```

instead of:

```
Maggie, [Not Fri or Sat] (071) 369 6969, (071) 369 6968
```

You should note that where a single digit is entered in this way it relates only to the digit before it. Therefore using 6969/0 would *not* produce 6969 and 6970, but 6969 and 6960.

To redial a number already used, press [Ctrl]+[D]

Help

The Help screen

Help is the last option on the menu. If you press [H] from the main Address Book menu, or [Fn][1][H] from either screen mode, scrollable command summaries are shown on the Portfolio's screen. You may then choose between:

Address Book Menu Help

This section briefly explains the Search, Cards and Dial options.

File handling

This is a general screed on the various options for filing and printing with the applications software. It also shows the default file extensions.

Dialing

Explains in reasonable detail the method and formats used to dial numbers from the Portfolio.

General Help

As with all the Applications software, you can select the general help screens by pressing: [Fn][2]

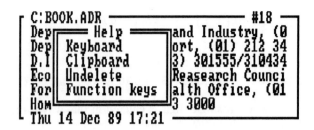

The General help box

You will then be able to scroll through the relevant summary help text by using the up and down arrows.

Keyboard

When the General Help menu shows on the screen, press [K] and the Portfolio's screen will produce a summary of the Portfolio PC key equivalents. Included in the same text are brief details of the effects of pressing the Atari ([⌒]|[⌄]), [Lock] and [Fn] keys.

The same information is included in Chapter 1 of this book, under the heading Keyboard.

Clipboard

Pressing [C] from the General Help menu causes the screen to show a summary of the functions of various options which can be chosen from the Clipboard Menu. In this book, detailed information about the Clipboard is given in Chapter 7.

Undelete

When [U] is pressed from the General Help menu, information is given on the use of the [Fn][4] key combination to recover deleted text.

When an item has been deleted, it can be recovered by pressing [Fn][4], if necessary repeatedly. The cursor should be in the position where the recovered text is to be placed.

Successive deletions may be recovered by this means, regardless of their origins. Recovery of data from one Application to another is enabled by switching Undelete save to On in Setup (see Chapter 7).

Function keys

This option, obtained by pressing [F], gives a summary list of the effects obtainable by using the function, control, and other keys. The text provided on screen covers the use of the keys in all the Applications software. In this book the same information is included in Chapter 1, under the headings **Function keys and their effects** and **General text editing functions**, as well as in the various chapters dealing with particular Applications.

The [Return] key mentioned in the Help text displayed by the Portfolio is the exact equivalent of the key termed [Enter] in this book.

4

The Calculator

The Portfolio's Calculator serves as a capable number processor, of particular value when you do not want to get involved with the Worksheet. It has five memories and displays all the calculations made.

The Calculator's function is ephemeral, in the sense that no files may be saved; Calculator data cannot be saved to the Clipboard and may not be transferred to other applications software. Therefore, you cannot recall anything, you exit from the Calculatoronce lost, though you can make use of the Calculator's memories. If you want to transfer numerical data to other applications software, or to save it to disk, you should use the Worksheet.

In order to save keying in an excess of figures, it is possible to edit a series of entries in the Calculator's display, so as to correct mistakes and show 'what if' results.

Several calculating modes are available, including fixed, scientific and engineering, and there are also a variety of functions:

factorials, percentage tools, one-key negation, square roots, brackets, powers, various number formats, printer output.

How to use the Calculator

To start in the Calculator press

[J|\] + [C]   or   [J|\] + [Z] [C]

or type app/c from the operating system to obtain the Calculator screen.

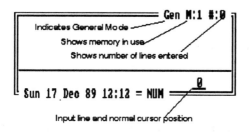

The Calculator Screen

When the Calculator is switched on, the keyboard is automatically put into numeric keypad mode, indicated by the abbreviation NUM at the bottom of the screen. It is therefore convenient to enter data and operators into the Calculator by using the red number keys which form the numeric keypad of the Portfolio, instead of using the normal keyboard numbers which are printed in black and situated along the top row. In fact the only 0 (zero) key which will function is the one printed in red.

Single calculations in General Mode

When the Calculator is first used it is set for General Format, as indicated in the screen frame.

Simple arithmetic in General Mode

Addition is easy:

Key in a figure, then +, and then the figure to be added to the first. Finally, press the = key.

E.g. 1 + 2 = 3

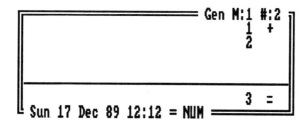

Diagram of screen after simple addition

Subtraction is much the same:

Key in the figure, then −, and then the figure to be subtracted from the first. Finally, press the = key.

Multiplication:

Key in the figure to be multiplied, then *, and then the figure to multiply by. Next, press the = key.

E.g. 10 * 2 = 20

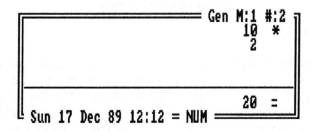

To divide:

Key in the figure to be divided, and then /, and then the figure to divide by and lastly, press the = key.

E.g. 10 / 2 = 5

In division operations, the result is not always exact, so if the following sum is done, the screen will show a number beyond the decimal point:

10 / 2.6 = 3.8461538461538

The number of digits displayed here is greater than that usually seen on an ordinary Calculator, but note that some figures can never be ex-pressed exactly in decimals, no matter how many digits are displayed.

Calculations with more than one operator

The use of brackets - chained calculations

When using the Calculator it is important to realise that there is an order of precedence in the basic addition (+), subtraction (-), multiplication (*) and division (/) operations. Multiplication and division are always calculated before addition and subtraction. The way to avoid errors, is to use brackets. Whatever is included in the brackets will be calculated first. At least 50 sets of brackets may be used in a calculation.

E.g. 2 + 3 * 4 = 14

Whereas (2 + 3) * 4 = 20

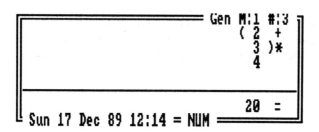

Screen showing the use of brackets

The same sort of thing occurs in division:

$10 + 2 / 2 = 11$

and:

$(10 + 2) / 2 = 6$

Use of the percentage (%) key

To add a percentage to a number:

Enter the number, then press the + key, enter the number of percent to be added, and finally press the % key.

E.g. 100 + 15 %, with no other keys pressed gives 115

To subtract a percentage from a number: Enter the number, then press the – key, enter the number of percent to be subtracted and press the % key.

E.g. 100 – 10 %, with no other keys pressed, gives 90

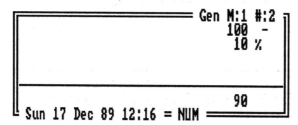

Diagram showing percentage subtraction

The Portfolio offers two other percentage functions:

Calculate Markup

This function calculates the percentage figure as a percentage of the final figure in the sum. It is especially useful in calculating commissions, where the number must be expressed as a percentage of the final selling price. E.g. Conusall Ltd. pays a wholesale price of £100 each for televisions. They must make 50% of the selling price in order to make a profit. Enter 100 then press * and 50, and lastly press the % key:

100 * 50 % = 200

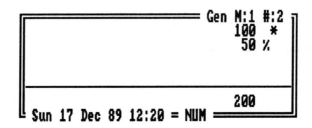

An example mark up calculation

Calculate Markdown

Like the markup function, markdown calculates a percentage of the final figure.

E.g. Bodge's D.I.Y. sell certain items at a V.A.T. inclusive price and they need to calculate what V.A.T., at the 15% rate, they would have to pay on a selling price of £59. Enter 59, then press /, then 15 and %. The calculation gives a 15% markdown, so the VAT at 15% is £59.00 – £51.30 = £7.70:

59 / 15 % = 51.30

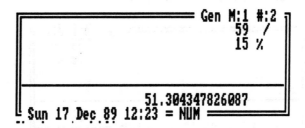

An example markdown calculation

In financial calculations, it is best to set the display to only two decimal places. Press [Fn][1] and then press F for Format; press F again to select Fixed and when you see the entry box, type 2. Then press Enter.

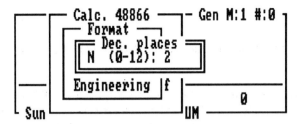

The format decimal places entry box

Other Operators

Powers

The ^ character, obtained by pressing [Shift]+[6], is used for calculating powers (i.e. the black 6 key).

E.g. pressing keys [1][0][shift]+[6][3][Enter] calculates the value of 10 to the power 3, which is 1000.00.

Pressing [3][*][10][Shift]+[6][3][Enter] calculates the value of

$3 * 10^3$ which = 3000.00

Root

The square root of a number, indicated by √, is obtained by entering the number and then pressing [Fn][7]. The result is shown on the entry line.

E.g. [4][Fn][7] gives 2.00.

The nth root can be obtained by using the formula:

nth root of x = x to the power ($1/_n$)

E.g. To obtain the cube root of 7 enter:

[7][Shift]][6][(][1][/][3][)][Enter]

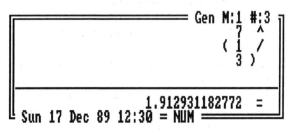

Screen showing the cube root of 7 calculation

Editing

Mistakes can be edited out and additional data entered by using the Calculator's editing facility.

Normally, the cursor rests on the input line below the bar and the data entered scrolls up the screen line by line with the operator, as each is keyed in. Prior to pressing [Enter] (which is the same as =), these lines of data can be recalled for editing or inspection.

When the up arrow [↑] is pressed the cursor moves above the line. By using the cursor keys for vertical and lateral movements, together with the [Del] and number pad numerics, the figures and operators in the cur-rent calculation can be edited and corrected. Or you may simply re-examine your entries and then return to the results line.

[Esc] will restore the current data deleted by [Del]. Once you have moved the cursor from a line which has been deleted, using [Esc] will not restore it. Additionally, [Ctrl]+[L] will delete a whole line of data and [Fn][4] can be used to recover it. The memories cannot be used during the editing process.

When the editing process is complete, press [Enter] (= on the number pad) and the data will be recalculated, the cursor returned to the input line and the new result displayed. Further data can be added to the input line if the editing is terminated by an operator.

Function keys

To obtain the various functions, simply press the [Fn] key, followed by a number. Certain operations, discussed elsewhere in this chapter and indicated below, will then be carried out directly.

[Fn][1]	Display the main Calculator menu
[Fn][2]	Get help for the current application
[Fn][3]	Not used
[Fn][4]	Recover deleted characters
[Fn][5]	Toggle screen frame on or off
[Fn][6]	Not used
[Fn][7]	Gives the square root of the number displayed - indicated by the √ sign
[Fn][8]	Add the number displayed to the default memory (M+)
[Fn][9]	Subtract the number displayed from the default memory (M-)
[Fn][0]	In the Portfolio Owner's Manual [F10] is supposed to recall and clear memory (MR or MC), but this key sequence does not exist! [Fn][0] is the key sequence for F10.

[Fn][1]+[0] will only produce the main Calculator menu, so press [Fn][0] once to recall the contents of the default memory. If the com-bination [Fn][0] is pressed again the default memory will clear to 0.

Main Calculator Command Menu

First obtain the main Calculator menu by pressing:

[Fn] [1]

or

[ ]|[ ]

from the Calculator screen.

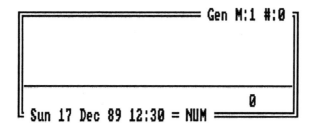

Main Calculator menu

The various options obtainable from the Calculator menu are described below, with examples where appropriate.

Memories . . .

From the main Calculator menu, press [M] and the Memories menu will be displayed. The Calculator has five memories. Each memory in use is shown in the top left of the screen frame. The memory in current use is shown in the top right of the frame. A number may be added to or taken away from any of the memories, and each memory may be recalled or cleared. If the memory number is not set, the default is Memory 1.

Plus

This option can be activated by pressing [P] from the Memories menu, or [Fn][8] from the Calculator screen when a menu is not displayed. The figure displayed on the entry line of the Caclulator screen can then be added to the default memory. When this has been done the Portfolio's screen will show M+ next to the figure.

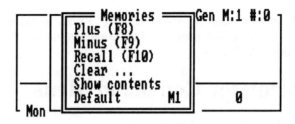

The Calculator Memories menu

Minus

In a similar fashion, the minus option, obtained by pressing [M] from the Memories menu, or [Fn][9] when no menu is displayed, will take the figure displayed on the entry line Calculator screen away from any number in the default memory. M- will then be shown next to the number on the screen. The default memory will also allow negative values, so that taking 3 away from a memory containing 2 will result in a total of -1 in that memory.

Recall

This option allows you to examine the contents of any memory. Press [R] from the Calculator Memories menu, and press [Enter] the number of the memory which you want to see.

The Memories menu then vanishes and the figure stored in the selected memory is shown on the entry line.

When a menu is not shown on the Calculator screen, pressing [Fn][0] will cause the contents of the default memory to be shown on the entry line, with MR beside it. But be careful, pressing [Fn][0] a second time will clear the default memory to 0. When this has been done, MC is shown on the entry line, beside the figure which has been cleared.

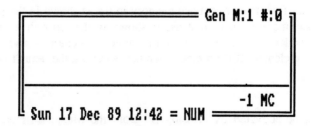

The screen display after pressing [Fn][0] twice

Clear . . .

All or any one of the Memories can be cleared to 0. From the Memories menu press
[C] and then enter A for All, or the number of the memory to be cleared.

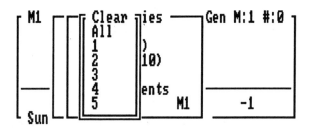

The Memories Clear option box

Show contents

From the Memories menu press [S] and the contents of all five Memories are shown
on the screen. [Esc] returns you to the Memories menu.

Default

This option is used to set the number of the memory which will currently be in use.
From the Memories menu press [D] and then enter the number of the memory which
is to be used.

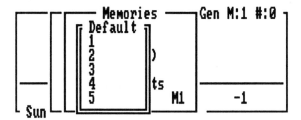

The Memories Default option box

Display

Display, is an option on the main Calculator menu. To obtain it, press [Fn][1] and
then [D] when the menu is shown. Its purpose is to allow the user to choose whether
or not to use a comma to separate every three figures beyond a decimal point, as in
1,000 and to allow a choice be-tween a comma or a full stop as a decimal point
indicator, as in 1.23 or 1,23 . When [D] is pressed an option box appears on the
Calculator screen.

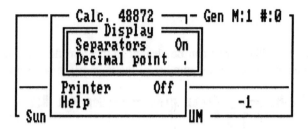

The Calculator Display option box

Pressing [S] will toggle the separators on or off. Pressing [D] will toggle between a comma and a full stop as the decimal point. If the comma is used as the decimal point it will not also be used as a triad separator, and a full stop is used instead. Therefore, the number display will be as shown below:

Separator switched On

1,000.00 if the comma is chosen as a separator; or

1.000,00 if the comma is chosen as the decimal point and the separator is toggled On.

You might feel that this is confusing, if so switch the separator off when you must use a comma as the decimal point.

Separator switched Off

1000.00 when Decimal point switched to full stop (.) or 1000,00 when Decimal point switched to comma (,) .

Format . . .

Four formats are available for figures in the Calculator and these appear on the Format menu. From the Calculator screen, press [Fn][1] and then [F]. The Format menu will then appear.

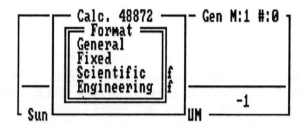

The Calculator Format menu

To select a format, just press the initial letter of the format required. Fill in the decimal places option box, press [Enter] and the Calculator will work in the number format chosen until altered again. The various number formats which you can select are:

General

This configuration enables calculations to be done with a floating decimal point. The figure 1000 will be shown as:

1000.00

or its equivalent, depending on the separator and decimal points selected.

Fixed

If this option is chosen the decimal point will be fixed to allow between 0 and 11 decimal places to be viewed on the screen. From the Format menu, press [F] and a dialogue box will appear. Enter the number of decimal places required and press [Enter]. A format of two decimal places is used for most calculations involving cash.

Scientific

Scientific notation will be used when [S] is selected from the Format menu. In scientific work it is frequently necessary to use large or very small numbers. Therefore it is useful to be able to present such numbers in a condensed form. Various base numbers can be used in scientific and engineering notation. The exponents expressed by the Portfolio's Calculator are to the base 10. E.g. the figure 10000 can also be expressed as 10 where 4 is the exponent to the base 10.

As an example, choose [S] from the format menu and press [2][Enter] when the dialogue box for the decimal display is shown. This will give you a display of two decimal places.

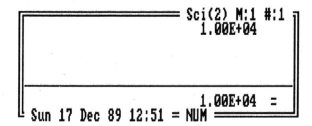

The Calculator screen in Scientific format

When the Calculator screen is shown again, press the keys for 10000 and press [Enter]. The result is shown as 1.00E+04 on the entry line.

You could select any decimal display between 0 and 11. This does not af-fect the display of the exponent, but simply allows you to see more digits behind the decimal point, as well as giving you the power of 10.

Try entering .0001. In this case, the exponent in the number, 10^{-4}, is negative; the figure is four places behind the decimal point, displayed as 1.00E-04.

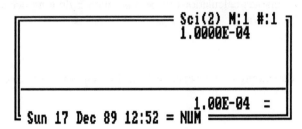

The screen after entering .00001 in scientific format

Scientific notation Calculators become really useful when they allow people to avoid a lot of long winded arithmetic or algebraic work. For instance, problems like:

x = (74000 x 0.00075)/170

are not immediately evident as powers of 10.

Try it. Key in (followed by 74000, then *, next .00075 and) ; next enter / and 170. Lastly press Enter. The figure 3.26E-01 is shown on the screen.

which, in general notation, would be expressed as .3265 If more decimal places are chosen at the Format selection, greater accuracy is achieved in the calculation. For instance, the same calculation done with a display of four decimal places would yield 3.2647E-01

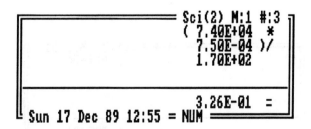

An example of a scientific calculation

When compared with a dedicated scientific Calculator, the Portfolio does not have so many built in functions and neither will it allow the direct entry of exponential numbers.

Engineering

The Engineering format is virtually the same as the scientific format, except that the exponent is fixed at 3. This means that numbers are expressed in terms of 100 instead of 10. Therefore, with two decimal places selected, entering 10000 results in a display of 10.00E+03 on the entry line.

Breakdown

The Breakdown command is a toggle between off and on. Its function is to allow a full display of the numeric breakdown during percentage calcula-tions. Obtain the Calculator menu by key presses [Fn][1]. The current state of Breakdown will be shown with the menu display.

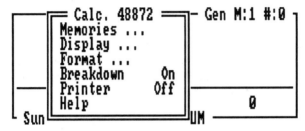

The Calculator menu with Breakdown switched On

As soon as [B] is selected breakdown is toggled on or off and you are returned to the Calculator screen immediately. If you want only to check the condition of Breakdown, just press [Fn][1] and then back out with [Esc].

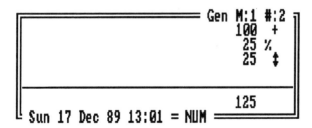

Breakdown On

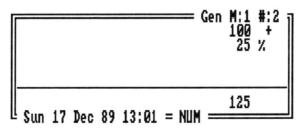

Breakdown Off

When Breakdown is switched to On, percentage calculations are shown as the data entered, the interim data and the result. The number which is shown alongside the double headed arrow is the amount which has been added to the original value to produce the result which has been calculated.

Printer

Printer output can be toggled on or off by pressing [P] from the Calculator menu. The current state of the Printer command is shown on the menu. In order to obtain printed material, you must have previously connected your printer to the Portfolio by an appropriate interface.

When the printer is on, and the cable is connected, all calculations are printed as soon as [Enter] is pressed.

Note also that if you set the page to 0 in the Setup menu, form feeds (FF) will be suppressed and your printed calculations will follow, one after the other, on the same page in the printer. If FF is not suppressed, the printer will move on to the next page after printing a single calculation.

Help

In common with the other applications software, the Help option on the menu serves as an *aide memoire*. Guidance is given for the Calculator's Memory, Display separators, Format, Breakdown and Printer options.

Pressing [Fn][2] brings the general Help menu to the screen with its Keyboard, Clip-board, Undelete and Function keys option.

5

The Diary

Introduction

Diaries tend to be very personal items, but apart from the purely personal data that a diary will inevitably contain, it can play an important part in scheduling one's use of time and as a real time event recorder.

The Portfolio's Diary will allow you to schedule and record both the personal and professional aspects of your life, as long as you take the warning to renew the machine's batteries regularly. More specifically, you can write and edit appointments for any time, any day. Additionally, the Diary will allow you to move appointments from one time or day to another and set single or repeating alarms. When set, the alarm will sound, even when the machine is not being used. The Diary can also be searched for various pieces of data and its files saved, printed or transferred to another computer.

The Portfolio's Diary functions in both Calendar and Diary modes. When you first select Diary, the Calendar Mode is displayed. If you press Enter the display alters to the Diary mode.

How to use the Diary

Method 1. Using the main Applications Menu:

From DOS press   [J|\J]+[Z][D]

Pressing these keys selects the main Applications menu and then the Diary.

Method 2. Bypassing the main Applications Menu:

From DOS press [⏎|⏎+[D]

Pressing these keys bypasses the main Applications menu and goes directly to the Diary.

Method 3. Typing a command from DOS:

From DOS type app/d to bypass all menus.

Any of these actions will cause the Portfolio to present the Calendar screen.

Calendar Mode

With the Calendar on the screen the block cursor should be blinking on the current date, assuming that this has been correctly set. Refer to the chapter on DOS to see how to set the date and time.

```
┌ C:DIARY.DRY ═══════════════════ 3 ═┐
│1990  Sun Mon Tue Wed Thu Fri Sat    │
│Jan:   7   8   9  10  11  12  13      │
│      14  15  16  17  18  19  20      │
│      21  22  23  24  25  26  27      │
│      28  29  30  31   1   2   3      │
│Feb:   4   5   6   7   8   9  10      │
└ Tue 26 Dec 89 10:58 ════════════════┘
```

Calendar startup screen

Movement Round the Screen

The following keys allow you to move the cursor through the scrolling Calendar:

[←]	back one day
[→]	forward one day
[↑]	back one week (up one line)
[↓]	forward one week (down one line)
[Fn][PgUp]	screen up 3 lines
[Fn][PgDn]	screen down 3 lines
[Ctrl]+[A]	move to first entry or appointment
[Ctrl]+[Z]	move to last entry or appointment
[Fn][Home]	return to current date
[Ctrl]+[U]	return to last cursor position
[Esc]	returns you to the DOS system

When you enter appointments and set alarms, they are indicated on the Calendar screen by means of various symbols which will be explained later.

Press [Enter] to change to Diary Mode.

Diary mode

When you press [Enter], the Calendar will vanish and the screen shows Diary Mode, with a display of the date on which the cursor was positioned in Calendar Mode when Enter was pressed. If you would like to return to today's date, press [Fn][Home].

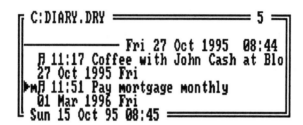

Diary Mode display with some appointments entered

Above the bar is a blank area for the entry of data. Below the bar there is a scrollable list of the appointments in the Diary in order of date and time. If your Portfolio is new, you won't have any entries!

Note that the date shown on the bar is the Diary date. When entries have been made in the Diary, these match the entry on which the cursor is currently resting. Watch them alter as you scroll up and down the list by means of the [↑] and [↓] keys.

How to make an entry in the Diary

If the appointment is for the date and time shown on the bar of the Diary screen, simply type in your entry and press [Enter].

For instance, if the screen looks like the one below:

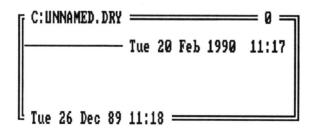

A startup screen

and you type in:

```
Coffee with John Cash at Bloom's [Enter]
```

the entry will be placed immediately in your Diary and appear below the entry bar:

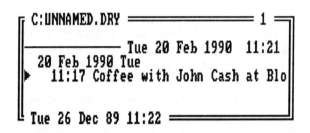

Entry placed in the Diary

If the appointment which you want to record is for another time and date, both the date and time must be entered ahead of the comment.

```
21/1/90 11.30 Sat on dog[Enter]
```

If you had another appointment on the same day, it could be inserted, by using the same date on the bar. You would therefore only need to type:

```
12.30 Take dog to vets [Enter]
```

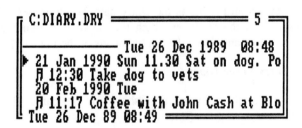

Screen showing the entry in position among others

Note that the time can be entered using either a full stop or a colon as a separator as 10:30 or 10.30

The date can also be set from Calendar Mode by placing the cursor on the date and pressing [Enter] to move back into the Diary mode.

You can use either / or - to separate the figures in dates. The order in which the day, month and year are presented is determined by the country code in the CONFIG.SYS file which DOS uses when it first starts up. You can alter it to suit yourself. For more detail. refer to the chapter on DOS.

When your appointment has been entered in the Diary, the entry line will clear and the appointment will take its place in order of date and time. Entries can be made to repeat automatically by using the Repeat option on the Diary menu. This is described later in the chapter.

Movement round the Diary screen

[→]	moves pointer eight characters right
[←]	moves pointer eight characters left
[↑]	moves pointer up list
[↓]	moves pointer down list
[Fn][PgUp]	screen up 3 lines
[Fn][PgDn]	screen down 3 lines
[Ctrl]+[A]	move to first entry or appointment
[Ctrl]+[Z]	move to last entry or appointment
[Fn][Home]	return to current date
[Ctrl]+[U]	return to last cursor position
[Esc]	returns you to DOS system

Editing Entries

If you point to an entry and then press Enter, that entry will appear above the bar and can be edited.

```
┌ C:UNNAMED.DRY ══════════════ 3 ═┐
│11.30 Sat on dog                 │
│──────────────── Tue 26 Dec 1989   11:51│
│  21 Jan 1990 Sun 11.30 Sat on dog │
│     12:30 Take dog to vets        │
│  20 Feb 1990 Tue                  │
│     11:17 Coffee with John Cash at Blo│
└ Tue 26 Dec 89 11:52 ═════════════┘
```

Screen showing data entry above the date bar ready for editing.

You simply use the delete and character keys in the usual way. It can help to place the Portfolio keyboard into insert mode, by pressing [Shift]+[Ins] to save overwriting parts of an existing entry. When you do this the screen frame will show INS at the bottom right corner.

```
┌ C:UNNAMED.DRY ══════════════ 3 ═┐
│11.30 Sat on dog                 │
│──────────────── Tue 26 Dec 1989   11:51│
│  21 Jan 1990 Sun 11.30 Sat on dog │
│     12:30 Take dog to vets        │
│  20 Feb 1990 Tue                  │
│     11:17 Coffee with John Cash at Blo│
└ Tue 26 Dec 89 11:52 ═══════════ INS ┘
```

Diary screen with INS showing.

When the editing is finished press [Enter] and the entry will again take its place in the list.

The following keys provide various options for deleting characters which have been typed into the Diary entry line.

[Del]	Delete one character at a time to the right
[Backspace]	Delete one character at a time time to the left
[Ctrl]+[E]	Delete to the end of the line right of the cursor
[Ctrl]+[B]	Delete to the beginning of the line left of the cursor
[Ctrl]+[L]	Delete whole line
[Ctrl]+[W]	Delete one word to the right of the cursor
[Ctrl]+[Backspace]	Delete one word to the left of the cursor

Deleting Entries

An entry can be deleted by placing the pointer opposite it by means of the [↑] and [↓] keys and pressing [Del]. The date and time are automatically removed if the deleted entry is the only one for that day.

If you delete an entry which shouldn't have been deleted, press [Fn][4] to recover it.

Function and control keys

The function keys are selected by pressing the Fn key and an appropriate number key.

[Fn][1] or [/|\]	Displays the Diary command menu
[Fn][2]	Requests help
[Fn][3]	Operates the clipboard
[Fn][4]	Recovers the previous character or block which has been deleted
[Fn][5]	Toggles screen frame on or off. Switching off the frame allows two more lines of text to be shown on the screen.

[Fn][6] - [Fn][0] are not used in the Diary.

Main Diary Menu

The Diary Menu allows you to search for data amongst the entries, move and repeat them, set alarms, use the filing system and print to a file or printer.

How to get the main Diary menu on the screen

If one of the Portfolio's Diary screens is showing, you can press [Fn][1] *or* [/|\]

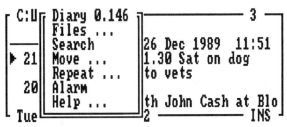

The main Diary menu

This menu only operates fully when the applications software is in Diary Mode. Although the menu can be displayed in Calendar Mode, inappropriate selections from it will not work. Therefore, you may not effectively use Move, Repeat or Alarm at this stage. As usual, to select an option you may press an appropriate letter, or position the cursor on the initial letter of the function required, and press [Enter].

Files . . .

From the main Diary menu, press [F] to get the files menu. All options in it will work from either mode.

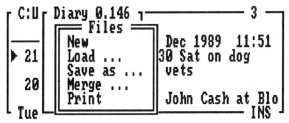

The Files menu

New

Pressing [N] will clear all data from the memory and start you off on a new, completely blank, file. In case you have altered the Diary entries and forgotten to save the altered file, the Portfolio provides a safeguard, so that you are given the chance to resave by entering [Y] or to discard by entering [N] in the selection box shown on the screen.

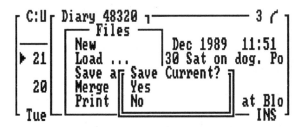

The Yes/No box

The new blank file name reverts to UNNAMED.ADR when [N] is selected.

Load . . .

Using [L] will give you the chance to load an alternative Diary file. A dialogue box will be shown with the default file name.

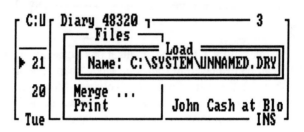

The Load dialogue box.

You can load the default file by pressing [Enter], or enter a new file name, directory, and drive, or any one of these. Using the [Del] key will allow you to erase an existing path and enter a new one.

If the file present in the Diary when you attempt to load another, has not been altered the new file will be loaded.

Accepting the default file name

An unfortunate feature of the Portfolio's filing system is that it ignores alterations to the current file when an attempt is made to load a file of the same name. Therefore, if the file present in the Diary, when you attempt to load the default file, has been altered *and still has the default file name*, the old file will be loaded without warning and *any information entered into the existing file will be lost.*

Using a new file name

If the current file has been altered and you enter a new file name in the dialogue box an option box is shown on the screen, so that you get the chance to save the current file before loading a new one. As with the New command, simply move the cursor to Yes to save or No to discard the current file and press [Enter]. Pressing [Esc] returns you to the Load menu.

If you are not sure of the files which are available for loading, they can be viewed on any drive in any directory:

Type [:][Enter] To view all files and subdirectories in the current directory.

Type [*][Enter] To view all Diary files from the current directory.

If you want to change the drive and or directory, type the path name into the dialogue box. If no file name is given, the wild card *.DRY is automatically entered and all the Diary files in that directory will be shown. All files and directories will be shown if you type in the path name followed by *.* . If the file list is long, you can scroll up or down the names in the box by using the cursor keys [↑] or [↓].

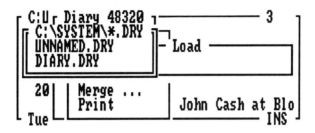

The file list superimposed on the dialogue box.

A file can then be loaded by placing the cursor on the file name and pressing [Enter].

If you use *.*, it is possible to load ASCII files other than Diary files. This can cause some weird effects, as in the illustration below, where an Editor file has been loaded into the Diary which has allocated a time to each line of text. Once you understand the format of the Diary files, you could write a complete list of appointments on a PC word processor and transfer them to the Portfolio for use in the Diary.

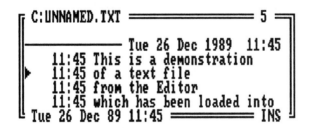

An Editor file loaded into the Diary

Save as...

As in the other applications, a file can be saved under its existing, or a new, name with this command. This could be useful if you wanted to save a tentative list of appointments temporarily. If the appointments were eventually confirmed, the temporary file could be Merged with the main one.

Press [S] from the Files menu and the Save dialogue box will be shown on the screen.

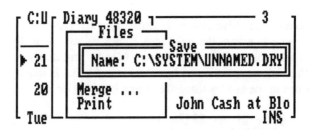

The Save dialogue box.

If [Enter] is pressed the file will be saved under the default name without warning.

You can also enter a new name for the Diary file and then press [Enter] to save it. If you try to save a file with a new name to one which already exists in the same directory, the Portfolio will ask if it should overwrite the existing file. If you answer yes, by pressing [Enter] the data in the file on the disk will be deleted. Otherwise move the cursor to No and press [Enter], or back out with [Esc].

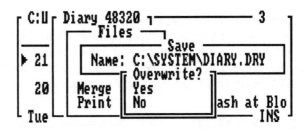

The Overwrite dialogue box

Entering [*] in the dialogue box will allow you to view existing files.

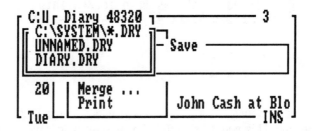

The dialogue box and listed files.

When you are saving Diary files under other names it is important to realise that any alarms which you might have set will not sound unless they are in the default file which must be C:\SYSTEM\DIARY.DRY

Merge . . .

Pressing [M] from the Files menu will allow you to merge a file on disk with one which is already loaded. Any new appointments which are merged will be sorted into date and time order, to combine with those which already exist.

When you select Merge, you may either enter a new name into the box, or enter * to see a list of available Diary files. These will normally be in the C:\SYSTEM directory, but you can Merge from another directory if you need to.

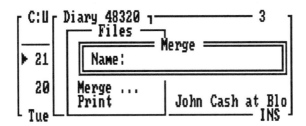

The Merge box awaiting an entry.

The current file name is not changed by the merging process, so you may need to use a new name when you save the merged file. Remember that alarms will only sound when they are in C:\SYSTEM\DIARY.DRY.

Print

Pressing [P] prints the current Diary file to a printer via the optional parallel or serial interfaces, or to a PRN file according to the options chosen oin Setup. Even if an interface is not fitted the printing box will be shown on the screen. If the Portfolio hangs (fails to respond to keyboard commands), press [Esc] and the screen will revert to whatever was displayed previously.

Character size, margins and page length are defined by using the Setup menu.

Search

The Search command will work from both the Calendar and Diary Modes. It is a good idea to set the pointer at the beginning of the data through which you want to search. Therefore, press [Ctrl]+[A] and the pointer will go to the first entry in the Diary.

To conduct a search, obtain the main Diary Menu by pressing [Fn][1] and then press [S]. A scrolling dialogue box is displayed and you may then enter the search word or character string.

For example, if the Diary contained reminders of several of your friends' birthdays, you could place 'birthday' in the box and press [Enter]. The computer would then search forward through the list and the pointer, in Diary mode, will stop opposite the first entry of 'birthday'. If you wanted to search for another birthday further on in the list, pressing [Ctrl]+[S] to repeat the search forward would find the next birthday, and so on through the entry list, until the Portfolio bleeps and the message 'String not found' is shown.

When the 'String not found' message is shown, it could mean that the data sought is actually under the point from which the search has started. This problem can be solved by doing another search in the reverse direction. To conduct a search backwards through the list, enter the character string in the dialogue box and then press the up arrow [↑], instead of Enter.

A backwards search of the Diary can be made by pressing [Ctrl]+[Z] to take the pointer to the end, entering the sought data in the dialogue box and then pressing [↑].

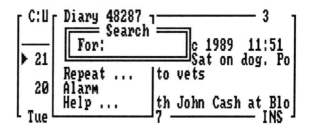

The Search dialogue box

If you carry out the search from Calendar mode, the cursor will be positioned on, and show only, the date of the first 'birthday' and you must press [Enter] to get into Diary Mode if you want to read the full entry for that birthday. Note that the search command will not work if you enter a time or a date in the dialogue box, it simply returns 'String not found'.

Move . . .

The purpose of this command is to move an entry to a new time or date, without the need to delete and reenter the appointment. Move is only appropriate to the Diary Mode and, although the option can be displayed with the menu, it will not work from Calendar Mode.

From the Calendar, get into Diary Mode by pressing [Enter], then position the pointer opposite the entry which you wish to reschedule. Press [Fn][1], then M. First, a time box will be shown. If you want to leave the time as it is, press [Enter]. Otherwise put in the new time and then press [Enter]. Next, the date box is displayed. You can leave the date as it is by pressing [Enter] again, or reschedule a new date by replacing the old date in the format for which your CONFIG.SYS file has been set. In Britain this would be dd/mm/yy or dd-mm-yy. Finally, press [Enter].

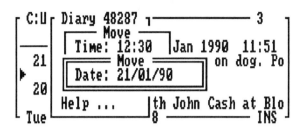

The Date box.

When you look at the list of Diary entries, you will see that the rescheduled appointment has been moved, and placed in order according to its new time or date.

Repeat ...

The Repeat command only works when used with the alarm. To set a repeat, select your desired entry in Diary Mode by positioning the pointer on it. Then press [Fn][1] to get the Diary menu, and [R] for repeat. You must then select an option from the repeat menu. To do this simply press a key with the initial letter of the option on it, or move the cursor to the relevant selection and press [Enter].

The Diary Repeat menu.

The various symbols used to indicate that a particular appointment will be repeated at the time indicated are placed by the alarm symbol by the selected entry in the Diary:

d	daily
w	weekly
n	daily, but not at weekends
y	yearly

The following line shows an entry with an alarm which repeats daily at 15:30 p.m.

d♫   5:30 Tea time

As mentioned above, it is possible to cancel the alarm and leave the repeat indicator in place, but a repeat without an alarm has no function. Any repeat symbol can be removed by using the clear command on the Repeat Menu.

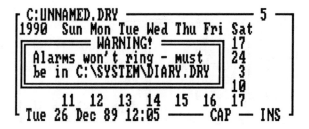

Diary screen with Repeat symbols shown, and alarms set.

Alarm

Alarm can be set as a reminder of important appointments which you have entered into the Portfolio's Diary. Unless set to repeat, an alarm will only sound once at the set time and date.

Alarms will only sound when they are set in C:\SYSTEM\DIARY.DRY

```
┌ C:UNNAMED.DRY ──────────── 5 ─┐
│ 1990  Sun Mon Tue Wed Thu Fri Sat  │
│ ┌═══════ WARNING! ═══════┐ 17  │
│ │ Alarms won't ring - must │ 24  │
│ │ be in C:\SYSTEM\DIARY.DRY │  3  │
│ └───────────────────────┘ 10  │
│      11  12  13  14  15  16  17   │
└ Tue 26 Dec 89 12:05 ──── CAP ─ INS ┘
```

The 'alarms won't ring message'

When an alarm is due, the Portfolio sounds a bleeper and the text in that entry shows on the screen. To stop the alarm press [Esc] and the computer will go back to whatever it was doing previously. If the Portfolio is switched off when an alarm is due the bleeper will still sound for a time and text will be shown on the screen. If an alarm is sounded and another becomes due before the first one has been acknowledged, the second alarm message is displayed over the first. Press [Esc] to acknowledge it.

To set an alarm, get into Diary Mode by pressing [Enter] if the Calendar is displayed on the screen. Position the pointer opposite the entry upon which you want to set the alarm, then press [Fn][1] or [⏎][↓] to get the main Diary menu. Press [A] to set the alarm. All entries in the Diary which have an alarm set on them show a musical note sign, like ♫ . An alarm can be removed by positioning the Diary pointer on the entry, pressing [Fn][1] and [A] again.

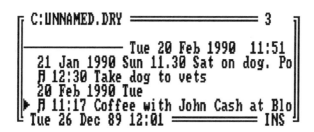

The Diary screen with only alarms set.

As mentioned previously, alarms can be set to repeat by using them in conjunction with the repeat feature.

By selecting the Save as... option in the Files menu, you can give any name you like to the Diary entry file, but only alarms in the main DIARY.DRY file will work. All other alarms are ignored and a warning is given on the screen before you exit from a file other than DIARY.DRY.

It might be as well for readers to note an experience which I had during testing. I managed to lose all the data in the Portfolio by setting the alarm for a time which coincided with my attempt to save the contents of the Diary to the RAM disk. The lesson here would seem to be to avoid a clash between such a saving operation and the sounding of the alarm. How to do this is rather a personal matter!

Help

The Diary Help option offers application specific aid with menu and file handling. To obtain help, press [H] from the main Diary menu. From a Diary screen, press either [⏎][↓] or [Fn][1], followed by [H]. Then make your selection for [M]enu or [F]ile handling.

Menus

This is a brief scrollable textual summary of the commands available from the Diary Menu. As with other applications, control characters are indicated by ^.

File handling

Deals with the various options available for filing and printing. This is virtually the same for all the Applications software.

General Help

Don't forget that you can get general help from any of the applications by pressing [Fn][2]. This allows you to scroll through a summary text dealing with the keyboard, clipboard, undelete and function key usage.

The use of the Clipboard is covered in a Chapter 7.

6

The Editor

Introduction

The Editor is a no frills ASCII word processor. Even so, it has enough power for most everyday uses. Simplicity has its own advantages. As there are no complicated sets of commands to remember, you can start entering text immediately.

If the text, which you type in to the Portfolio's Editor, is sent straight to a printer, it will appear on paper as it did on the computer's screen, a condition described as WYSIWYG (What you see is what you get.) Even so, it is possible to enhance the hard copy in various ways, by inserting printer control codes, as explained in Chapter 10.

Many of the more sophisticated word processors used with computers do not store their text in the form of ASCII code, but they usually allow for conversion to the ASCII standard for interchange with other programs. To this extent, it is an advantage for a small machine like the Portfolio to save its data in ASCII format, because it is then immediately available for transportation to other programs and other computers. More details about the ASCII standard are included in Appendix A.

How to Use the Editor

You can start the Editor by following any of the usual routes into an application program.

Method 1. Using the main Applications menu:

From the operating system screen (DOS) press [J|\J+[Z][E]

This selects the main Applications menu and then the Editor menu.

Method 2. Bypassing the main Applications menu:

From DOS press [⏎]⎇+[E]

When you do this the machine will bypass the main Applications menu and the Editor screen will appear.

Method 3. Typing a command from DOS:

Type `app/e`. The editor screen is immediately shown and you can start typing a trial sample of your text into it.

Entering Text

The screen shown below is ready for the entry of text.

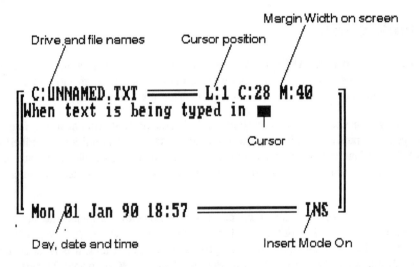

The Editor screen ready for further text entry.

When text is being typed in, a new paragraph can be started by pressing [Enter]. The [Del] key will erase mistakes, singly and to the right of the character upon which you position the cursor.

The current file name and drive are shown at the top of the screen on the left side. On the right of this, the Portfolio shows the line and column numbers (measured in character spaces) on which the cursor is positioned, e.g. as L:1 and C:28. The right margin setting is also shown after M: and in the above illustration it is 40 characters. This means that when Wordwrap is switched on the text will automatically wrap round and appear on the line underneath when the last complete word has been typed on a line set to 40 characters. Further details of this are given in the menu section below. As in the other Applications programs, the ≈ indicates that the current file has been altered since it was loaded. The day, date and time are shown at the bottom of the screen. If INS is also showing, the Editor is in insert mode, which means that space is automatically made for any text which is typed in between the existing text. The alternative mode (when INS is not shown) allows overtyping of any text present.

Specimen text 1

The following passage is included at this stage, so that you can get some hands on experience. It also provides something upon which to practice the menu and other commands.

Obtain the Editor screen and make sure that Wordwrap is On. To check Wordwrap, press [ꓕꓼ] when the Editor screen is showing. You will see Wordwrap in the Editor menu. If On is shown, simply press [Esc]. If On is not showing press [W] to switch it on. Also check to see that INS is showing in the bottom right hand corner of your screen. If it is not, press [Ins] to switch it on. Then type in the following text:

```
1st February 1990.[Enter]
Enter]

Dear Sir,[Enter]
     I am writing in response to your enquiry about our Russian
Blue cats.[Enter]
```

The spaces below 'Dear Sir' are obtained by pressing the space bar, or [Tab] and a space. Further presses of [Enter] will create more blank lines between the date and 'Dear Sir'. Then, when you type the last piece of text, the upper part will scroll off the screen. Don't worry, you can get it back !

```
┌ C:UNNAMED.TXT ════ L:1 C:1 M:40 ┐
│1st February 1990.◀               │
│◀                                 │
│Dear Sir,◀                        │
│          I am writing in response to │
│your enquiry about our Russian Blue │
│cats.◀                            │
└ Thu 01 Feb 90 19:00 ═══════ INS ┘
```

Part of a letter typed in from the Portfolio's keyboard.

Editor Frame

Pressing [Fn][5] switches the frame on and off and allows the screen to show more text.

The Default File

Whatever document was saved from your last session with the Editor will be reloaded by default. When you use the Editor for the first time, the screen will be blank and the current file will be UNNAMED.TXT. To leave the Editor, press [Esc]. At this point, if there has been an entry, a box on the screen asks if you want to save the text. If you answer Yes, the sample text which has been typed will be saved in the UNNAMED.TXT file. If you answer No, any new text which has been typed in will be lost.

The next time the Editor is used, the UNNAMED.TXT file will be loaded and, if you have saved it, your sample text will appear on the screen. If this is the file you want, good! If not, the screen can be cleared by pressing [Fn][1], then [F] to get the files menu, then [N] for New. After these actions, the screen will clear, although the file name will still be the default, UNNAMED.TXT. As explained below, a unique file name can be assigned by pressing [S] (Save as ...) from the files menu.

Movement through the Text

Use of the up, down, right and left cursor keys will allow you to make appropriate movements, one character at a time, through the text. Other keys allow movement through greater numbers of characters.

[↑]	1 character up
[↓]	1 character down
[→]	1 character right
[←]	1 character left
[Ctrl][→]	1 word right
[Ctrl][←]	1 word left
[Fn][PgUp]	7 lines up
[Fn][PgDn]	7 lines down
[Ctrl][A]	Beginning of the file
[Ctrl][Z]	End of the file
[Fn][Home]	Start of the current line
[Fn][End]	End of the current line
[Ctrl][U]	Moves to previous cursor position

Key Strokes which Delete Text

[<--] (Backspace)	Delete one character to the left
[Del]	Delete character under cursor and move right
[Ctrl][Home]	Delete all characters to start of line
[Ctrl][B]	same
[Ctrl][End]	Delete all characters to end of line
[Ctrl][E]	same
[Ctrl][L]	Delete whole line
[Ctrl][<--] (Backspace)	Delete one word left
[Ctrl][W]	Delete one word right.
[Fn][4]	Recovers deletions

Function keys

[Fn][1] or [/]\[\]	Shows main Editor menu
[Fn][2]	Shows Help menu
[Fn][3]	Clipboard menu
[Fn][4]	Recovers deletions
[Fn][5]	Switches screen frame on or off
[Fn][6]	No function
[Fn][7] - [Fn][0]	Not used in the Editor
[Shift]+[6]	Enter control character

Moving Text

The Editor allows you to move text within the current document, or to copy data, including text, from other files. In addition, reports and items produced by the Editor can be exported to other devices. One could therefore regard the Editor as a central component in the coordination and transmission of information.

Using the Clipboard to Copy or Move text

The Clipboard is the tool which allows information to be transmitted between each element of the Applications software, except the Calculator. While its general use is covered in Chapter 7, an example is given here to show how you can employ it to move text.

To obtain the Clipboard, press [Fn][3]when the Editor screen is showing. This will cause the Clipboard menu to appear.

The Clipboard menu

Four options are available:

Cut

Remove a block from the currently displayed data and take it into the Clipboard memory.

Store

Copy a block from the currently displayed data and take it into the Clipboard memory.

Cut can be considered an equivalent to the Move command of other word processors and Store is the equivalent of Copy. The essential difference between the two is that Cut removes part of the current text and Store merely copies it, leaving the original intact.

Paste

Deposit, or paste, a copy of the Clipboard data into the currently displayed data.

Mark

It is essential to use this with both Cut and Store. The command marks the beginning of the data to be copied into the Clipboard.

The Clipboard menu

Method of use

Refer to the Specimen text 1 above from which we shall copy the words Russian Blue cats into the Clipboard for later use.

1. With the text displayed on your screen, position the cursor on the R of *Russian*, then press [Fn][3]. When Clipboard menu shows on the Portfolio's screen, press [M].

2. Move the cursor to the full stop at the end of *cats* and press [Fn][3] again.

Select [S] to Store (copy) the text.

This results in the words *Russian Blue* cats being copied into the Clipboard's memory. If you want to move text, select [C] to cut it out.

3. Move the cursor to the position where you want the copied (or cut) text to appear, press [Fn][3] and then [P] to paste it in. For the sake of this exercise, you could choose the end of the text.

The CLIPBORD.DAT file.

If you press [J]\[J]+[S] from the DOS screen the Setup menu is shown. Pressing [A] from this menu will show the Applications menu, which lists Clipboard save as On or Off.

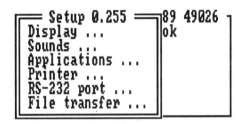

The Setup menu

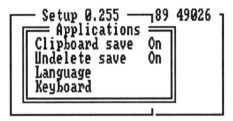

The Applications menu

When Clipboard save is On any data saved to the Clipboard is stored in a file called CLIPBORD.DAT (C:\SYSTEM\CLIPBORD.DAT) when you leave the current Application program. This means that you can recall the data from the file and paste it into any other Application program.

If Clipboard save is Off data can be saved to the Clipboard and may be recalled within the current application, but when you move to another program the data will be lost.

Therefore, it is vital to make sure that Clipboard save is switched On when you want to transfer information between Applications.

Try another experiment. Type your address into the Address Book and copy it from there to the top of the Specimen text 1 letter.

Using [Ctrl]+[W] and [Ctrl]+[<--] to move text

In addition to using the Clipboard, text can be moved from one place to another within the Editor by using the delete and recover keys.

As indicated above, pressing [Ctrl]+[W] will delete a word to the right of the cursor and [Ctrl]+[<--] will delete a word left. You can, of course, delete successive words by repeating the key press. It is also possible to recover deleted words by using [Fn][4].

Therefore, you can delete words in one part of the text, move the cursor to another part and use [Fn][4], pressed a number of times if necessary, to recover and reposition them. [Fn][4] will only work once for each word and it cannot be used to repeatedly copy the same word as can the Clipboard Store command.

Use of the Alt key to type in special characters

If you look at the ASCII character tables at the end of this book, you will see that the IBM character set contains a number of characters in excess of those which are used in everyday alphanumerics. It is therefore possible to mix, for example, the Greek Alphabet with normal text. To do this you must use the Alt key and embedded numberpad (the red numbers on the Portfolio's keyboard).

First look up the decimal character code in the ASCII table, included in Appendix A. The Greek letter Omega has a code of 234. To enter this with your text press [∪|∪]+[Lock] to switch on the numberpad, then hold down the [Alt] key and enter [2][3][4] on the number pad (use the red number keys). Ω will then appear on your screen and can be printed on paper by any printer which is capable of reproducing the IBM extended character set.

Notice that, when the Alt key and numberpad are used for entering characters of the IBM extended character set, the Portfolio's cursor changes from ■ to _ .

```
┌─ C:ERFORM.TXT ════════ L:1 C:1 M:60 ═┐
│                                      │
│           Y = β X  +ε                │
│            i     i    i              │
│                                      │
│                                      │
│                                      │
│                                      │
└─ Tue 26 Dec 89 09:14 ════════════════┘
```

$$Y_i = \beta X_i + \varepsilon_i$$

A mathematical formula entered by using the Alt key and number pad.

The above formula was obtained by the following two lines of key-presses:

```
[Y][Space][Space]
[-][Space][Alt]+[2]+[2]+[5][X][Space][Space][+][Space]
[Alt]+[2]+[3]+[8][Enter]
[Space][i][Space][Space][Space][Space][Space][i][Space]
[Space][Space][Space][i][Enter]
```

These keypresses exclude the initial spaces entered in order to place the formula somewhere near the middle of the screen.

Notice that certain graphics characters are also included in the ASCII tables. These may also be entered with your text, so that boxes and other effects can be employed to highlight certain features.

Main Editor menu

The main Editor menu enables one to perform various filing operations, search and replace text, set the right margin, word wrap and mode. It also allows you to obtain on screen help to use the menus and for file handling. The menu appears when either the [Fn][1] or [ ]|[ ] keys are pressed.

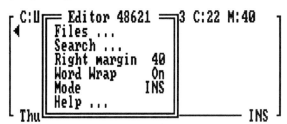

Main Editor menu

Files . . .

The use of files is also covered in Chapter.... To obtain the Files menu, press [Fn][1] or [ ]|[ ] to get the Editor menu, then [F] for the Files menu.

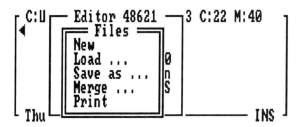

The Files menu

New

This command clears the screen. If the current text has not been altered, the screen will clear immediately. The presence of the ≈ sign in the screen frame indicates that the text has been altered, and then an option to save it is provided.

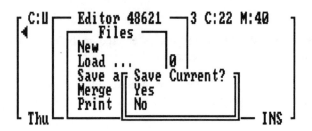

The Yes/No box

Place the cursor on Yes or No, as appropriate, and press [Enter]. The document will then either be saved (Yes) with its existing name, as shown at the top left of the screen, or abandoned (No). If it is abandoned, the previous version will not be erased from the computer's memory, but if the document is saved with its existing name, the previous version will be overwritten and consequently lost. The screen then clears and you may start a new document. Note that the Editor also displays the file name UNNAMED.TXT.

Load . . .

Accepting the default file name

You may use this command to load a piece of text, which has been previously saved under a file name, from any drive connected to the Portfolio. The default (RAM) drive is C: and the Portfolio memory card drive is designated A:. If you press [L] from the Files menu, the screen will show the default drive, directory and file name. This may be, for example, drive C:, and file UNNAMED.TXT .

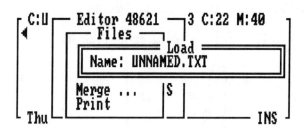

The Load dialogue box

If you want to load the file whose name is shown in the box, just press [Enter].

Using a new file name

If you want to load in a new file, the [Del] key can be used to remove all or some of the information in the box. The new information is then typed into the appropriate position. For instance, you could overwrite the drive name C: by inserting A: to read a file from a memory card, or B: to read a file from an external drive. (Don't try this unless you have a memory card or an external drive connected.) You could enter a new file name by erasing \UNNAMED.TXT and entering \MYFILE.TXT. In practice, the .TXT can be omitted because the computer will automatically put that bit of the file name in after a name which does not contain the file extension.

Directory display

A directory name could also be edited. The base, or root, directory is the first \ shown after the drive. Therefore C:\ shows the drive and root directory. Any other name after that which terminates in \ is a subdirectory. Thus C:\LETTERS\ might be the directory in which you keep all your correspondence. For more on directories, see Chapter 2. Finally, you have one more choice. You can look at all the files in the directory shown.

Type [:][Enter] to view all files and subdirectories in the current directory.

Type [*][Enter] to view all .TXT files from the current directory.

Typing *.* will also cause the machine to display all the files and subdirectories in the current directory. For instance, if the Load dialogue box was showing C:\, typing *.* will cause the display box to show the SYSTEM subdirectory and any files in the root directory, such as CONFIG.SYS.

If the dialogue box was showing C:\SYSTEM*.* all files and subdirectories in the SYSTEM subdirectory would be listed.

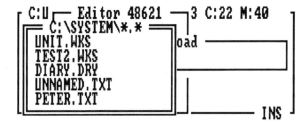

Directory display of System subdirectory

If you type *.* from a root directory, such as C:\ or A:\, you can display the content of other subdirectories, simply by placing the cursor on them in the display box and pressing [Enter].

You can scroll up or down the display list by using the cursor keys. As with all the other boxes, if the file name is longer than the dialogue box, you can scroll left or right, with the cursor keys. If the cursor is positioned on the name of any valid text file and [Enter] then pressed, that file will be loaded into the Editor and its name will automatically become the default name.

The act of loading a new file automatically erases any existing file from the computer's memory. If you attempt to load a new file without saving an existing file which has been altered, the Portfolio gives you an option to save the existing file. If you want to put two files into the Editor at the same time, use Load to get the first one in and Merge to load the second, third, etc.

When you have already loaded one file which you have then edited, attempting to load another file will usually cause the Portfolio to produce an option box asking whether you want to save the first file. This safeguards your new work.

Unfortunately, if the file already loaded has the same name as that which you are attempting to load, no option to save is offered. It is, therefore, possible, under these circumstances, to erase your most recent work by inadvertently loading the default file showing in the Load dialogue box.

You can avoid this problem by developing the habit of giving each edited file a unique name when you start working on it. This will guarantee that the automatic option to save comes into operation if you forget.

If, for example, you were working on a file called GREEN.TXT which had been previously saved, and you then chose the Load option and immediately pressed [Enter], the old GREEN.TXT file would be loaded over the file in memory and all your current work would be erased. This is due to the fact that when the Load option is selected, its dialogue box shows the current file as the default.

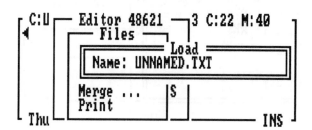

The Load dialogue box showing the default file.

Editor and other Text Files

How do you know which file is a text file? Well, the files which end with .TXT are text files, but you can also load .ADR and .DRY files without any complications, because they also conform to the ASCII standard. But if you alter any of the .DRY or .ADR files, and save them again, the alterations will show up in the Diary and Address Book applications when the relevant file is loaded.

Diary and Address Book files can, therefore, be edited by using the Portfolio's Editor and any of these files can be fed into a desktop PC via the appropiate interface. Once there they can be archived, or manipulated as required.

Save as...

This is another file storage option for the Editor. Using it will enable you to save your document for future use, under its existing name, or a new one. From the Editor screen, press [Fn][1], then [F] to get the File menu. If you then press [S], the Save as... dialogue box is shown and you are asked to enter a filename.

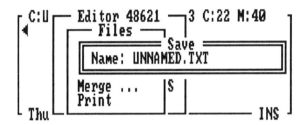

The Save dialogue box

The current drive, directory and file name will be shown in the box and you might need to alter these in order to avoid a conflict with some existing data which you want to keep. If you are editing a file which you loaded previously, and wish to save it under the same name, simply press [Enter] and the file will be saved.

If you want to give your document a new file name, then you have to edit the dialogue box and insert your new name. The old file name can be removed by using the [Del] key. Don't forget that the current drive number and directory will be shown in the box as well.

You need only enter the name, not the extension. The Editor will add .TXT to the name you enter. For instance, if you gave a file the name of BINGO the full name would become BINGO.TXT, and if no more information was entered this file would be saved in the default drive and directory.

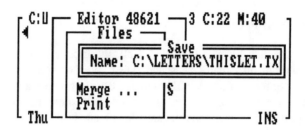

The Save as... dialogue box

The files list can be displayed in the same way as with the Load command, by entering:

[:] or [*.*] to display all files and subdirectories at that level

or

[*] to show all *.TXT files

After you have saved a file, the system returns you to the same document in the Editor, so you can either continue to work on it, or start a new one with the New command.

Merge . . .

The Merge command is provided so that two documents can be joined together. If you have loaded the first document in the Editor, the second file can be merged with it, so that they form one. Once merged, documents can be Saved as... one file.

From the Editor, press [Fn][1] and then [F] for the Files menu. Next press [M] for Merge and a dialogue box is presented. If the box shows a default file, you can simply accept this by pressing Return. To enter a new file name, use the cursor keys and [Del] to erase the name in the box and then type in the name of the file which you want to be merged, followed by [Enter].

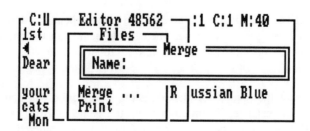

The Merge dialogue box

In the event that you have forgotten what the exact name of the file is, you can examine the contents of the directory by typing *[Enter] instead of the file name. All the *.TXT files in the directory will then be shown and you can merge any one of them with the one already loaded by placing the cursor on its name and pressing Return. The directory and file names can be edited in the usual way if necessary.

After you have done a merge, the newly merged file must be saved if you want to keep it, so use the Save as... command. If you use the name of an existing file the merged file will overwrite it and the original will be lost. It may, therefore, be necessary for you to give the new file a different name from that which was first loaded. When the merged file is saved under its new name, the files from which it was formed will remain in the computer, unaltered.

Specimen text 2

The following text can be merged with the few lines of your first sample text. Type in:

```
This shorthaired breed is characterised by green eyes and a
blue-grey coat overlaid by a silvery sheen.
```

When you have entered this, press [/|\][F][S] to get Save as... and save the file with a name, like RUSSIAN2.

The Specimen text 1 should have been saved in the UNNAMED.TXT file, so you can now load this. Once you have it on screen, position the cursor on the last line and press [Enter] once or twice to create a blank line or two which will serve as a space between paragraphs and then press [/|\][F][M] to get the Merge dialogue box. You can then type in RUSSIAN2[Enter], or [*][Enter], and position the Cursor on the RUSSIAN2.TXT file name to be merged before pressing [Enter] again. Either one of these two actions will cause the RUSSIAN2 file to be merged with your existing text.

This kind of merge procedure can be very useful to those who have to regularly compile letters consisting of a varied assortment of paragraphs which are not consistent from letter to letter. The merge operation can be used repeatedly on the screen.

Print

Pressing [P] will send the current file to a printer via the parallel or serial interfaces, when fitted, and set with the Printer Destination option of the Setup menu. Text can also be saved to a formatted printer file, and stored on one of the Portfolio's disk drives, by setting the Destination option of the Setup Printer menu to File.

Further information about printing and formatting text is given in Chapter 10.

When printing is in operation a Printing... message is displayed on the screen.

Search

The Search option enables you to search through text for any word or phrase, or series of characters or numbers.

There are three subdivisions of the Search menu: Search, Replace and Goto.

Search will find text without altering it.

Replace finds and replaces text.

Goto will place the cursor on a line n spaces from the top of the document.

Bear in mind that the Search and Replace commands work from the current cursor position. It is, therefore, good practice to position the cursor at the beginning of your text by using [Ctrl]+[A], before starting a search.

The Goto command correctly positions the cursor n lines from the top of the document, whatever the current cursor position.

To get the Search menu on screen, press [Fn][1] to obtain the main Editor menu, and then press [S].

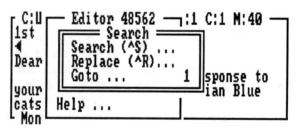

The Search menu

Search . . .

Press [S] again and a dialogue box is presented which requests the characters for which you want to search.

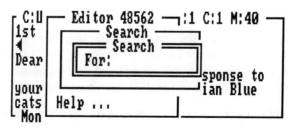

The Search dialogue box

Search is not case sensitive. For instance if you enter Test, it will find all occurrences of test, (e.g. TEST, test) whether or not they have an upper case t. Fill in the dialogue box and press [Enter] or [↓] to search forwards. The search stops when the first set of characters is found. If you want to search the rest of the document in the same direction, press [Ctrl]+[S] to find the next occurrence of the same text, and so on until the string not found message is displayed.

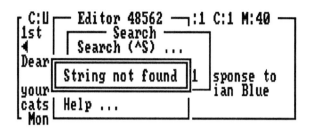

The String not found message

To search backwards from the present cursor position, press [↑] after filling in the dialogue box.

Alterations to the text can be typed in each time the search stops, but for repetitive alterations it is easier to use the Replace command.

If no previous search has been conducted, the dialogue box can be displayed simply by pressing [Ctrl]+[S] when the Editor screen is displayed. After that you may proceed with the search as described above.

Replace . . .

From the Search menu, press [R]. A dialogue box, identical to that for Search, is presented. Enter the text you want to replace and press [Enter] or [↓] to go forwards, or [↑] to go backwards through the text. When the search finds the first piece of identical text, the Replace box is shown.

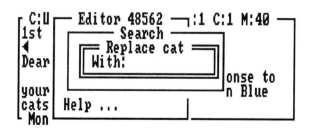

The Replace box

Fill in the box with the text with which you want to replace the original and press [Enter]. The search text will be removed and the replaced text will take its place.

For example, to replace test with TEST, key in test[Enter] in the search dialogue box and when the Replace box is shown type in TEST [Enter].

After the first replacement has been done, the operation may be repeated for each occurrence of 'test' simply by pressing [Ctrl]+[R]. If you want to search and replace for another word, or words, press [Fn][1] and [S] to get the Search options again. On this occasion the box shows the words last entered, so these must be edited as appropriate.

Goto . . .

This option allows you to move the cursor to a specified horizontal line number. From the Search menu, press [G] and you will be prompted to enter the line number. Enter the figure and press [Enter].

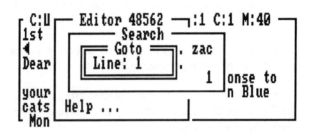

The Goto prompt box

The lines of text in the Editor do not display their numbers, so you will have to make a count from the top of the text, including any blank lines, to the line where you want to place the cursor.

If you want to move up or down the text relative to the present cursor position, precede the number in the box with - to go up and + to go down. For instance, if you wanted to move back up through the text 5 lines, you would type in -5.

Pressing [Ctrl]+[G] will repeat the last Goto move.

Right Margin

Press [Fn][1] to get the main Editor menu. On it, by the Right margin command, you will see the present margin setting.

If you want to alter the setting, press [R] and a dialogue box will appear.

Any figure between 5 and 250 can be set. After you have entered a figure, press [Enter]. In other words, a line on the Editor can be up to 250 characters wide, but many printers are not able to accept this width. Normal tractor paper is 8.5 inches wide and, with blank margins of .25 inches right and left, the width available is 8 inches. The number of characters which can be printed varies according to their size. Thus, after allowing for margins, 8.5 inch wide paper will take 8 x 10 (80) characters of the size 10 characters per inch (cpi), 8 x 12 (96) characters of the size 12 cpi and so on. Extra wide printers and paper are available. For instance, the Epson FX 100 printer will take paper 13 inches wide.

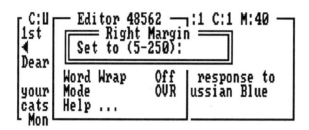

The Right Margin dialogue box

How to avoid lateral scrolling of the screen text

Due to the difference between the width to be printed on paper and the 40 character width of the Portfolio's screen, you may feel that it is best to employ a dual formatting technique when using the Editor.

Initially, fix the margin at a width which is convenient for viewing all the text on screen without lateral scrolling. A setting of about 37 is suitable when the screen frame is switched on. Also, make sure that Word Wrap is switched On. Then, when the time comes to print the document, it is possible to load the file from the RAM or other disk and restore the right margin to one which is suitable for printing it on paper, by resetting the Right margin to a width suited to the printed characters and paper width.

Word Wrap

Word Wrap is a word processor feature which allows text, in the form of complete words, to be automatically placed on the next line down when the present line, set with the Right margin command, has been filled up. When Word Wrap is switched off, the Right margin setting does not limit the on screen width of the text, but a line can be ended by pressing [Enter]. Normally, Word Wrap would be switched to On.

Press [Fn][1] to get the main Editor menu. The present state of the Word Wrap is shown, On or Off. If you press [W] you simply toggle the other option and the Portfolio immediately reverts to the Editor screen.

When Word Wrap is On all returns (inserted by pressing [Enter]) are shown as left hand pointers. When word wrap is Off returns are not shown.

```
┌ C:UNNAMED.TXT ═══════ L:1 C:1 M:40 ═┐
│ 1st February 1990.◄                  │
│ ◄                                    │
│ Dear Sir,◄                           │
│          I am writing in response to │
│ your enquiry about our Russian Blue  │
│ cats.◄                               │
└ Mon 01 Jan 90 19:26 ═════════════════┘
```

The Editor screen with Word wrap switched On

```
┌ C:UNNAMED.TXT ═══════ L:1 C:1 M:40 ═┐
│ 1st February 1990.                   │
│                                      │
│ Dear Sir,                            │
│          I am writing in response to │
│ your enquiry about our Russian Blue  │
│ cats.                                │
└ Mon 01 Jan 90 19:27 ═════════════════┘
```

An Editor screen with Word wrap switched Off

Mode

Mode can be either OVR or INS, that is, overwrite or insert. With OVR set any text which you type on a line which already has text on it will replace characters already there. If INS is set the text will be inserted into the text from the place in which the cursor is positioned when you start. In other words, a space is automatically made for it and it will be added to any text already there.

To see Mode, press [Fn][1]. The menu shows its present state. To toggle the other option, press [M]. The machine then returns you to the Editor screen.

Insert or Overwrite can also be set by pressing the [Ins] key.

Help

Pressing [H] from the Editor menu causes the Help screen to be shown. You can then select help on file handling or menu use by pressing [M] or [F] and scrolling through the displayed text with the up and down cursor keys.

Editor menu Help

This briefly explains the Search, Replace, Goto, Right Margin, Word Wrap and Mode commands.

File handling

Choosing this option allows you to read through the list of commands for filing and printing.

General Help

The General help box can be obtained by pressing [Fn][2] when the Editor screen is shown. The usual options of Keyboard, Clipboard, Undelete and Function key help can then be selected for perusal.

7

Setup, Clipboard, data and file transfer

The Setup menu

The Setup functions of the Portfolio allow the user to control miscellaneous functions in accordance with personal preferences, file transfer and data output.

Once the options available with the Setup menu have been adjusted, they can usually be left as they are for some time.

The methods used for displaying the Setup menu are similar to those for the Applications.

Method 1. Using the main Applications menu:

From DOS press [ ]|[ ]+[Z] [S]

By this means the main Applications menu is selected and pressing [S] causes the Setup menu to be displayed on the screen.

Method 2. Bypassing the main Applications menu:

From DOS, press [ ]|[ ]+[S]

After this, the Setup menu will appear on the screen.

Method 3. Typing a command from DOS:

When the DOS C> prompt is shown, type app/s [Enter] to get the Setup menu.

```
 ═ Setup 0.255 ═89 48965 ┐
Display ...          ok
Sounds ...
Applications ...
Printer ...
RS-232 port ...
File transfer ...
```

The Setup menu

Display . . .

Pressing [D] when the Setup menu is on the screen, causes the Display menu to appear.

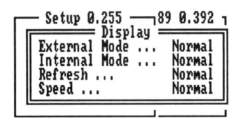

```
┌── Setup 0.255 ──┐89 0.392 ┐
         Display
External Mode ...    Normal
Internal Mode ...    Normal
Refresh ...          Normal
Speed ...            Normal
```

The Display menu.

The options shown indicate the types of display which are available with the Portfolio's screen.

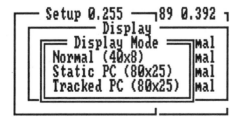

```
┌── Setup 0.255 ──┐89 0.392 ┐
         Display
  ═ Display Mode ═mal
 Normal (40x8)     mal
 Static PC (80x25) mal
 Tracked PC (80x25) mal
```

The External Mode option box

The *External Mode* is available for software not built into the Portfolio. When programs of this type are run, the screen display automatically used is that which has been set in the Setup Display menu's External Mode options.

The *Internal Mode* display is the one which is used by DOS and the Portfolio's built in applications.

If no external software is being used, the External and Internal Display settings should be left on Normal. Otherwise, for both External and Internal displays, three choices are available. The settings for these two modes can differ from each other.

Normal

The normal display is a 40 column by 8 line screen.

Static PC

This display uses the usual PC 80 character by 25 line screen. The Portfolio's 40 x 8 screen acts as a window on this larger virtual screen and the user moves round it manually by using the Alt and cursor keys.

Tracked PC

Again, the display simulates the normal PC 80 column by 25 line display, and the Portfolio screen is a window on this. But instead of the user having to manually move round the PC screen, the window automatically follows cursor movements

Keys which move the screen window in Static and Tracked PC modes:

> [Alt]+cursor key   One column or one line
> [Fn]+[Alt]+cursor key   20 columns or 6 lines

If an external program finishes when the External and Internal modes are set differently, the message:

`Press any key to continue`

is shown on the screen. When this has been done, any information left on the screen by the external program can be read by using the [Alt] and a cursor key.

The difference between Tracked and Static PC modes

The appearance and behaviour of the Portfolio's screen when using the Editor or Worksheet resembles that of the Static PC screen, except for the cursor key response.

The following example will help to clarify the difference between the two modes. A short external public domain program, called DTA, will run on the Portfolio, or a PC, but uses the PC 80 column x 25 line screen display. DTA displays directory files, but gives more information than is available with the DOS DIR command.

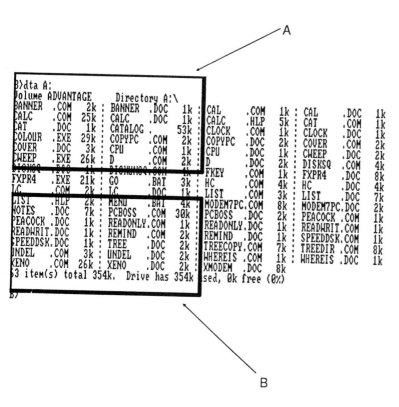

The DTA PC display is inside the outer frame; the Static display is shown by 'A' and the Tracked display by 'B' – see text below for details

The outer frame represents the 80 x 25 PC screen which shows a directory listing produced by DTA.

Inside this, screen A shows the position of the Portfolio screen with the Display set to External Mode Static PC. This screen, which acts as a window on the full PC screen, starts off in the position in which it is located in the diagram and can then be moved to any other position by use of the [Alt] and a cursor key.

Screen B represents the Portfolio screen set to Display External Mode Tracked PC. The starting position of this screen is at the bottom, because this is where the cursor is positioned by DTA. DTA displays a full PC screen of information at a time and the Tracked PC screen moves with the cursor position which is dictated by the DTA program. As long as this screen of information is displayed by DTA, the Portfolio tracked screen can be moved around by using the [Alt] and cursor keys, but if the external program had already scrolled information off the 80 x 25 PC screen the Tracked screen would have moved down with the cursor and it would not then be possible to view that information.

Both Static and Tracked PC Modes can also be used, if necessary, with internal Portfolio programs.

Refresh . . .

Some external programs use a PC's screen memory to display information and this information only becomes visible on the Portfolio's screen when it is refreshed from the relevant area of memory.

Pressing [R] when the Display menu is shown, causes the Refresh options to be displayed. These allow you to choose which of three refresh modes is to be used.

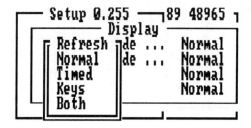

The Refresh options

Normal

Press [N] to choose this setting. It should be selected when only the internal software is being used. No refresh is performed because the internal software does not use that area of memory.

Timed

This option, selected by pressing [T], is linked with the Speed option in the Display menu. The screen is refreshed at whatever interval Speed has been set to.

Keys

This is the recommended selection for running external programs. Press [K] and the screen will be refreshed whenever the current external program waits for a key press, but not otherwise.

Both

Pressing [B] causes both Timed and Normal to operate together. This means that the screen is refreshed at the regular intervals set with Speed and also when the external program waits for a key press. A sort of belt and braces setting!

Speed . . .

Press [N] for normal speed which means that the Portfolio screen will be refreshed every 128 seconds, or [F] to refresh the screen twice every second.

It is recommended that Fast is only chosen when the external program really does need the screen to be refreshed this rapidly. Choosing this fast speed uses more processor time and causes the Portfolio to perform other operations at a slower rate.

Sounds . . .

The Portfolio will emit sound when keys are pressed, alarms are due and when internal or external programs sound a buzzer. Press [S] when the Setup Menu is shown to make Sounds selections.

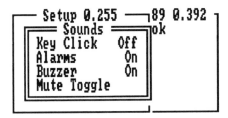

The Sounds menu showing the defaults

All three options may be switched on or off individually or together.

Key Click

The Portfolio's keys will provide a sound feedback, in the form of a click, when pressed. To toggle this click on or off, press [K] when the Sounds menu is shown.

Alarms

One's attention is drawn to the Portfolio, when Alarms is switched on, by a bleeping noise. Whether Alarms is switched on or off the alarm message will be displayed on the screen. However, when the lid is shut, it would be difficult to see! Switch Alarms On or Off by pressing [A] when the Sounds menu is shown on the screen.

Buzzer

The buzzer sounds in response to error messages produced by the built in applications programs and in response to commands issued by external programs. The buzzer is switched on or off by pressing [B] from the Sounds menu.

Mute Toggle

This option allows you to switch Key Click, Alarms and Buzzer all on or off at once. To do this, press [M] when the Sounds menu is displayed.

Applications

This Applications menu allows you to elect certain defaults which will affect the operation of the Portfolio and its Applications software. Press [A] from the Setup menu to see it.

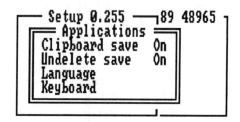

The Setup Applications menu

Clipboard save

Clipboard save is set to On or Off by pressing [C] when the Setup Applications menu is on the screen. When Clipboard save is switched on, data from the Clipboard, used with the relevant Applications software, is saved to the C:/SYSTEM file CLIPBORD.DAT when the user withdraws to DOS or changes Applications.

The maximum size of CLIPBORD.DAT is 8K and much of this RAM can be saved if the Clipboard is emptied, or if the Clipboard save option is switched off after the Clipboard has been used.

Undelete save

Another data file used by the Applications software is called UNDELETE.DAT. This one holds all the data which is deleted by the various delete commands and keys. Eventually, when full, this file will have a maximum size of 2K. So if you want to prevent your RAM disk being occupied by this data, the file can be deleted from DOS in the usual way, or the Undelete save option can be set to Off by selecting [U] when the Setup Applications menu shows it to be switched on.

Language

The Portfolio's built in Applications software and DOS will operate in English, French and German. When [L] is pressed from the Setup Applications menu, the available options are shown.

Simply press [E], [F] or [D] to make your choice.

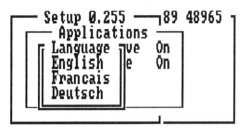

The Language options menu

```
Le volume dans unité c n' a pas de label Répertoire de c:\

system <REP> 1-01-80 3:01
unnamed adr 152 18-03-90 20:29
di prn 115 3-10-90 17:38
config sys 35 0-00-80 0:00
dta com 3895 16-10-88 15:00
french txt 0 19-03-90 11:42 6

Fichiers 43776 octets libres
```

A files list displayed by typing DIR from the DOS screen, after selecting [F]

The figures above show that the commands vary with the language chosen. Therefore, if you cannot remember what key presses to select from a foreign language it might be difficult to move around the various menus. The way out of this situation is to Esc out of the menus to DOS and then start Setup as usual, by pressing [⌡|⌡]+[S], then [P] which is the same for both French and German. After this press [S] if in German, or [L] if in French. Then the Language options menu appears and you can press [E] for English.

Keyboard

An English keyboard, with software in French or German would be an anomaly. The Portfolio's developers have therefore provided for the French or German keypress equivalents, but the physical appearance of the keys will remain the same. So, you would need to be thoroughly conversant with AZERTY or QWERTZ keyboards to know which keys to press!

```
(c) D╔══ System 50983 ═══╗
Adre ║ Bildschirm...       ║
Rechn║ Signale...          ║
Zeitp║ Programme...        ║
Textv║ Ausdrucken...       ║
Syste║ RS-232...           ║
Kalku║ Dateien bertragung..║
```

The Setup Applications menu displayed after selecting [D]

Printer

This choice is fully dealt with elsewhere in this book. The Setup Printer menu allows appropriate options to be made for different printer controls, page format and interfaces.

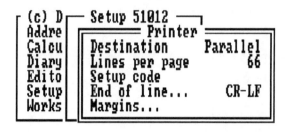

The Setup Printer menu

RS-232 (serial) port . . .

Serial communications ports of the RS-232 type are commonly fitted to PCs and provide a means whereby data can be transferred to and from the computer, often in connection with another computer. This sort of interface is extremely useful when it is necessary to communicate at a distance, via telephone lines or even radio links. It is also very useful when data has to be sent from one type of computer to another. For instance, if you were upgrading from an Apple IIe to an IBM AT, you could send your valuable records from the Apple to the IBM via serial interfaces and a hard wired modem (a cross wired direct connection).

For the purposes of this discussion assume that the data would be sent in some conventional form, such as ASCII codes. It is possible to transmit programs between computers and they will work if the computers are compatible, like IBM clones, but not if they are dissimilar.

There is a thriving body of people, usually called sysops, who operate computer bulletin boards for the population at large. These carry all sorts of information and can usually be accessed free via a modem connected between the RS 232 port of your computer and the telephone line. Unfortunately, telephone charges must be paid as usual! A modem is a device able to translate computer signals into a form suitable for transmission over communication (e.g. telephone) lines.

The RS-232 ports of two communicating computers could be connected by a single, appropriately cross wired, hard modem cable, a cable from each computer to a modem with each modem connected to a telephone line, or some other method, by which data could be transmitted between them. Naturally, it would be necessary to plug one end of the cables into the computer and the other end into the modem. Plug types and sexes vary with different computers. The Portfolio's RS-232C compatible Serial Interface plugs into the right side of the machine. The other side of the interface has a 9 pin D shell connector whose wiring differs from the 9 way D IBM standard.

Data is transmitted through an RS-232 port sequentially, one character (or byte) at a time. In other words, very small pieces of data are sent out of, or taken into, the computer, one after the other down the same wire. This is a very simple account of the process and further hardware connections, which perform other functions, are involved in a working RS-232 interface for the cable.

The RS-232 interface is the hardware, but it is necessary to run suitable software with this interface in order to transmit data successfully. This would involve running a communications program on the Portfolio and also one on the computer with which it was communicating. At the time of writing, no commercial software is available for the Portfolio's optional serial interface, though there is plenty for IBM PC's, Apples and a host of other machines. Recently, a simple dumb terminal for the Portfolio has been made available through the public domain.

Nevertheless, the Setup menu makes provision for the serial port to be configured.

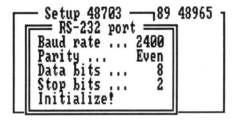

The RS-232 port configuration menu

To gain access to this menu, press [R] when the Setup menu is showing on the screen.

Baud rate...

The Baud is a unit of measurement, used to gauge the speed at which data is transmitted over communications lines. The figure given actually represents the number of bits per second. Therefore when data is sent at 9600 Baud it is travelling a lot faster than it would at 300 Baud. In terms of convenience and telephone charges, this can mean a lot.

If you press [B] from the RS-232 configuration menu, the Baud rates available on the Portfolio will be shown on the screen and a choice can be made by pressing one of the initial numbers or appropriately positioning the cursor and pressing [Enter].

```
 ┌── Setup 48703 ──┐89 48965 ┐
 │ ┌── RS-232 port ──┐        │
 │ ┌ Baud rate ┐ 2400 │      │
 │ │1200       │ Even │      │
 │ │600        │    8 │      │
 │ │300        │    2 │      │
 │ │150        │     │       │
 └─└───────────┘─────┘───────┘
```

Baud rates available on the Portfolio

Parity . . .

The default Parity setting is shown on the RS-232 port menu. If you need to adjust it, press [P].

Parity refers to an error checking protocol, carried out by the hardware, whereby an extra check bit is sent with a character block. The two systems in communication must have the same parity settings and you can select None, Even or Odd by pressing the appropriate key on the Portfolio, when the Parity selection box shows on the screen. One would normally set the parity on the Portfolio to that used by the system to which it is going to be connected.

Data bits

If [D] is pressed when the RS-232 port menu is on the screen, the two options for the data bit setting are shown. The selection is made by pressing [7] or [8]. A Byte of data (equal to a character) may contain up to 8 bits, but the ASCII character set only uses 7. Most computers can use 8 Bits per Byte so that they can send data codes which use all 8 bits. The factory default setting on the Portfolio is therefore 8, but the option of 7 is given in case a remote system dictates this to you.

Stop bits . . .

To obtain the Stop bits options, press [S] when the RS-232 menu is displayed. You may choose [1] or [2]. Stop bits mark the end of the transmission of a single character. Choose a setting on the Portfolio which corresponds to that of the host system.

Initialize

Initialize is selected from the RS-232 menu by pressing [I]. It is necessary to use initialize when any of the RS-232 menu settings have been altered, when the serial interface is connected to the Portfolio, before returning to the Setup menu.

RS 232 menu factory default settings and options

Configuration	Default	Other optional values
Baud rate	9600	4800, 2400, 1200, 600, 300, 150, 110
Parity	None	Even, Odd
Data bits	8	7
Stop bits	1	2

File Transfer

The File transfer menu appears on the screen when [F] is pressed on the Setup menu. Its purpose is to give the user options to Transmit, Receive or Serve the commands of the host PC during the transfer of files via the optional parallel interface which can be fitted to the Portfolio. The various menu alternatives are chosen by pressing the key representing the initial letter of the command required.

Using the Parallel Interface

The Portfolio's parallel interface is a necessity for any owner who wants to transfer data and programs between it and a desktop PC. It is also necessary if one needs to output data to a parallel printer.

The interface plugs into the expansion socket on the right side of the Portfolio's base. In addition, software on 5.25" and 3.5" disks, for the PC, and a manual are supplied. The interface can be connected to a printer by means of a normal IBM parallel printer cable, or to the parallel port of a desktop PC via a special cable with a 25 pin D type male connector at either end. It is also possible to use the parallel printer cable for file transfer if the Centronics plug is fitted with an adapter to convert it to the 25 pin male D type connector.

To use the interface for printing, the Portfolio is switched off and the interface is then connected to it. Next the printer cable is connected between the parallel interface and the printer, which must also be switched off. The Portfolio and printer should then be switched on. All printing and printer settings should be adjusted as required. Data can then be sent to the printer from the applications software, as detailed in Chapter 10 and as given in the sections detailing use of the applications software and operating system. Further information on printing is given in the interface manual.

For file transfer, it is first necessary to connect the various pieces of hardware; Portfolio, parallel interface, cable and PC. This must be done with Portfolio and PC switched off. When the connections have been made, the two computers are switched on. Data transfer, although carried out by use of the PC's parallel card, is in fact a serial process with a transmission rate of only 200 characters per second.

The file transfer software on the PC can be started from hard or floppy disk by typing the program's name, FT.

```
A>ft
Press the first letter of the option you require
     Transmit  Receive  Server  List  Quit
```

The File Transfer software menu as it appears on a PC's screen

On the Portfolio, the Setup File transfer menu is selected and a [T], [R] or [S] chosen.

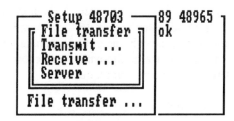

The Portfolio's Setup File transfer menu

The simplest method for file transfer involves the choice of Server on the Portfolio and either Transmit or Receive on the PC software menu. Also, files present on the Portfolio can be listed on the PC's screen by choosing [L].

Therefore, having made these suggested menu settings, if one wishes to transfer a file from the Portfolio to the PC, [R] is pressed on the PC. Next, the file name and location on the Portfolio must be entered at the PC end, together with its desired destination on the PC's disks.

When [Enter] has been pressed after the last entry, the file will be sent from the Portfolio to the PC. Only copies of the files are transferred and the masters remain on the computer of origin.

If you want to send a file from the PC to the Portfolio, the procedure is the same, except that [T] is pressed on the PC's keyboard.

Command lines can be used with the file transfer software, instead of menu selections. These take the form of:

```
FT <source file name><destination file name> /t/r/s/l/e/f/d/?
```

Drives and directories can be included with the file names. The usual rules for shortening, as applicable to the DOS COPY command, also apply.

The command:

```
FT B:\LETTERS\JACK.TXT  C:\SYSTEM\JACK.TXT /t
```

would cause the file JACK.TXT to be sent from disk B:, directory LETTERS on the PC to directory SYSTEM on disk C: on the Portfolio. Provided that both computers are set in the correct disks and directories, the file could be sent simply by typing:

```
FT JACK.TXT /t
```

Switches, included after the last file name, can be used as well.

Switch	Function
/t	Transmits files to the Portfolio
/r	Receives files from the Portfolio
/s	Server mode. Use without file names to set Server
/l	List Portfolio files
/e	FT prompt language set to English
/f	FT prompt language set to French
/d	FT prompt language set to German
/?	Get help

File Transfer Switches

The File Transfer software can also be run from batch files

Further information, including error messages, is given in the manual sold with the Parallel interface.

The Clipboard

The Clipboard is a valuable utility which allows information to be transferred between all the applications programs, except the Calculator. For instance, a set of calculations produced by the Worksheet could be transferred to the Editor and included in a report, or an address from the Address Book could be placed in the Editor at the end of a letter. It is also possible to enter items into the Editor and, provided the format is suitable, transfer them to the Address Book or Diary. Data can also be copied or moved within an application. If you had a text paragraph which was in the wrong position in the Editor, it would be possible to transfer it to another location and thus avoid the need to retype it.

To bring the menu driven Clipboard into use press [Fn][3].

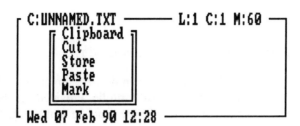

The Clipboard menu

The operation of the Clipboard allows two basic functions to be carried out:

Moving data

and

Copying data

When data is *moved* the original is lost, when it is *copied* the original remains and the copy is a duplicate.

Clipboard commands

In order to move or copy a piece of data, it must first be marked, then cut or stored and finally pasted. Therefore the menu commands following will be described in this logical sequence, rather than the order in which they appear on the Clipboard menu.

Mark

It is essential to place a marker at the beginning of any data which you want to move or copy to another location in the Portfolio. In order to mark a piece of data, for example a piece of text in the Editor, move the cursor to the beginning of the data to be marked. Next press [Fn][3] and then [M].

After the marker has been placed in the data, the Clipboard menu will vanish. The cursor must then be positioned at the end of the data concerned. You can move the data to another location, or store a copy of it in memory for copying. When the cursor is at the end of the data and you are ready to continue, press [Fn][3] again and the Clipboard menu will reappear on the screen. Next, choose either Cut or Store.

Cut

Cut is the command to use when you want to move the data to a new location. When the Clipboard menu appears on the screen again, press [C]. The data which you have selected will then vanish from the screen.

Store

To copy, but not remove the data from the original, use Store. When the Clipboard menu is presented on the screen, after you have marked the beginning of the data and pressed [Fn][3] for the second time, press [S]. When Store is used, the original data remains, but a copy of it is placed in the computer's memory.

Paste

The final part of the Clipboard process is pasting. When either Cut or Store are used, the data is fixed in the final position by using Paste.

Put the cursor in the final position to which you want to move or copy the data. Press [Fn][3] and, when the Clipboard menu shows on the screen, press [P]. The moved or copied data will then show on the screen.

A piece of data which has been Stored can be copied to a new location as many times as is necessary.

Other Clipboard features

The Clipboard save option in the Setup menu can be set to on or off. If it is set to On the data from the Clipboard is saved in a special file, called CLIPBORD.DAT . When you move to a new Application the Clipboard can recover information from this file and transfer it into the new Application.

If the Clipboard save option is switched Off, the Cut or Stored data will be lost when you move out of the current Application.

Like any other file, CLIPBORD.DAT can be discarded by DELeting it from DOS, or its contents can be viewed by loading it into the Editor. Details of these operations can be found in chapters 2 and 6. When the Clipboard save option is switched On again, a new file will be created when the Clipboard is used.

The Clipboard can also be cleared within the current Application program by doing a dummy run. Press [Fn][3], then press [M] when the menu appears. Leave the cursor in the same position and press [Fn][3] again. When the menu is shown on the screen for the second time, press [S]. This has the effect of copying nothing and clearing the Clipboard's memory allocation

As long as Clipboard save is switched On, prior to pasting the data, you can transfer to a new Application and a new document. The Clipboard works within the same Application, even when Clipboard save is switched Off.

An example of Clipboard use

In this example, an address previously entered into the Address Book will be copied
to the end of a letter in the Editor.

First, make sure that Clipboard save is switched on. From the DOS screen, press
[J|\J[Z] to get the main Applications menu, then press [S] for Setup (or go straight to
the Setup menu by pressing [J|\J[S]), then [A] for Applications. At this point the
menu will show whether or not the Clipboard save is switched On or Off. If it is
switched Off, switch it On by pressing [C]. When you are sure that the Clipboard
save is switched on, return to the main Applications menu by pressing [Esc] twice.

Choose [E] for Editor and type your letter as usual. When you have finished, save
you letter in a file with an appropriate name and press [Esc] to get back to the main
Applications menu.

Next, select [A] from the main Applications menu to get into the Address Book, and
you will see the list of names. Place the cursor on the one you have selected and
press [Enter]. This will automatically position the cursor at the beginning of the card
containing that name and address. Press [Fn][3] and then [M] to mark the beginning
of the name and address. The Clipboard menu will disapear from the screen. Move
the cursor to the end of the address and press [Fn][3] and then [S]. The Portfolio will
save a copy of the name and address to CLIPBORD.DAT for future use. You can
press [Esc] to return to the main Applications menu and then choose [E] to get to the
Editor, or simply press [J|\J[E] to move straight from the Address Book to the Editor.

The letter which you have typed will be loaded automatically as the default
document. Move the cursor to the end of the letter, where you want to insert the
address, and press [Fn][3]. When the Clipboard menu is shown, press [P] and the
address will be inserted into your letter.

8

The Worksheet

What is a Worksheet ?

The Portfolio's Worksheet is a number crunching facility, of the type otherwise known as a spreadsheet. It can be thought of as a two dimensional grid, consisting of 255 rows down and 127 columns across. All the columns are designated by letters and the rows by numbers. Each box of the grid, into which you can enter text, figures and formulae, from the computer's keyboard, is called a cell. Like the squares on a chess board, any cell on the grid can be located by means of its unique row and column number, known as the cell reference. For example A1 is the upper left square, A2 the one underneath and B1 is the one next to A1.

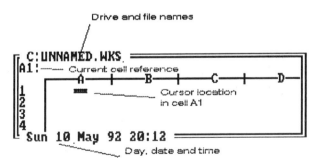

Part of the Worksheet to show edge numbering

The illustration shows the path name in the upper left of the frame, with the cell reference beneath it. When you alter anything in the Worksheet the ≈ character will show in the upper right of the frame. At the bottom left are shown the day, date and time.

Figures can be subjected to various calculations, by straightforward arithmetic, or the insertion of formulae and certain functions which are built into the software.

Spreadsheets have much more power than simple calculators because a large number of figures and formulae can be entered on one sheet and be subjected to a variety of mathematical operations. Another major advantage of spreadsheets is that, on the basis of one alteration, all the calculations in the grid can be automatically updated. Thus, forecasting the effect of a 10% or 15% rise on a set of prices, mortgage payments or a cashflow projection can be very easy.

The increasing popularity and general development of personal computer use has undoubtedly been helped by the value of spreadsheet software to a spectrum of enterprises. Apart from routine calculations, companies of all kinds have found them of use in modelling a variety of financial scenarios. It is, for instance, possible to see what the effects of an increase in various overheads such as wages, raw materials, sales volume, sales prices, and capital projects will have on the viability of one or more divisions of a corporation.

On the domestic front there are all sorts of possibilities for the application of spreadsheet experimentation, such as monthly budgets, household income, expense sheets, mortgages, school and university expenses, as well as adventure holidays, hobby expenses and garden productivity, to name just a few.

The screen as a window

With the Portfolio's small screen (or even on a full PC VDU) it is not possible to see all of the Worksheet at once. The screen should therefore be regarded as a window which you can use to view various sections, by moving it to different areas of the Worksheet.

Compatibility

The Portfolio's spreadsheet is highly (though not completely) compatible with that of Lotus 1-2-3 Release 1A. The Lotus standard has been very widely adopted by other software manufacturers, which means that the Portfolio version is also able to communicate directly with a number of other, usually cheaper, spreadsheets sold under different labels. Twin, VP-Planner, Javelin and Ability are examples of Lotus look-alikes. If you run one with another name, on a desktop computer, check to see if it is compatible with Lotus 1-2-3. The significance of compatibility is, that by using either a memory card, or the linking cable and parallel interface supplied as an accessory to the Portfolio, you should be able to swap Worksheet files backwards and forwards between a desktop PC and the Portfolio. These files usually have the suffix .WKS, so if you see a PC file called, for example, MYCASH.WKS, you should be able to load it straight into the Worksheet.

Planning

As with any intellectual activity, it is important to have a good idea of your main objectives when constructing a worksheet. If these are relatively complex, write them down on paper.

After this stage, you can begin to plan the contents of the rows and columns in more detail, still with paper and pencil, but taking account of the whole area of the worksheet which you are constructing. By considering each set of data by itself, you could, for instance, group certain sets of input and output data together in regions where they would make a better presentation when the results were being studied by some person other than yourself.

Where possible, use formulae and the worksheet functions to clarify the planning and ease any future alterations of the mathematical processes. Note, also, that there is a convention whereby the time element of data runs horizontally across the worksheet from left to right.

It is worth including a few informative notes, as a reminder, where there is likely to be any misunderstanding about the function or use of the worksheet. Since cell A1 is easily reached and frequently used, the top left hand corner of the worksheet may be the best position to use for this purpose.

How to use the Worksheet

Obtaining the Worksheet screen

Method 1. Using the main Applications Menu:

From DOS press [⌂]|[⌂]+[Z]+[W]

This selects the main Applications Menu and then the Worksheet.

Method 2. Bypassing the main Applications Menu:

From DOS press [⌂]|[⌂]+[W]

Pressing these keys bypasses the main Applications Menu and presents the worksheet screen immediately.

Method 3. Typing a command from DOS:

From the C> prompt type app/w and the worksheet screen will appear.

Hands On!

There is no substitute for practical experience, so experiment with the Portfolio's Worksheet as you read through the rest of this section of the book.

From the main applications menu, press [W] for Worksheet. If the Portfolio's Worksheet has not been used previously, you may be confronted with a set of blank cells. If it has been used, by default the sheet last saved from it will probably be reloaded. Automatic reloading is set by the Autoload option of the Worksheet Defaults menu. The worksheet can be cleared of figures by pressing [Fn][1] to get the Worksheet menu, then [F] for files and [N] for New.

Try playing around with a few figures to get the hang of the system. By means of the cursor and certain other keys, you can move the cursor around in the grid, and wherever it is currently located you can enter figures or labels.

Keys which move the cursor.

[→]	one cell right
[←]	one cell left
[↑]	one cell up
[↓]	one cell down
[Tab]	one screen right
[Shift][Tab]	one screen left
[PgUp]	two thirds of one screen up
[PgDn]	two thirds of one screen down
[Home]	moves the cursor to cell A1
[End]	With a cursor key moves to first or last in a group of cells. Press [Fn]+[End], then [↑],[↓],[→] or [←] to make the move.

Remember that you need to press [Fn] when using the keys marked in blue (Home, PgUp, PgDn and End).

Try positioning the cursor in the A1 cell (top left) and enter the label Add. Move the cursor down to A2 and enter 12. In A3 enter 24 and in A4 enter 36. Finally in A5 enter @SUM(A2..A4) and move the cursor to the next cell down. Bingo, cell A5 contains the total (72) of the numbers you entered. If you make a mistake, use the [Del] key to delete the contents of the cell and then re-enter. You have entered:

A1	a title
A2	a value
A3	a value
A4	a value
A5	one of the Worksheet's built in functions which has totalled all the values between cells A2 and A5. The cells A2 to A5 are described as a Range. @sum, like the other @ functions, is considered a formula by the Worksheet.

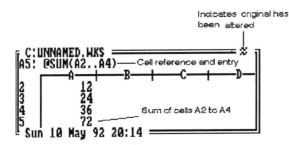

The entries, as they appear on the Portfolio

Easy entry of values when using formulae

When using @SUM, you typed the range of cells as (A2..A4). There is an alternative, and possibly easier, method to include a cell range with a formula.

Let us put the total in cell C5 this time.

Enter @SUM(in cell C5, then press []. A box will show on the screen and it can be moved around by means of the cursor keys. Move it to cell A2 and press [↑] . The box is then anchored at cell A2. Next, expand the box downwards to include cells A3 and A4. Notice that the cell names following @SUM(correspond to those included in the box. Finally, type the end bracket [Enter]. The whole formula will now show as @SUM(A2..A4)

Individual cells can be specified. Choose a cell for the formula and enter the first part of it, including the opening bracket. Press a cursor key and move the box to the first cell to be included. Next, press an operator, such as + - * / or , and the cell reference will appear in the entry position with the formula, followed by the appropriate operator. This can be repeated for any number of cells. To conclude, type in the closing bracket and then press [Enter].

This technique, known as Range Painting, can be used for any formula where one or more cells, including columns, rows or blocks, has to be specified.

Text

The Portfolio's Worksheet automatically recognises all characters as text, except:

0 1 2 3 4 5 6 7 8 9 + - (@ # and the decimal point

Formulae

A formula is an instruction which causes a Worksheet to take values from one or more named cells, do a calculation and show the result in another cell.

When formulae are used, you can include cell references, like A1, B2, etc., operators such as + - * / , functions like @SUM, and numbers. Formulae may contain up to 240 characters.

When a formula begins with a letter, prefix it with a + so that the Worksheet does not mistake the formula for a label.

Functions

Not to be confused with function keys, which are different, these are built in to the Worksheet and can be considered as shorthand versions of complex formulae. Functions begin with @.

Values

A value is a number. Any number between plus or minus 9.999 to the power 99 can be used.

Precedence and operators

The Worksheet's preference and operators are given below in decreasing order:

^	powers
+ -	unary plus and unary minus
* /	multiply and divide
+ -	add and subtract
> < = <= >= <>	relational operators
#NOT#	logical NOT
#AND# #OR#	logical AND, logical OR

Circular reference

A circular reference situation arises when a cell contains a formula which refers back to itself. Under these circumstances the computer may not perform properly because it is trying to read and write to the same cell. An error is therefore indicated. In some cases a circular reference can be used to increment a cell's value automatically.

Either way, the top left corner of the Worksheet will show a small circle under the cell reference.

Absolute and Relative cell references

Absolute and relative cell references are expressed in the way formulae are written for the Worksheet. Details are given in the section of text in this chapter dealing with the Copy command.

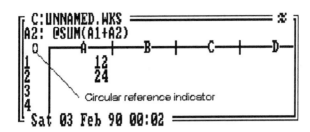

*Screen showing a circular reference. Cell A2 contains the formula @SUM(A1+A2).
A1 contains a value of 12 and A2 is indicating a value of 24, even though it has no
value entered into it.*

Using the Function Keys

As in other Portfolio applications, the function keys can be used to carry out some
operations directly.

[Fn][1] or [/] or [J|\]	Show current application main menu
[Fn][2]	General help
[Fn][3]	Go to the Clipboard Menu
[Fn][4]	Recover the last deletion
[Fn][5]	Switch screen frame on or off
[Fn][9]	Recalculate the current Worksheet. Forces a single recalculation if the recalculate option has been turned off.
[Fn][0]	Flip between windows

[Fn][6] - [Fn][8] are not used for the Worksheet.

Using the Worksheet Menus

To get the main Worksheet menu from the screen showing columns and rows, press:

[Fn][1] *or* [J\|\] *or* [/]

Lotus 1-2-3 uses the [/] key to get to the menu so, unlike the other applications, this
key can also be used from within the Portfolio Worksheet for this purpose.

As in the other applications software, you can back out of menu choices and the
Worksheet as well by pressing [Esc].

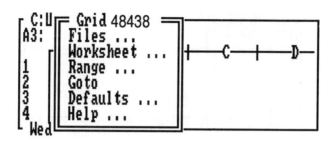

Main Worksheet Menu, showing free memory after the word Grid

Files . . .

To get the Files menu press [F] from the main Worksheet menu.

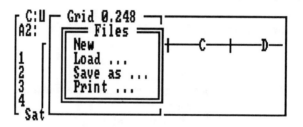

The Files menu

There are only four files options for the Worksheet.

New

Pressing [N] while in the files menu will clear any existing Worksheet and start a new one which is called UNNAMED.WKS

If the Worksheet has been altered, and not saved, the Save Current box will be displayed on the screen so that you do not abandon the altered data inadvertently.

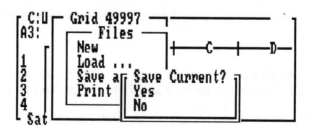

The Save Current? screen

Load

This option loads any existing Lotus 1-2-3 compatible Worksheet; namely, those with the suffix .WKS or .WK1 .

Press [L] from the Files menu and a query box for the name of the file is shown on the screen.

Accepting the default file name

To accept the name in the box, just press [Enter]. Take care to avoid loading the old default file from disk when you have already altered, but not saved, the default file of the same name in memory. If you do this your newly altered information will be obliterated.

Entering a new name

Enter the new name in the dialogue box and press [Enter]. Type in only the name if the file is in the current directory, otherwise the full path name. If the current file in memory has been altered an option to save it, before loading the new one, is offered.

Examples:

1. To load the file SALES.WKS which is in the current directory and drive.

Type SALES[Enter] (If the file is located in the root directory on drive C:, the full path name for this file is C:\SALES.WKS)

2. To load the file SALES.WKS from subdirectory SYSTEM on drive B:

Type the path name B:\SYSTEM\SALES.WKS[Enter] (If the file is located on drive B:, directory SYSTEM.)

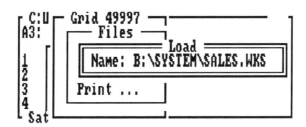

The Load dialogue box

Using Wildcards

Wildcards may be used to get a file listing for a particular directory.

Type [:][Enter] or [*.*][Enter] to view all the files and subdirectories in the current directory.

Type [*][Enter] to view all .WKS files from the current directory. .WK1 files are not listed, but can be viewed by using [:]. The drive and directory can be changed and files in it viewed by entering the drive/directory, followed by *. Entering B:\SYSTEM* when the default is C:\ is, therefore, permissible.

Save as ...

Press [S] from the Files menu. The dialogue box is displayed, inviting you to enter a file name. This gives the option to save a newly created or modified Worksheet under a new file name. The following choices exist:

Save a file with the default name displayed in the box. Just press [Enter]. The warning about saving default files, given in the Load section, also applies here.

Save a file with a new name to the present directory. Type the name of the file and press [Enter].

Save a file to another drive or directory. Type the full path name and press [Enter].

View a list of .WKS files in the current directory. Type [*][Enter]

View a list of all files and subdirectories in the current directory. Type [:][Enter] or [*.*][Enter].

Print ...

Pressing [P] from the Files menu causes the screen to show a query box requesting information about the Range of cells to be printed and the Width, in characters, to be printed on the page.

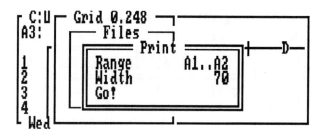

The Print query box

Range

To set the Range press [R], then type in names of the top left and the bottom right cells at the limits of the group of cells which you want printed, and press [Enter]. The two limiting cells must be separated by two full stops. You can also use the expanding box to enclose the area to be printed. The box will first be located on the leftmost cell shown opposite Range. Therefore, if A1..DW23 is showing, the box will first be located on A1.

If the area to be printed runs from cell A1, all you need to do is to expand the box, using the cursor keys, to include the whole of the area you want to print. Then press [Enter] and the query box will be shown with the Range set.

If you do not want to start from cell A1 the box can be moved to a new location. When the box is first shown press [.][Esc] and the box will disappear. Then press a cursor key and the box will reappear and move with the cursor key. When the box reaches the new location from which you want to start the print Range, press [.] and then expand the box by means of the cursor keys. Press [Enter] at the end of the Range and the query box will again be shown on the screen with the Range set.

Width

The number in the Width section represents the number of character widths which will be printed across the page. To change it, press [W] and enter the desired number. If you select a width greater than that which your printer is capable of, the remaining figures for that row of the Worksheet will be printed on the row underneath. Therefore do not exceed the permitted width for your printer.

The width of the paper is, of course, constant, but the amount of space occupied by the text varies according to the size of the printed characters. Allowing for a 0.25 inch margin on either side, on 8.5 inch wide paper, use the following table to set the widths.

Characters per inch	Set dialogue box to
10	80
12	96
15	150 (condensed printing)

In order to print anything more than the standard character set, you will need to make sure the printer is properly configured. This can often be done by setting switches on the printer, but you might need to send a Control code to the printer where external switches are not provided. For large Worksheets it might be better for you to use condensed printing at, say, 15 cpi, if you have this facility on your dot matrix machine, to allow for a greater number of printed columns across the page.

Sending control codes to the printer

Method 1. Using the Setup menu.

This should be done before you start using the Worksheet. Alternatively, you can save your data and escape from the Worksheet. When the DOS screen shows, press [J]\[J][S] and the Setup menu will be shown on the screen.

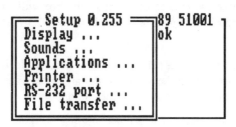

The Setup menu

Next, press [P] and the various printer default settings will appear.

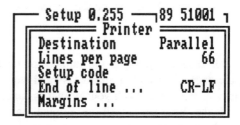

The Setup Printer menu

At this stage, you should only be interested in altering the Setup code. Press [S] to check this. If you do not want to change the code. press [Esc] to escape and, if necessary, [Esc] repeatedly to get back to the DOS screen.

To set a new character code, look up the relevant control character for your printer and, after erasing any unwanted material from the Setup Code box, enter your code in 3 figure ASCII decimal form, separating each ASCII control character by a back slash. For example, the code Esc SI which is the Epson FX code for commencing condensed printing would be entered as \027\015 .

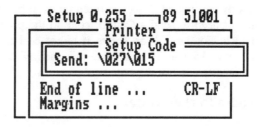

The Setup Code box showing the code for Esc SI

Method 2. Entering a printer code in cell A1.

This is not an officially recognised technique, but it works if you want to use the Epson code for condensed print (Esc SI) and has the advantage that each Worksheet can be formatted individually. You will use a worksheet cell for a printer code and it cannot then be employed for labels or any other purpose.

When you employ method 2, make sure that there are no printer control codes in Setup which can interfere with those which you may place in the Worksheet.

The principle used here is the same as in the Editor. When using the Editor to format a document, printer control codes are entered as characters in the body of the text . In the case of the Worksheet, the printer control codes are entered in a cell. When information in the Worksheet is sent to the printer, the flow commences with cell A1. Therefore, this cell should be used for the control codes.

Take care not to use formulae or cells which refer any other cell to any cell which holds printer control codes.

To use the same code given in Method 1, Esc SI, look up the relevant ASCII control codes which are ^[for Esc and ^O for SI. Enter these in cell A1 by pressing [Shift][6][[[ ] for Esc and [Shift][6][O] for SI. The codes will be transmitted to the printer when the Worksheet is sent to it, and an Epson FX printer will respond by changing to its condensed character set. All following data will then be printed out in this font until it is changed by either altering the control code, or switching off the printer. By using [Shift][6], you are simply telling the Portfolio that a control character is being entered and this will usually be represented on the screen by a ^ preceding the character which you type after it.

Be warned that this method does not work with other control codes which use printable characters. In fact, the Portfolio objects so much that it shows a system failure warning on the screen. In this case one can recover from the catastrophe by pressing [Esc].

ASCII tables are included in Appendix A at the end of this book. For more information, refer to Chapter 10.

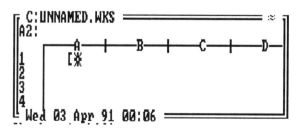

Cell A1 with Esc SI entered.

Sideways?

There is also the possibility of using programs like Sideways and Sidewriter which will print your Worksheet at a rotation of 180 degrees, (i.e. sideways!) so that you gain the advantage of 11.5, rather than 8.5, inches width on an 80 column printer. To use these programs directly with the Portfolio it will probably be necessary to add extra memory, but the Worksheet can be transferred to a desktop PC and printed sideways from that. There is a little more information about this in Chapter 11.

Go!

Lastly, if you press [G] your Worksheet will be sent straight to any printer which is connected to the Portfolio by a parallel or serial interface and cable. If Setup Printer Destination is set to File, the Worksheet will be sent to a .PRN file as a formatted document which can be printed later by means of a DOS command.

Worksheet . . .

From the main Worksheet menu, press [W] to get the Worksheet options menu. The Worksheet options menu offers six commands which enable functions such as automatic recalculation, protection of areas containing titles, insertion and removal of rows and columns, selection of window areas and deletion of data to be carried out.

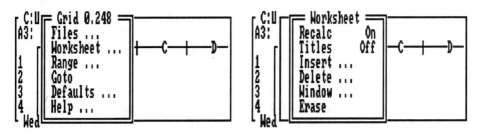

The main Worksheet command and Worksheet options menus

Recalc

This is a toggle for on or off and Recalc is an abbreviation of recalculation. Its current state is shown in the menu and pressing [R] will change it to whatever state is not shown. If On is shown pressing [R] will cause it to change to Off and vice versa.

If Recalc is set to On, any new figures entered into the Worksheet will cause a global recalculation, so that all the other figures will be automatically corrected to take account of the new figures entered.

Under certain circumstances, as when many figures are being put into a complex Worksheet, checking the input is made easier by switching Recalc to Off, so that all figures remain the same. When a function, such as @SUM, is entered with Recalc switched Off the indicator S is shown in the top left of the Worksheet screen. If Recalc has been switched to Off, a single global recalculation of the grid can be forced by pressing [Fn][9] or the Recalc mode can be set to On again by pressing [R].

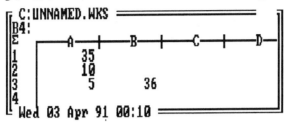

The top part of screen showing the Σ indicator

Titles

Titles is also a toggle for On or Off. When On it functions to prevent erasure of titles which you want to keep on the Worksheet. Also, these titles will be shown in the appropriate row or column, even when you move the cursor away from the cell in which the title is located. The current state of Titles is shown on the menu. If it is shown as On, pressing [T] will cause it to go Off and vice versa.

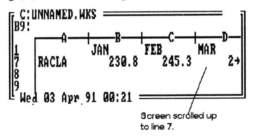

The appearance of Titles, switched On, when the screen is scrolled. Note that the titles relevant to the row or column are still displayed.

To use this option, while in the Worksheet enter your titles in the first rows and columns as usual, then move the cursor to a place below the rows and to the right of any columns which you wish to preserve.

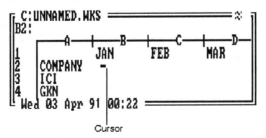

The screen with cursor in position for switching Titles On

Next press [Fn][1]. When the menu comes onto the screen, press [W] and then [T] to toggle the Titles to On. When you have done this you will not be able to move the cursor into the protected area by means of the cursor keys, but the Goto command will place the cursor in that area if instructed to do so. If you want to insert any new titles, you can switch Titles to Off, enter your new titles and then reposition the cursor to protect the same rows and columns again before switching Titles to On.

Insert . . .

The Insert command allows blank rows and/or columns to be introduced, at the current cursor position, between others already on the Worksheet.

To use the Insert command, first place the cursor on the row below, or the column to the right of, the position where you want to place the new blank working area. Press [Fn][1] while the Worksheet is shown on the screen. When the menu appears, press [W] and then [I] when the next menu is shown. The screen will show an option box, asking whether you want to insert a row or column. Select one or the other, by pressing the [R] or [C] key. Another small double framed box is then displayed in the position where the row or column will be inserted. By using the cursor keys, this may be expanded to cover one or more rows or columns. When [Enter] is pressed the number of blank rows or columns selected will be inserted in the Worksheet. It is possible to stretch the box both vertically and horizontally, but you can only insert rows or columns; not both together. The blank areas can then be used like any other blank area of the Worksheet and all the other rows and columns will be adjusted automatically so that formulae will always use the correct references to cells.

Delete . . .

The purpose of this command is to allow whole rows and columns, and their contents, to be deleted from the Worksheet.

The controls work in a similar manner to those of the Insert command. First position the cursor on the row or column to be deleted. It is possible to delete more than one row or column and if you want to do this, put the cursor on the top row or on the far left column of those to be deleted. Press [Fn][1] to view the main menu and then [W] for the Worksheet menu. When that menu is shown press [D] to get Delete. An option box for row or column is seen next, and you should press [R] or [C], as appropriate. The cell on which your cursor has been placed will then be surrounded by a double framed expandable box. To delete a single row or column, simply press [Enter], or to delete more than one row or column, stretch the box in the required direction and then press [Enter].

Window . . .

The window option allows you to flip backwards and forwards between two areas of the Worksheet which cannot both be shown on the screen at the same time. For instance, if you were working on cells in the region of B50 and needed to regularly see data in cell Z4, you could arrange the window so that both these parts of the Worksheet could be viewed alternately on the screen, simply by pressing [Fn][0].

To use this facility while in the Worksheet, place the cursor in the cell where you want to create the window, press [Fn][1], then [W] to get the Worksheet main menu, and [W] again for window. An option box will be shown on the screen and you should press [M] to mark the required cell. This sequence has designated the window to which you will be able to return from any other area of the Worksheet.

When you move away from the marked cell, by using either the cursor keys or the Goto option, pressing [Fn][0] when the Worksheet screen is shown, or [F] from the option box, will cause the screen to move back to the window containing the marked cell. If you press [Fn][0] again the screen will return to the previous position. You may move around the Worksheet and [Fn][0] will always flip between the marked cell and your present position.

Only one window can be created at a time, but by using the Window and Mark options you can redefine the position as often as necessary. The window command can be used with the Goto option to move rapidly around the Worksheet.

Erase

Using Erase causes the whole Worksheet to be wiped clean! So Erase must be used with due care. When the Worksheet is erased all the parameters are reset and the name of the Worksheet reverts to UNNAMED.WKS .

To use Erase, while in the Worksheet, press [Fn][1] , then [W] for the Worksheet menu. Next press [E] . If the Worksheet is one which has been loaded and not altered, it will immediately be wiped clean.

If you have altered, or done any work on it, a box, asking whether you are sure, is shown. You must then answer Yes or No, by pressing the [Y] or [N] keys or positioning the cursor and pressing [Enter].

If you want to keep the contents of the Worksheet, it should be saved by using the Save as... option on the Files menu. Erase does not delete a Worksheet file which has been previously saved and any data in such a file can therefore be recovered.

Parameters reset when the Worksheet is erased

Data and formulae are abandoned
Viewing windows are discarded
Text realigned to the left
Column widths reset to 9 characters
Current file name retained
Numeric format reset to General

Range . . .

The Range menu contains a series of facilities which allow you to copy, erase, set the widths and numeric formats of ranges of cells.

To obtain the Range menu from the Worksheet, press [Fn][1] and then press [R] .

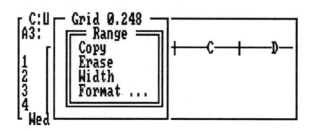

The Range menu

Copy

This is an easy way to duplicate the contents of a block of cells for insertion into another part of the Worksheet. The block copied may be just a few cells or a large number of rows and columns.

To use Copy, from the Worksheet, first position the cursor at the corner of the block of cells you want to copy, then press [Fn][1] to get the main Worksheet menu, then [R] for range and finally [C] for copy. On the screen you will then see the current cell surrounded by a double framed expandable box. The box can be stretched up or down and sideways by using the cursor keys. Expand the box to cover the range of cells which you want to copy. Whichever way you go, the original cell will always form one corner of the box. The range of cells selected is shown on the top right of the screen.

When you are satisfied that the box encloses the range of cells to be copied, press [Enter] and the cursor will go to the cell in which you started.

Next, move the cursor to the top left cell of the new range, where you want to insert the data. An expandable box will appear. If you are copying a block, there is no need to remember the exact range of the destination cells, simply press [Enter] again and the data will appear on the Worksheet.

Points to note about the Copy command

1. If a block of cells wider than a single column or a single row is copied, it can only be inserted in a new area once with each use of copy. As mentioned above, when such a block is copied the exact range of the destination cells need not be specified, as long as the destination box is located at the top left corner of the destination range.

2. If a single row or a single column of cells is copied, it can be replicated at the destination as many times as the remaining space on the Worksheet will allow. In this case you have to expand the destination box to cover all the rows or columns where you want the original column or row to be inserted.

3. A range of cells to be copied can be specified without using the box. For example, if you wanted to copy a range of cells from B10 to C25, just enter the letter and number of the starting cell on the keyboard, then two decimal points and finish by entering the letter and number of the cell at the end of the range - B10..C25. Press [Enter] and Copy To: will appear. Designate the cell range in the same way, or simply enter the starting cell of the range, where the data is to be copied to, and the Portfolio will fill it in automatically.

4. Cell references: When copying formulae, it is important to recognise that different types of cell references exist. It follows that when you are first defining the formula, you should decide what type of references are to be included, though it is possible to alter them at a later time.

A. Relative cell references

Relative cell references do not have a special designator, e.g. in cell B10 the formula B8*B9 is entered.

The Worksheet reads this as 'take the value of two cells above and multiply it by the value of one cell above. Place the result in the current cell'. The values in cells B8 and B9 are seen relative to B10. Therefore if the formula in B10 is copied to Z20, the values in Z18 and Z19 will relate to Z20 in the same way.

B8*B9 is a relative cell reference.

B. Absolute cell references

Column and row references are preceded by a $ sign and look like this: $C$5

Sometimes it is essential that, no matter where a formula is copied to, it always relates to only one or two specified cells on a worksheet. These may, for example, contain unique data. In the Worksheet below, cell C5 contains the current number of shares in the Orful Unit Trust, while the current price per share is always entered in cell C6. If the formula $C$5*$C$6 in cell C7 is always to reflect the current value of the investment in the Orful Unit Trust it must refer absolutely to the figures in C5 and C6 no matter where it is copied to in the Worksheet.

To make a cell reference absolute, simply add $ before the row and column position of the cell.

C. Mixed cell references.

It is possible to make only row or column references absolute and the other part of the cell definition relative. For instance, row A can be made absolute, but any cell in it relative. A cell definition for an absolute column and relative row would look like this: $A2, and a cell definition for a relative column and an absolute row is shown thus: A$2.

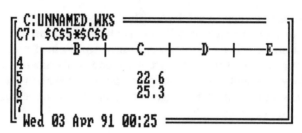

Worksheet with labels to illustrate absolute cell references

All cell references are treated as relative unless otherwise specified by the character $.

Erase

Erase is used to delete the contents of a block of cells anywhere on the Worksheet. As with the copy command, the block may be just one cell, or several rows and several columns.

First, position the cursor at one corner of the rectangular block of cells to be erased, then press [Fn][1], when the main Worksheet menu shows, press [R], to get the Range menu, and then [E]. A stretchable double-framed box is shown at the point on the Worksheet where you have positioned the cursor. By using the cursor keys you can expand the box in any direction and the range of cells actually covered is shown at the top right of the screen. When you are satisfied that the cells to be erased are correctly defined, press [Enter] and they will be deleted from the Worksheet. Data and formulae contained in the erased cells are abandoned.

Width

By using this command the width of a range of columns can be set to between one and 34 characters.

Press [Fn][1] and then [R] to get the Range menu. Next press [W] for the Width command. The default setting is then shown enclosed in a box. Enter a figure for the column width to be set and press [Enter]. This causes a range selection box to be displayed in the place where the cursor was positioned on the Worksheet. By means of the cursor keys, this is used to define the number of columns to be altered.

The cell range is shown at the top left of the screen, but as explained, the command only operates on the columns shown. Columns can be defined from the keyboard, simply by typing in a cell range.

When the range has been correctly defined, press [Enter], and the cells in the columns defined will be reset to the new width.

Format...

Format can be used to set the numeric format of one or a range of cells. The various options given below are allowed, and the numeric format for the current cell is shown at the top left side of the screen, along with the cell location and its contents.

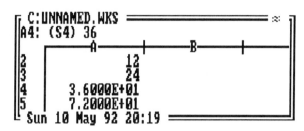

Worksheet screen with the current cell set to 4 decimal places in Scientific Format

Type of Format	Screen Indicator	Example.
Fixed	(F3)	1000.000 (fixed at 3 decimal places)
Scientific	(S2)	1.00E+03 (fixed at 2 decimal places)
Currency	(C2)	£1,000.00
,	(,3)	1,000.000(triad comma separator and 3 dp)
General	(G)	1000
Percent	(P2)	100000.00% (fixed at 2 decimal place)

N.B. Percentages should be entered on the Worksheet as decimals. 20% would therefore be entered as .20

To use the command whilst in the Worksheet, first position the cursor at one corner of the block of cells which you want to format, then press [Fn][1] to get the main menu. Next press [R] for the Range menu and [F] for Format. The Format menu will appear on the screen and you should press the initial letter of the format required.

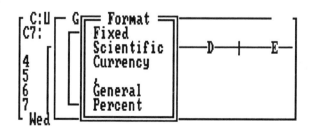

The Range Format menu

Except for General format the screen will first show an entry box for you to set the number of decimal places. Enter the figure of your choice and press [Enter]. Next the double framed 'range painting' box will appear at the position of the cursor and, by moving the cursor keys, you can stretch this to define the range of cells which you want to be formatted. Alternatively, you can enter the cell range directly by typing from the keyboard. When you have defined the range, press [Enter] and the numeric format of the defined cells will be changed to that which you have selected.

When the format selection procedure has been completed, the Worksheet returns to the screen. Numeric formats for the whole Worksheet are set by means of the Defaults menu but, as mentioned in that section it may be necessary to utilise the Range command instead of Defaults:Format.

Goto

The Goto command will probably be one that you will use quite frequently and it is very simple to operate. The purpose of Goto is simply to allow rapid and direct movement from one part of the Worksheet to another. With Goto the cursor can also be moved inside a protected area which contains titles and these can then be edited. You cannot move the cursor into the protected area by means of the cursor keys.

To use Goto while in the Worksheet, press [Fn][1] to get the main menu, then [G] to select the Goto command. A dialogue box is then shown on the screen and you should enter in it the row and column definition of the cell, between A1 and DW255, which you want to move to. When a definition within this range is entered, followed by [Enter], the cursor will be moved to the cell selected and you may continue working in that area.

Defaults . . .

The Defaults command is used for baseline (default) settings for various Worksheet parameters affecting all the cells.

The defaults should be entered when setting up a new Worksheet, and they then operate on the whole Worksheet, although certain areas may be reset later.

Parameters which can be set with the Defaults Menu.

Parameter	*Options*
Decimal Point	. or ,
Text Alignment	Left, Right, Centre
Column Width	1 to 74
Autoload Yes/No	Yes or No
Numeric Format	Fixed, Scientific, Currency, triad divider (,) ,General, Percent
Currency Characters	Any three characters

From the Worksheet, press [Fn][1] and the Defaults command menu will be shown on the screen, together with the current default settings.

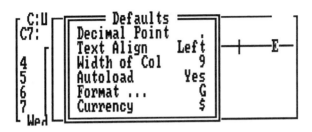

The Defaults menu

Decimal Point

The Defaults menu shows the option , or . currently selected for the decimal point. If the decimal point selected is . then the triad (or thousands) separator will be , If you press [D] while the menu is visible, the alternative option is switched on. In this case the decimal point would then become , and the triad or thousands separator .

| eg. | 1,000.25 | Defaults menu shows decimal point as . |
| | 1.000,25 | Defaults menu shows decimal point as , |

The triad or thousands separator is switched on or off by means of the Format command (see below).

Text Align

There are three options for aligning text on the Worksheet: Left, Right and Centre.

When the Defaults menu is shown, pressing [T] will cause the Text Align option box to appear on the screen. Then make your selection for the default text alignment by pressing the appropriate initial letter, [L], [R] or [C], on the keyboard.

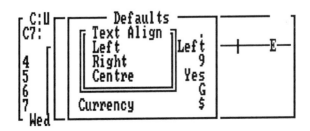

The Text Align option box

Text entry and alignment in single cells

The following characters tell the computer that the entry into a cell, even if numeric, is to be treated as text. Entries are aligned as indicated below and should be preceded by the relevant characters:

'	Left aligned
^	Centred
"	Right aligned

If a character is preced by a backslash (\), it will be duplicated across the width of the cell.

Column Width

Column Width sets the default width of all columns, as a number of characters, for the whole Worksheet.

Press [W] when the Defaults menu is shown and a dialogue box will appear on the screen. Simply enter the maximum number of characters, between 1 and 34, which you will need to put in any column of the Worksheet, and then press [Enter].

Autoload

When the Autoload option is set to Yes the last file used will automatically be loaded when the Worksheet is selected from the main Applications menu.

The current state of Autoload is shown on the Defaults menu. To toggle between Yes and No, press [A]. When you have done this the Worksheet grid is automatically returned to the screen.

Format

You may choose any one of six options for the default numeric format of the Worksheet grid. The current default is shown by Format on the Defaults menu.

To obtain the Format menu, press [F] when the Defaults menu is shown. The various options are then shown on the screen:

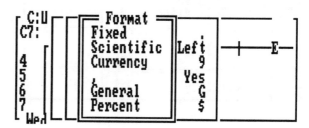

The Format menu

To select a numeric format, press the key for the appropriate initial letter. Any choice, except General format, will then cause a dialogue box to be displayed on the screen.

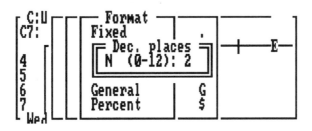

A Format entry box

Enter into it the number of decimal places which you want shown on the Worksheet. Any figures beyond the number of displayed decimal places are rounded up if over 5 or rounded down if less. Therefore, when the number of decimal places is set at 2, 200.404 shows 200.40 and 200.406 shows 200.41.

If the numeric format chosen is General, the Worksheet will show the numbers in decimal format, except where all the digits in a number cannot be fitted into the cell. In that case the display will revert to Scientific format. If the cell is less than 5 characters wide, Scientific format cannot be displayed and the cell is then shown filled with asterisks (*). When this happens, use the Range Width command to increase the cell's width.

As noted previously, percentages should be entered on the Worksheet as decimals. 20% would therefore be entered as .20

If your Portfolio will only load the Worksheet in General format

Unfortunately, some early Portfolios will not save an altered Defaults:Format Worksheet. Therefore, even though it may have been changed, the Worksheet is always loaded in General format. To remedy this situation, you can alter the numeric format by using the Range:Format command to cover as many cells as necessary.

The currency format takes the currency symbol from the default currency character set by the Currency command (see below).

Currency

To use the currency command, press the [C] key when the Defaults menu is displayed. Then type the currency symbol and press [Enter]. Up to three characters may be used at this stage. The default currency symbol is displayed by the Defaults menu.

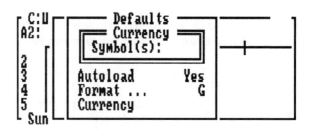

The Currency entry box

Examples of Currency Symbols:

Symbol	Currency	Keys to use
£	Pounds sterling	[Alt]+[Shift]+[£]
$	US Dollars	[$]
C$	Canadian Dollars	[C][$]
L	Italian Lira	[L]
NKr	Norwegian Krona	[N][K][r]
Dm	German Deutschmark	[D][m]

Help

The last option on the menu is Help. If you press [H] the Help menu will appear on the screen and one can make selections that will produce a pré'cis on Worksheet menus, File handling or @Functions.

The @Functions list (see later) is of particular value as quick and brief reminder.

Pressing [Fn][2] will bring up the general Help menu for queries about the keyboard, Clipboard, undelete and function keys.

Worksheet Functions

Special or complicated operations in the Worksheet can be performed quickly and simply by means of the built in functions. Functions are really sophisticated formulae stored within the Worksheet program. All the functions begin with @. Some, like @PI, place a particular value in a cell. In this case entering @PI in a cell will cause the number 3.141593 (the value of Pi) to be displayed in a cell with six decimal places. Others, like @SUM will do calculations on a range of numbers, or, like @CHOOSE, make choices based on data which you have entered.

The functions described below are all compatible with the same functions in Lotus 1-2-3, and Worksheets with these functions which are transferred from the Portfolio to a desktop PC running 1-2-3 should be completely interchangeable.

As already mentioned all functions begin with @, followed by the name of the function, and some require one or more arguments. Contrary to appearances this is not a computer punch up, but is the value, or list of values which the function operates on.

Note that the arguments which a particular function can use will depend on the function concerned. A function which requires arguments is written like this:

`@FUNCTION(argument1, argument2,..argumentn)`

Possible arguments	Example
Single value	a number e.g. 50
A cell address	B10
A formula	B10 * 25
A single cell range	B10..B25
A list of values, cells	10, 20, 30, 40
or ranges	B1, C12, C15, D10
	A10..A30, B5..B10, C1..C3

Abbreviations used in descriptions of arguments

exp	a numeric expression or a reference to a cell which displays a numeric value.
cell	a single cell reference e.g. A25
range	an inclusive cell range described as e.g A25..A50
list	a list of items which conform to the descriptions of exp and range. All items must be separated by commas. If the decimal point is a full stop.

Arithmetic functions

Most of these functions use one argument, a single value not a range.

@ABS(exp)

The absolute value of exp. The absolute value of a number is its value without a plus or minus sign. This function is useful if you want to display a number as an unsigned or positive number, perhaps in circumstances where an expression may produce a negative number. Numeric values, cell references and mathematics expressions can all be used as exp.

e.g. @ABS(-25) returns 25

@ABS(A10) would return 2.12 if cell A10 contained the number -2.12

@ABS(-300+25)-C10) would return 378 if cell C10 contained the number -103.

@EXP(exp)

The value of the constant e raised to the power exp. This function calculates the value of x where e is the base of the natural logarithms.

e.g. @EXP(5) returns 148.4132

@INT(exp)

The integer of an *exp*. Integers are whole numbers, so only the whole number part of *exp* will be returned. Numbers or cell references can be used.

e.g. @INT(5.123) returns 5

@INT(D10) would return 12 if cell D10 contained the number 12.111

@LOG(exp)

The logarithm, base 10, of exp. If exp is less than 0, ERR will appear in the cell.

e.g. @LOG(5) returns .69897

@LOG(B4) would return 3.477121 if the number 3000 was in cell B4 and @LOG(B4) in another cell.

@LN(exp)

Produces the natural logarithm of exp. If exp is less than 0 the cell will show - ERR.

@MOD(exp1,exp2)

Is the modulus (or remainder) of expression1 divided by expression2.

e.g. @MOD(5,2) would produce 1

@MOD(F10,F12) contents of cell F10 divided by the contents of F12 and the remainder is placed in the cell to which @MOD(F10,F12) was assigned.

@ROUND(exp1,exp2)

Exp1 is rounded to the number of decimal places specified by exp2. If a negative value is entered for exp2 it will be rounded to the nearest @ABS(exp2)^10.

e.g. @ROUND(2356.5678,1) would give 2356.5

@ROUND(45670.009,-3) would give 46000

@ROUND(5678.1,0) Would give 5678

@SQRT(exp)

Gives the square root of exp. If exp is negative ERR is shown.

e.g. @SQRT(16) gives 4

@SQRT(F12) gives the square root of the value in cell F12.

@RAND

The value returned is a pseudo-random number between 0.0 and 1.0. 0 may be included, whereas 1.0 is excluded. @RAND should be entered on the Worksheet.

e.g. @RAND entered while writing this text gave .589867

Trigonometric functions

@ACOS(exp)

Returns the arc cosine of exp; the angle in radians which has the cosine exp. The value of exp must be between -1 and 1, or an error message - ERR will be shown.

e.g. @ACOS(.9) returns .451027

@ACOS(B7) would give the arc cosine of the value in B7

@ASIN(exp)

Gives the arc sine of exp; the angle in radians, which has the sine exp. Again, the value of exp must be between -1 and 1, otherwise ERR will be shown.

e.g. @ASIN(-.4) returns -0.41152

@ASIN(H6) would give the arc sine of the value in H6

@ATAN(exp)

Gives the arc tangent of exp; the angle in radians, which has the tangent exp.

e.g. @ATAN(.412) returns .390808

@ATAN(H10) would give the arc tangent of the value of H(10)

@ATAN2(exp1,exp2)

Returns the arc tangent of exp1 divided by exp2; the angle in radians, which has the tangent exp1 divided by exp2.

e.g. @ATAN2(4,6) returns 0.982794

@COS(exp)

Returns the cosine of the angle exp. The angle must be entered in radians.

e.g. @COS(3.12) returns -0.99977

@SIN(exp)

Returns the sine of the angle exp which must be given in radians.

e.g. @SIN(2.5) returns 0.598472

@SIN(H4) would return the sine of the value in H4

@TAN(exp)

Returns the tangent of the angle exp. The value of exp must be given in radians.

e.g. @TAN(3.25) returns 0.108834

@TAN(H3) would return the tangent of the value in cell H

Normal arithmetical operations may be performed with these functions. For example, @TAN(2.5)+@TAN(3.0) may be entered into the same cell and will give the final result of the calculation, in this case -0.88957.

Statistical Functions

These functions operate on a list of arguments, and the arguments must be separated with commas. In a range, functions ignore all blank cells, so that if cells B6 and B7 are empty @SUM(B6..B7) will result in 0. If you use individual cells as arguments in a function blank cells containing value 0 are considered to have a value and, for example, @COUNT(B6,B7) will result in 2, even though B6 contains a 0 and B7 is completely blank.

@AVG(list)

Computes the arithmetic average of the values in the list and displays the result in the cell where the function is entered.

e.g. @AVG(100,300,12,5) a list of numbers (or cells)

@AVG(C5..C50) a range of cells (or numbers)

@AVG((120/5),(54*2),(2+3)) a list of mathematical expressions

@COUNT(list)

Shows the number of entries in a specified list or range which are numeric values, formulae or cells which contain numbers or text. The result is displayed in the cell where the @COUNT entry is made. When individual cells are in an argument (list) even blank cells have a value, but not when they are included in a range.

e.g. @COUNT(4,5,6,9,12,14) gives a value of 6

@COUNT(B10..B22) gives a value of 13 if all cells in the range contain a numeric entry, even if some of these have an entry of 0. If, say, cell B12 was blank, the result would be 12.

@COUNT(B10,B11,B12,B13,B14,B15,B16,B17,B18,B19,B20,B21,B22) would return a figure of 13, even if cell B12 was blank, because each cell in the argument is mentioned individually.

@MAX(list)

Shows the largest value in the list.

e.g. @MAX(1,2,3,49,12,) returns 49 @MAX(32,A24,C12) returns the largest of 32, the value in A24 and the value in C12

@MIN(list)

Shows the smallest value in the list.

e.g. @MIN(1,2,3,49,12) returns 1

@MIN(32,A24,C12) returns the smallest of 32, the value in A24 and the value in C12

@STD(list)

Gives the standard deviation of all values in the list. Blank cells will be ignored, but not 0 entries. An error message ERR is shown if all the cells in the list are blank.

Standard deviation is a measurement of the variance from the mean of a range of entries in a numeric sample. The method involves squaring deviations from the mean value of the sample, averaging and then taking the square root. Therefore, this function can involve a great saving in labour and can be of considerable mathematical significance. For practical purposes the samples would probably be much larger than those given in the examples below.

e.g. @STD(4,5,6,7,12,59) returns 19.61929

@STD(32,C12,A5) would give the standard deviation of 32, the value in C12 and the value in A5

@SUM(list)

Totals all the values in the list. Although included under the statistics heading, this function is probably one of the most generally useful of those available. The result is presented in the cell where the function is entered.

e.g. @SUM(C10..C22) sums the contents of all the cells in the range C10 to C22.

@SUM(-22,35,45) returns 58

@SUM((3+11)/6) returns 2.333333

@VAR(list)

Gives the statistical variance from the mean of all the values in the list.

e.g. @VAR(1,3,6,10) returns 11.5

@VAR(30,C15,D10) gives the variance of 30, the value in C15 and the value in D10

Financial functions

Generally, financial functions are used to calculate the values of investments and to forecast and analyse various financial scenarios.

@NPV(int,range)

Returns the net present value of an investment. The present value of a cash flow is its value today, the net present value would reflect its value less the initial cost. The interest rate is represented by 'int' and the cash flow amounts are entered in the 'range' section as a range of cells which must be in a single row or column. Interest rates must be entered as decimal figures. For instance, an interest rate of 15% would be entered as 0.15 .In the 'range', negative values are considered as outgoing amounts and positive values as incoming cash. Blank cells in a range are treated as 0 cash. The initial entry in the range represents the initial outlay and each further entry, the payment made at the end of an interest period.

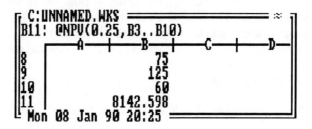

A Worksheet showing range with payments and cell with int

e.g. @NPV(0.25,B3..B10) returns the net present value of an initial cash outlay, shown in cell B3, followed by cash repayments entered in cells B4,B5,B6,B7,B8,B9 & B10, at an interest rate of 25% .

@FV(pmt,int,term)

Shows the value, at the end of (term) periods of an annuity (pmt) invested at an interest rate of (int) %. For instance, in the case of an investor, the annuity (pmt) could be considered as the yearly premium, the interest rate (int) as the rate of interest per year and the (term) as the number of years for which the investment continued.

e.g. @FV(1000,0.1,5) returns 6105.1 which is the value of an investment of 1000 units (£, $ etc.) at an interest rate of 10%, paid into the fund yearly by the investor for 5 years. The investor will therefore have paid 5000 units into the fund at the end of this time and will receive 6105.1 units in return.

@IRR(exp,range)

Internal rate of return allows the question 'What rate of return does the project earn ?' to be asked. In other words, the IRR is the interest rate which would produce a net present value (NPV) of 0 on the the cash flows included in 'range'. The 'exp' part of the argument is an estimated figure and the rate returned by IRR is the decimal equivalent of the interest rate per period.

e.g. @IRR(0.15,B1..B5) returns 0.229712 (=22.9712%)

In this formula, the interest rate is estimated at 15% (=0.15) and the contents of cells B1 to B5 form the range. In this example, the contents were:

B1 -800, B2 500, B3 300, B4 200, B5 200.

We are, therefore, asking whether an investment of 800 units ($, £, etc.) from which dividends of 500, 300, 200 and 200 units were paid yielded 15% per period. The answer to this question is no, it yielded 22.9712% per period .

@PV(pmt,int,term)

This is the present value function, which calculates the current value of an annuity by using the amount of the payment, the interest rate per period and the number of periods.

e.g. @PV(500,0.09,5) returns 1944.826

Therefore, the present value of an annuity of 500 units, at 9% interest per period over 5 periods is 1944.826 units. This shows what the payment is worth when interest is x % per period for n number of periods.

@PMT(prin,int,term)

Calculates the number of periodic payments (term) needed to repay a capital sum (prin) at a certain interest rate (int). This is therefore a function which can be used for calculating loan or mortgage repayments.

e.g. @PMT(15000,.145,10) returns 2932.031

This example shows that a mortgage loan of 15000 units, at an interest rate of 14.5% repaid over 10 periods would cost 2932.031 units per period.

Selection functions

These functions are used to search, by using one value to select another value from a list.

@CHOOSE(exp,list)

Commencing with position 0, this function selects the item at position exp in a list. Exp must be an integer.

e.g. @CHOOSE(2,10,12,14,15) returns 14 , which is in the third position on the list.

@CHOOSE(B2,C3,C4,C5,C6) would take the value of B2. If the value in B2 is 3, the function will display the value in cell C6.

@HLOOKUP(exp,range,idx) and @VLOOKUP(exp,range,idx)

Horizontal and vertical lookup functions use one value to lookup another in a table on the Worksheet. With @HLOOKUP, the idx part refers to rows and in the case of @VLOOKUP it is concerned with columns. Therefore, @HLOOKUP seeks a value in a range of cells where the values used for comparison are across the first row and the values sought are in one or more rows underneath. @VLOOKUP uses a value in the first column to lookup other values in columns to the right.

Here is an example of @HLOOKUP, using the following spreadsheet:

	A	B	C	D	E
3	10	50	100	500	1000
4	0	2.5	5	10	15
5	0	7	10	15	20

@HLOOKUP(50,A3..E5,2) returns 7 which is the figure in the second row below the 50 in B3. @HLOOKUP(499,A3..E5,1) returns 5, which is the figure in the first row below 100.

The function looks up the last cell in the first row of the range, in this case A3..E5, whose value is less than or equal to the figure given in exp. The first row of the range must contain several values for comparison and these must be arranged in ascending order from left to right with no duplicates. The following spreadsheet illustrates the use of @VLOOKUP:

	A	B	C	D	E
3	10	0	0		
4	50	2.5	7		
5	100	5	10		
6	500	10	15		
7	1000	15	20		

@VLOOKUP(100,A3..C7,2) returns 10, which is the figure two columns to the right of the 100 located in cell A5

Logical Functions

This group of functions allows the use of logical mathematics in the Worksheet. What is logical mathematics? I suppose one might describe it simply as the mathematics of True and False! True is represented as 1 on the Worksheet and False as 0.

@IF(exp,then,else)

If exp is true (in which case it returns a value of 1) the argument is 'then'. If exp is false (and therefore returns a value of 0) the argument is 'else'.

e.g. @IF(L10>100,10,1) If the number in cell L10 is greater than 100 a value of 10 will be included in the cell where @IF is placed and a value of 1 when the number in cell L10 is 100 or less.

@ISERR(exp)

Checks the cell location given to see whether it contains a workable formula.

e.g. @ISERR(F12) returns 1 if cell F12 contains 23/0 because the Worksheet treats division by zero as an error and a cell containing this formula would show ERR. It is also possible to enter a formula directly as the (exp). Some spreadsheet programs allow a list to be entered after the @ISERR, but the Portfolio Worksheet does not.

@ISNA(exp)

Shows 1.0 (TRUE) if the cell referred to by exp shows NA (not applicable) and 0 if the cell does not contain NA. The NA message can be generated in a cell as a conditional response to logical operators and also as a direct response to the insertion of @NA in a cell.

e.g. @ISNA(B5) in C4 will show 1 if cell B5 contains @NA and 0 if it does not.

@TRUE and @FALSE

@TRUE returns a value of 1 and @FALSE returns 0. These two functions are mostly used in connection with other logical functions to produce conditional messages.

e.g. @IF(C3<>0,@TRUE,@FALSE) returns a value of 0 if the contents of cell C3 are equal to 0. If the contents of C3 are greater or lesser than 0 a value of 1 is returned.

It is worth emphasising here that the order in which the @TRUE and @FALSE are placed in such a function is all important. For instance @IF(C3<>0,@FALSE,@TRUE) returns 1 if the contents of C3 are equal to 0 and 0 if they are not equal to 0.

Other Logical Operators

<	less than
<=	less than or equal to
=	equal to
>	greater than
>=	greater than or equal to
<>	not equal to

Special Functions

@NA

Will place the message NA (not available) in the cell. The function can be used when a required value is not available.

e.g. @NA placed in cell B5 will cause cell B5 to show NA.

@ERR

The message ERR indicates that a calculation is not possible. Division by 0, such as 23/0 or @SQRT(-3), or an attempt to use a formula which includes a non existent cell value will all produce an ERR message. @ERR may be used in connection with logical functions also. Refer to that section for further information.

@PI

Returns the value of Pi (3.141593). The function can be used in any formula which requires Pi and extends to 13 decimal places.

Functions for date and time

When you want the Worksheet to interpret a date as a serial number, use @TODAY and @DATE. On the other hand, @DAY, @MONTH and @YEAR will convert a serial number date into a date label. All the date functions behave as though time started on December 30th 1899 and ends on December 31st 2049.

@DATE(year,month,day)

Calculates the number of days between the date entered with the function and December 30th 1899.

e.g. @DATE(89,05,01) returns 32629

@DAY(exp)

Does the opposite of the @DATE function. @DAY examines a number and determines what day of the month it is.

e.g. @DAY(32629) returns 1

@DAY(L10)

Will return an ERR. Cell locations may not be included.

@MONTH(exp)

Examines a number and determines what month it is.

e.g. @MONTH(32629) returns 5

@TODAY

Shows the number of the date currently known to the computer. For instance if the date is May 1st 1989 and your Portfolio knows this (by means of its calendar software etc.), a number of 32629 is returned.

@YEAR(exp)

Examines a number and determines the year.

e.g. @YEAR(32629) returns 89.

If you use @DAY(@TODAY), @MONTH(@TODAY) and @YEAR(@TODAY) in separate cells of the Worksheet it will give you a date record of that day's date in the form DD MM YY.

Summary List of Lotus 1-2-3 Functions recognised by the Portfolio Worksheet.

Arithmetic functions

@ABS(exp)	Absolute value of exp
@EXP(exp)	e to the power of exp
@INT(exp)	Integer of exp
@LOG(exp)	Logarithm, base 10, of exp
@LN(exp)	Natural logarithm of exp
@MOD(exp1,exp2)	Modulo (remainder) of exp1 divided by exp2
@ROUND(exp1,exp2)	Rounds exp1 to exp2 decimal places
@SQRT(exp)	Square root of exp
@RAND	Generates a random number between 0 and 1.0

Trigonometric functions

@ACOS(exp)	Arc cosine of exp
@ASIN(exp)	Arc sine of exp
@ATAN(exp)	Arc tangent of exp
@ATAN2(exp1,exp2)	Arc tangent of exp1/exp2
@COS(exp)	Cosine of angle exp
@SIN(exp)	Sine of angle exp
@TAN(exp)	Tangent of angle exp

Statistical functions

@AVG(list)	Arithmetic mean of values in the list
@COUNT(list)	Number of non blank cells in the list
@MAX(list)	Largest value in the list
@MIN(list)	Smallest value in the list
@STD(list)	Standard deviation of the values in the list
@SUM(list)	Sum of the values in the list
@VAR(list)	Variance of values in the list

Financial functions

@FV(pmt,int,term)	Future value of annuity
@IRR(exp,range)	Internal rate of return
@NPV(int,range)	Net present value
@PV(pmt,int,term)	Present value
@PMT(prin,int,term)	Mortgage calculator

Selection functions

@CHOOSE(exp,list)	Selects item at position exp in list
@HLOOKUP(exp,range,idx)	Horizontal lookup of a table
@VLOOKUP(exp,range,idx)	Vertical lookup of a table

Logical functions

@FALSE	Returns 0.0
@IF(exp,then,else)	True/false conditional test and action
@ISERR(exp)	Tests for ERR
@ISNA(exp)	Tests for NA
@TRUE	Returns 1.0

Special functions

@ERR	Generates an error value
@NA	Generates not available value
@PI	Returns the value of the constant Pi

Date and time functions

@DATE(year,month,day)	Returns a day number
@DAY(exp)	Day of the month (1 - 31)
@MONTH(exp)	Number of the month (1 - 12)
@TODAY	Number of days since 31 December 1899
@YEAR(exp)	Determines year when given day number

Lotus 1-2-3 functions not supported by the Portfolio

Database and Statistical:

@DAVG; @DDB; @DCOUNT; @DMAX; @DMIN; @DSTD; @DSUM; @DVAR

String Handling:

@CHAR; @CLEAN; @CODE; @EXACT; @FIND; @ISNUMBER; @ISSTRING; @LEFT; @LENGTH; @LOWER; @MID; @N; @PROPER; @REPEAT; @REPLACE; @RIGHT; @S; @STRING; @TRIM; @UPPER; @VALUE

Miscellaneous:

@CELL; @CELLPOINTER; @COLS; @CTERM; @HOUR; @MINUTE; @ROWS; @RATE; @SECOND; @SLN; @SYD; @TERM; @TIME

If an attempt is made to load a spreadsheet into the Portfolio which contains any of these functions, the Worksheet will warn you that "Some data cannot be loaded". The formulae which contained functions which are incompatible with the Worksheet are converted to; @ERR.

9

Worksheet Practice

Three sample worksheets are included here for those who feel a little practice would be useful. These worksheets are not meant to be paragons of mathematical expertise, but are, perhaps better regarded as samples of what can be done by a mathematically naive parasitologist! Use them for practice, examine the method and thinking involved, improve on them and send your bright innovative ideas to the author at P.O.Box 790, London, N21 1LB, to educate him further and for possible publication and inclusion in the public domain.

Before you start to enter the worksheets, clear any existing data. The correct sequence of keypresses, starting from the DOS screen, is [/]\[\]+[W] to get the Worksheet. [/]\[\] to obtain the main Worksheet menu, then [F] for Files and [N] for New.

Aword about titles: if you want to keep the relevant Worksheet column and row titles on the screen all the time, set Worksheet Titles to On, as directed in Chapter 8.

When you have constructed your new Worksheet, do not forget to save it with a unique name, by using the Files Save as... command.

Weekly Oil Fuel Record

Objective

During the winter I like to kid myself that I know how much oil fuel we are using. In fact what I really do is go outside and adjust the level of fuel in the gauge tube at the side of the tank, take a look at it and estimate the amount we have left. Perhaps it would be true to say that over a period of a year I have a fairly reasonable idea, based mainly on instinct, as to whether we are using a great deal more than usual.

Maybe this is what you do as well? How much better off would we be if we went outside once a week, measured the level of oil fuel, then entered it into a Portfolio Worksheet? This could be designed to automatically keep a record, calculate the cost on a weekly and a monthly basis and forecast more accurately how long the remaining oil would last.

This is the thinking behind this little worksheet. Perhaps you could design one that retains the simplicity, but also presents the data in some way which is more meaningful?

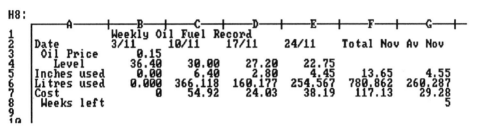

The Weekly Oil Fuel Record Worksheet

Method of use

To use the Oil Fuel Record, each week you type in the date and then the reading, in inches, of the oil level shown by the gauge tube. You must also have one cell which contains the current price of the oil fuel per litre. The formulae contained in the other cells will then do the rest. The cells below the entries you have typed will show the number of litres used for that week and the cost. At the end of the month there are figures showing the total number of inches which the gauge has fallen, the total number of litres used and the cost for the month. In addition, the average weekly fall in the fuel gauge, the average weekly fuel consumption and cost are given. There is also a cell which forecasts the number of weeks for which the fuel remaining in the tank will last.

The Worksheet presented here only lasts one month, but it could easily be extended to cover the whole winter. In that case the forecast for the remaining fuel and the averages could be made more accurate. If you refill the tank with oil in mid-winter, the Worksheet formulae and figures must be adjusted to compensate for the rise in the level of the gauge tube.

How to construct the worksheet

Labels

Although the worksheet has a logical sequence of cells, it is sometimes easier to enter all the labels first. The default location for text in the Worksheet's cells is left and that for figures, right. This sometimes looks at odds, so I centre justified the text in this Worksheet. To do this, press []|[\]|[D][T][C] when the blank Worksheet is showing. Also, set the default numerical format to Fixed 2, by pressing []|[\]|[D][F][F] and [Enter] when the box with the default 2 is shown.

Location	Entry	Comment
B1	Weekly Oil Fuel Record	
A2	Date	
B2	3/11	This is text, together with the next three entriesso precede the entry with ['] for left, [^] for centre or ["] for right justification.
C2	10/11	
D2	17/11	
E2	24/11	
F2	Total Nov	
G2	Av. Nov	
A3	Oil Price	
A4	Level	
A5	Inches used	
A6	Litres used	
A7	Cost	
A8	Weeks left	

The remaining data and formulae:

B3	0.15

B3 is the current price in pence of oil fuel per litre.

B4	36.4
C4	30.0
D4	27.2
E4	22.75

Row 4 contains the cells in which you enter the level, in inches, of the oil tank gauge reading.

B5	+B4-B4

B5 is the starting cell and the reading must be zero.

C5	+B4-C4

If cell C5 is copied to D5 and E5 the formulae will be relative and therefore correct.

At this point press []|[\]|[R][C] . The Copy From box should be positioned on cell C5, then press [Enter]. Next move the box to cell D5, press [.] and expand it to cover E5 as well. Press [Enter] again and the formula from cell C5 will be copied to the other cells.

When you have done this, the two cells to which you have copied the formula from C5 should contain the following data.

```
D5          +C4-D4
E5          +D4-E4
```

Next, enter the following.

```
F5          @SUM(B5..E5)
F6          @SUM(B6..E6)
```

Note in F6, for a subsequent month you would also include the first week. But in the first month, the inclusion of the first week, when no fuel was used, would make the average incorrect.

```
B6          +B5*57.206
```

The magic figure! A 1 inch drop in level in a 4 foot by 6 foot fuel tank is equal to about 12.5 gallons or 57.206 litres. Substitute a figure appropriate to your own tank if necessary. You can copy this formula from cell B6 to cells C6, D6 and E6, in the same way as you did for cells C5 and D5, E5, in the row above.

The formulae in C6, D6 and E6 should appear as:

```
C6          +C5*57.206
D6          +D5*57.206
E6          +E5*57.206

G5          @AVG(C5..E5)
G6          @AVG(C6..E6)
```

The remark for cell F6, about the first week, also applies to cell G6.

```
B7          +$B$3*B6
C7          +$B$3*C6
D7          +$B$3*D6
E7          +$B$3*E6
```

With regard to cells B7 - E7, the reference to cell B3 is made absolute, to allow this cell to be copied to cells C7, D7 and E7, yet still include the correct oil price.

If you were adding further months to this Worksheet, provision would have to be made to accommodate oil price changes. This could be done by using row 3 for the oil prices and referring the cells in row 7 to the relevant oil price, as necessary.

```
F7          @SUM(B7..E7)
G7          @AVG(C7..E7)

G8          +E4/G5
```

If you wish, row 6 can be set to three decimal places and row 7 to Currency by using the Range Format... commands.

A Litres/Gallons Price Converter

Objective

How many garages do you see where the price of petrol is shown in litres, but not gallons? You know the best price for a gallon of petrol, but do not have the mental agility to convert it rapidly to litres. Or, you might be young enough to work in litres, but have never really got to grips with imperial measurements.

Enter this on your Portfolio, and you will only have to worry about your Portfolio getting snatched from the car while you are out of it paying for what you now know is the best local price for petrol!

Method of Use

The Converter is very easy to use. First, you decide what unit the garage is using to price its fuel, gallons or litres, and pick the appropriate column heading on the worksheet. From then on you will ignore the other column.

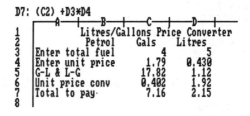

The Price Converter Worksheet

In the appropriate column, you then enter, in either cell C3 or D3, the total fuel which you intend to buy. Then you enter, in the same column, that is in cell C4 or D4, the price per gallon or the price per litre.

If you set the Enter total fuel in each column to 1.00 and have this worksheet as the default file, all you need to do when you drive into the garage is to press [J|\J+[W] and then enter the price of a gallon or a litre of petrol to get the direct price comparison.

After this you can read the cells below. Row 4 tells you the total amount of fuel in litres, if you entered it in gallons, or in gallons if you entered it in litres. Row 5 gives the price per litre if you entered the price per gallon and the price per gallon if you entered the price per litre. Finally, in row 6 you can read the total amount you will have to pay for the fuel entered in row 2.

Most of the Worksheet can be seen on the screen of the Portfolio if you remove the frame by pressing [Fn][5]

How to Construct the Worksheet

The titles on the left fill both columns A and B. The text can be centred in the cells, by using the Defaults menu Text Align command. Use the Defaults menu Format command to set the default to Fixed, at 2 decimal places.

Location	Entry
B1	Litres/Gallons Price Converter
B2	Petrol
C2	Gals
D2	Litres
A3	Enter total fuel
A4	Enter unit price
A5	G-L & L-G
C5	+C3*4.456
D5	+D3/4.456
A6	Unit price conv
C6	(+C3*C4)/C5
D6	(+D3*D4)/D5
A7	Total to pay
C7	+C3*C4
D7	+D3*D4

Cells C6 and D6 will show the ERR error message until the data is entered.

If you press [J|\][R][F], the cells in rows 4, 6 and 7 can be set to the Currency format, which will allow the £ sign to be shown. There is some advantage in setting the prices in cells D4 and C6 to 3 decimal places, so that the display shows a third place decimal for litre prices.

Unit trust portfolio valuation

Objective

If you own shares or have an investment in trust units, it is essential to keep an eye on the way they are performing. This is best done methodically, by recording a valuation at regular intervals.

This worksheet enables you to enter the bid price and derive a current valuation for each of the trusts in which you have an investment, and for your portfolio as a whole. In addition, you can build up a permanent record of the current valuation figures for future reference.

Only four imaginary trusts are included in the example, but this number could be extended very considerably, up to the limitations which the Worksheet allows.

Method of use

After setting up the Worksheet with all the initial data, all you have to do is to enter the current bid price per unit and date. The calculations are then done automatically. You can then copy the final reading and date to a new location to make a permanent record if you wish.

Trust name	Date bought	No. of units	price	Total paid	Current bid price	Current value	Loss/ Gain	Value at June 6th
	Unit Trust Portfolio Valuation							
Gold & General	12/8/87	1000	£0.50	£500.00	£0.33	£330.00	-170.00	£330.00
High Income	8/11/87	1200	£0.67	£804.00	£0.87	£1,044.00	240.00	£1,044.00
Yukon Mines	5/6/85	800	£1.90	£1,520.00	£2.09	£1,672.00	152.00	£1,672.00
Japan Hi Yield	6/6/88	1250	£0.95	£1,187.50	£1.57	£1,962.50	775.00	£1,962.50
		Total		===========	Present	===========	===========	===========
		cost		£4,011.50	value	£5,008.50	997.00	£5,008.50

The Unit trust portfolio valuation Worksheet, including the data copied from the current value column to the Value at June 6th column with the Clipboard.

How to construct the Worksheet

Adjusting the cell formats with the Worksheet Defaults menu.

For our present purpose, it is convenient to set the cell width to 12, rather than the default of 9. Press [Fn] [1] or [/] to get the Worksheet main menu and then select [D] for Defaults. The Defaults menu will show the current width, probably 9. Then press [W] from the menu and enter 12 in the box, followed by [Enter]. All the cells are then adjusted to a width of 12 characters automatically. Note that it is only possible to adjust the widths of whole columns of cells in the Worksheet. The Portfolio will not allow you to adjust the widths of some cells to one width and those below it to another width.

While in the Defaults menu, make sure that the currency character is set to £ . If it is not, press [C] and then key in [Shift][Alt][£]. Also, though a matter of personal preference, I set the Default Text Align to Centre, by pressing [T], and then [C], while in the Defaults menu. The text in individual cells can be aligned by preceding it with ' ^ or '' .

Although we shall be using the Range command to do some cell formatting later, it is convenient to initially set the default format to a fixed two decimal places so, while still in the Defaults menu, press [F] for Format and when the box shows on the screen, enter [F] and set the decimal places to 2.

Entering the titles

Next put in the titles. Move the cursor to the following cells and type in the title shown after them, pressing [Enter] after each entry. If you want to duplicate text, like =, across a cell, you can do so with \. Locate the cursor on the cell concerned, type [\][=][Enter], and the = character will be duplicated across the cell width.

Use Range Format to set the width of the A column to 14. Locate the cursor in cell A1 and press [/][\][R][W]. Then enter 14 into the Width box and press [Enter] again. This increases the width of this column, so that all the titles will fit.

Location	Entry
B1	Unit Trust Portfolio Valuation
A3	Trust Name
A5	Gold & General
A6	High Income
A7	Yukon Mines
A8	Japan Hi Yield
B2	Date
B3	bought
C2	No. of
C3	Units
D2	Offer
D3	Price Each
E2	Total
E3	Paid
F2	Current
F3	Bid Price
G2	Current
G3	Value
H2	Loss/
H3	Gain
D9	Total
D10	Cost
E9	===========
F9	Present
F10	Value
G9	===========
H9	===========

Entering the Date bought

If you begin the date entry with a figure, the Worksheet will think that this is part of a calculation. Since the date entry is not, tell the Portfolio this by preceding every date entry with ['],[^] or [''], depending on where you want to position the text in the cell.

Location	Entry
B5	12/8/87
B6	8/11/87
B7	5/6/85

B8   6/6/85

Entering the basic numerical information

Move the cursor to the cells listed below and enter the number indicated under the column heading No. of Units:

Location	Entry
C5	1000
C6	1200
C7	800
C8	1250

Move to the next column, headed Offer Price and enter:

D5	0.5
D6	0.67
D7	1.9
D8	0.95

Entering some formulae

The figures given in the column Total Paid are calculated automatically by formulae which can now be entered, as follows:

Location	Entry
E5	+C5*D5

Once you have entered this formula, you can use the Range Copy command to fill in the rest of this column. Having positioned the cursor on cell E5, press [/][\][R][C][Enter]. Press the down cursor key to position the Copy To.. box on cell E6, press [.] and expand it to cover the column to include cell E8 and then press [Enter]. The formula in cell E5 will be copied relatively to the other cells and should appear in them as:

E6	+C6*D6
E7	+C7*D7
E8	+C8*D8

Cells E5 to E8 now show the value of your original investment for each unit trust.

Current price data

For this exercise, let us pretend that we have today's bid prices for the individual units in various trusts. Enter the following figures, which represent the price per unit, as indicated below:

Location	Entry
F5	0.33
F6	0.87
F7	2.09
F8	1.57

More formulae

The current value of the holding for a particular trust is the number of units held, multiplied by the current offer price per unit.

Location	Entry
G5	+C5*F5

This formula can again be copied, by using the Range Copy command, as previously, to cells G6 - G8, so that the formulae in these cells are:

G6	+C6*F6
G7	+C7*F7
G8	+C8*F8

The loss or gain formulae are also simple. Loss or gain is calculated by subtracting the amount paid from the current value. This seems like doing the sum back to front, but it has the advantage of producing a negative figure for a loss and a positive figure for a gain.

Location	Entry
H5	+G5-E5

Using the Range Copy command, copy the formula in cell H5 to cell H6 - H8, so that they contain:

H6	+G6-E6
H7	+G7-E7
H8	+G8-E8

The total cost and present value of the whole unit trust portfolio are calculated by summing the relevant columns.

Location	Entry
E10	@SUM(E5..E8)
G10	@SUM(G5..G8)
H10	@SUM(H5..H8)

The entries in these cells can be made by using range painting. In each case, first position the cursor in the cell in which you want the result to appear (E10 first, then do it with G10), then type in @SUM(and press [↑] and move the box to the first cell to be included in the calculation (cell E5). Then press [.] and expand the box to cover all the cells to be included (down to E8). Type in the closing bracket to complete the range, and then [Enter]. The total for the column should appear in the correct cell.

Finally use Range Format to precede the cash entries with a £ sign. Position the cursor in cell D5 and press [/]\[][R][F][C]. Use 2 decimal places and press [Enter]. Next, use the cursor keys to expand the box across to include cell G5 and then down to G10. Finally, press [Enter]. If column H is formatted to currency it will lose the ability to show a negative sign where there has been a loss.

Use of the Clipboard to make a permanent record of the current value

Once obtained, it may be desirable to make a permanent record of the Current Value column and other columns. The Lotus 1,2,3 Worksheet enables its users to duplicate entries in this way by direct commands, but the only way to do this with the Portfolio Worksheet is to use the Clipboard.

First, position the cursor in the cell at the top left corner of the block to be copied. Press [Fn][3] to obtain the Clipboard menu and then Mark the start of the block by pressing [M][Enter]. Move the cursor to cell at the end of the block to be copied and press [Fn][3] again. This time select [S][Enter]. Then move the cursor to cell I2 and press [Fn][3]. Select [P][Enter] and the figures in the cells selected will be duplicated, beginning in cell I2. Note that you have only copied the figures as text, not the formulae. If you move the cursor to cell I2, permanent details, such as the date of this valuation can now be entered. For instance, you could enter Value at, then below, in cell I3, Jun 6 89.

10

Using Printers with the Portfolio

Do you need a printer ?

In the ideal world of information technology, perhaps it really is possible to distribute our data electronically, to store it in permanent memories and gain access to it at will. But for those who have to get by on restricted resources with one, or a few machines, which are liable on occasions to break down, get infected with viruses, or scrambled in some other way, the printed word on paper has a degree of permanence which gives one a greater feeling of security than all the guarantees in the world.

The printed medium is still an extremely important means of communicating information. In the case of the Portfolio business user, this probably means that there will be a steady output of letters, reports and memoranda.

From the personal point of view, one has to admit that a small machine like the Portfolio has a somewhat restricted means of communicating visual information to its owner. It is, therefore, virtually essential to provide some means by which the user can see an area of the work in hand which is larger than an 8 by 40 character screen. Those who use desktop personal computers will be able to transfer various documents from the Portfolio to the larger area of a video monitor, but eventually we all need printed output, or hardcopy.

For most people, a printer is almost as essential as the computer.

Classification of printers

If you agree that it is essential to have access to a printer, then it is important to know something about those which are available.

It is important to decide whether it will be desirable to print text, without graphics, like that produced by a typewriter, or now or in the future, to use the printer for the production of diagrams, graphs and fancy labels. This doesn't imply that the Portfolio is likely to be the most useful machine for the production of graphics, but when spending a significant amount of money it isn't a bad idea to consider as many eventualities as possible. Maybe you will want to use the printer with another computer.

What quality of output will be needed? Simply that which is adequate for your records, or good enough to print documents which can go straight to clients or the world at large ?

Printers are generally grouped according to the method by which they produce the printed copy. There are five basic types:

Daisywheel

Works in a similar way to the conventional typewriter. Uses a wheel with the characters on it. The wheel is turned and hit by a hammer to print the character on the paper.

Cost:	Low to high
Quality of print:	High quality text
Speed:	Relatively slow
Versatility:	Text only. Not very versatile, but different type sizes, styles and character sets are available by changing from one daisywheel to another.

Dot matrix

Has a print head, usually with either a 9 x 9 or 24 x 24 group of pins. The head forms the character by firing a selection of pins to form the appropriate pattern. The pins hit the type ribbon and the character is thus transferred to the paper.

Cost:	Low to high
Quality of print:	Poor to very good
Speed:	Quite fast. Draft speed varies between 135 and 400 characters per second. Letter quality from about 25 to 200 characters per second.
Versatility:	Very versatile. Machines with 9 or 24 pin heads available. Can produce graphics and various print styles. Many printers offer more than one font from their own hardware. Most popular type of printer for everyday use.

Ink Jet

Squirts small jets of ink on to the paper, though some use solid particles instead. The ink is in the form of dots which make up the shape of the characters.

Cost: Low to moderately high
Quality of print: Varies with different machines, but can be very good. Ink will smudge when fresh and the paper may crinkle with the wet ink when large areas of graphics are printed.
Speed: Draft speed 50 to 400 characters per second. Letter quality speed 20 to 200 characters per second.
Versatility: Very versatile. Results can be as varied as with the dot matrix printer and, depending on the machine, good quality colour printing is also available.

Thermal

Uses a column of heating elements to form dots on the paper like a dot matrix printer. These printers use either special paper which turns black when heated, or a thermal transfer ribbon and plain paper.

Cost: Low to medium
Quality of print: Poor to good.
Speed: Quite slow. Draft 60 to 270 characters per second. Letter quality 40 to 170 characters per second.
Versatility: Quite versatile. Modern types work with plain paper.

Laser

Similar in some respects to a Xerox photostatic type photocopier, laser printers produce whole pages rather than whole characters with options of landscape or portrait printing.

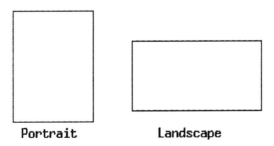

Portrait   Landscape

Paper orientation

Many actually use light emitting diodes rather than lasers. Most have a high resolution of 300 dots per inch - some have a much lower resolution.

Cost:	Medium to high. Fairly expensive to run. Often bargains available, but watch out for obsolete models and low memory capacity.
Quality of print:	Excellent.
Speed:	Very fast, 3 to 25 pages per minute.
Versatility:	Very versatile can produce graphics comparable with the best printed material. Some use the Postscript page description language.

Note that in the above I pitch low cost at around £200 or so and high cost at £2000 - £3000.

Plotters

It is also possible to buy plotters which employ special pens to produce high quality graphs and diagrams on paper when appropriate software is used by the computer.

Some points to consider when buying a printer

The range of available printers is so wide that it is beyond the scope of this book to consider more than just a few possibilities. Therefore, the discussion here will concentrate on a limited selection of types which seem likely to be of most use to Portfolio owners; dot matrix and daisywheel printers.

Most printers are made for desktop use and are, therefore, not very portable.

Text only or graphics and text.

Daisywheels generally produce high quality text without any graphics capability. A dot matrix printer which will give, at least, acceptable text with a graphics capability. Because of its versatility and the ability of recent models to produce high grade text, most people I know would choose a good quality dot matrix printer.

One with a 24 pin head is likely to give better quality text, and may be faster, than one with a 9 pin head, though it might be more expensive. A dot matrix printer should have the ability to produce letter quality (LQ), or near letter quality text (NLQ). Bear in mind that even though you may not have a desk top PC and a requirement to output graphics at present, you might want to buy one in the future.

Price and quality

A printer of reasonable quality can now be bought for less than £400. Make up your mind how much you can afford to pay and do a comparison of different dealers' prices for the same printer models. Look at the tables printed in the *PC World* magazine supplements and reviews, such as *Focus on printers*. These usually contain comparative information for many types, makes and models. Epson and NEC are but two of the manufacturers who produce reliable budget priced dot matrix printers, and Juki make some of the cheaper reliable daisywheel types.

There seems to be little point in buying an expensive product which is either unpopular or difficult to obtain or service.

Improvements and changes occur quickly, so that within a few years models can become obsolete. Therefore, make sure that you do not pay full price for a printer which is about to be discontinued. You should get such a machine at a considerable discount, but also get an assurance that the manufacturer (not just the dealer) will continue to supply spares for a number of years into the future.

See actual samples of all the different kinds of graphics and text which the printer can produce. Do not rely on photocopies. Take your Portfolio to the shop, not forgetting the parallel interface, hook it up to several printers and print out a formatted letter with varied text styles, and a worksheet. On the same printer draft quality printing may be up to six times faster than NLQ on dot matrix printers.

A general rule applicable to well known manufacturers is that price rises in proportion to higher printing speeds and the quality of output.

Maintenance costs and reliability

Routine maintenance on a dot matrix or daisywheel printer amounts to little more than wiping the paper dust off the machine and renewing its ribbon and paper supplies.

Printers use lots and lots of paper, but this depends on how much work you do. Those who need to print vast numbers of invoices, or great amounts of proof copy will probably require a heavy duty printer which will last longer than one which is cheaper, and hopefully not require a lot of maintenance.

The print head on dot matrix printers is usually renewable and the printwheels can be interchanged at will on daisywheel machines. If anything else needs doing, it is usually a job for a skilled engineer. The specification for a printer should give some idea of reliability in the form of a MTBF, (median time before breakdown) or design life, but MTBF may be given as hours or numbers of characters, and varies according to the amount of time for which the printer is used per working day.

Ribbons

Dot matrix printers usually use a multistrike nylon ribbon which goes round and round until the print gets so faint that you have to renew the ribbon. In some cases it can be reinked at a much lower cost, but, in my expereince, this tends to be a rather messy operation.

Daisywheel printer ribbons often come in the form of a single strike carbon film tape, but multistrike types are available.

Ribbon prices vary with the manufacturer and model of printer. Frequently, the original manufacturer's prices are higher than those of the suppliers of compatible ribbons.

But for a realistic evaluation one needs to know how many characters the ribbon can produce and then to calculate how many characters per £ you are getting for each ribbon type. Take care that fabric ribbon replacements for dot matrix printers are of a high quality. A poor quality fabric can damage the print head and, therefore, may impose hidden costs.

Paper

Some printers will take 60 or 80 g/sq m plain paper - known in the business as cut sheets, like a typewriter. Others have a tractor attachment which enables them to using listing paper with holes punched in the side. Certain models have the ability to use both kinds of paper without modification. Tractor attachments or cut sheet feeders are usually available as extras - at a price.

Apart from ordinary paper, most printers will print on self adhesive labels which are available mounted on a tractor backing one, two or three across. This is worth keeping in mind because it is possible to edit your address files, so as to make them suitable for label printing.

Interfaces

In order for a computer to transmit data to a printer it must be fitted with an interface. Likewise, in order for the printer to receive data from the computer it must have an interface. Both interfaces must match and must, of course be connected to each other properly. As supplied, the Portfolio does not have an interface. Most printers have an interface fitted to them when supplied. There are two alternative types of interface, parallel and serial. So a parallel printer needs a parallel interface at the computer end.

A parallel interface and printer cable with a 36 contact Centronics and a 25 pin D type plug is available as an optional extra for the Portfolio. My own feeling is that it should be supplied as standard, because you cannot print anything, or even transfer data to a desktop PC, without an interface. Parallel printers are so common that it is virtually essential that the printer you buy has this basic facility, that is, a parallel interface and a centronics type socket into which you can fit the other end of the Portfolio interface cable.

Atari also supply an optional serial interface for the Portfolio. This is necessary when using a modem. Some printers also have a serial interface, and if you wanted to use one of these the Portfolio would also have to be fitted with a serial interface (sometimes known as an RS 232).

Carriage width

Printers can be bought with either 80 column or 132 column wide carriages. The 80 column machines are designed to take paper to a maximum width of 8.5 inches the 132 column machines will take any paper up to a width of 13 inches. The 13 inch carriage is useful for printing wide worksheets, but software is now available for printing a worksheet sideways on the 11 inch length of listing paper pages.

Except for special purposes, it seems likely that most private users will find the 80 column models most convenient.

Specification

Take the trouble to read the specification for any printer which you are thinking of purchasing. Anything worth having will give a range of figures and descriptions.

Headings for information which may be included in a printer specification:

Print Method
Print Speed
Print Direction
Number of Pins in Head
Line Spacing
Matrix Size
Character Sets
Column Width
Maximun Characters per Line for Different Modes
Paper Types
Number of Copies Printed at One Pass
Paper Path
Interface Types
Ribbon Type and Life Expectancy
MTBF
Environmental Limitations
Power Requirement
Size
Nature of Casing

Character sets

Some printers are not able to print the full IBM character set. This can be a serious handicap, because you will not be able to reproduce some of the more unusual, but worthwhile, characters built into the Portfolio. For instance, the IBM set contains letters of the Greek alphabet and graphics characters, which may not be used frequently, but are very useful when writing or commenting on technical literature.

Most printers enable you to select a number of European language sets. These are not complete, but consist of certain groups of characters with special accents or symbols.

Secondhand or New ?

In my opinion, the risks involved in buying a secondhand printer outweigh any advantages there might be in terms of price. One simply doesn't know how much or how little it has been used. This view would apply particularly to printers bought at auctions. On the other hand, if a reputable dealer is prepared to give a comprehensive guarantee for an acceptable period, it just might be worth considering the proposition.

Given a moderate budget, my personal choice is for a 24 pin dot matrix printer such as my own NEC P2200 24 pin dot matrix printer. For my requirements, which include printing letters, catalogues of about 1000 books, invoices, graphics, and a lot of draft copy, it seems to be efficient and economical to run. The current price of this model is about £250. It is moderately robust, very versatile, and produces good draft and letter quality type in various sizes, with a choice of fonts, as well as very passable graphics. It has a high degree of Epson compatibility, ribbons are not too expensive and it can use ordinary listing paper, or cut sheets.

Having said all this, I must emphasise that I have no brief from NEC. There are many other good printers available! I just went for the best deal I could get at the time.

Using a Printer

As with any machine, before you attempt to use a printer learn the main controls. In the first instance, this recommendation refers particularly to the settings, switches, paper feed and ribbon position. A maladjusted printer whose tractor feed is screwing up paper at a rate of knots, with consequent damage to the print head and other components, is a terrible sight for any owner! Avoid the temptation to rush in. Read and understand the printer manual before switching on.

A few pointers are given below for your guidance.

Hardware - Printer controls

Check list of switches:

On/off. Printer power switch. To stop printing in an emergency, switch off.

Online or Select. The indicator light for this switch must be on for it to take data from the computer. When the printer is not online, it is offline. When offline it will not accept data from the computer, but is still switched on and using electricity.

Line Feed (LF). Pressing the switch will usually advance the printer one line. Keeping the switch pressed down might advance the paper continuously.

Form Feed (FF). Advances the paper one page length. The printer usually needs to be offline for this switch to operate.

Paper Out. Might bleep and flash a light. Means what it says. You are at the end of the paper and the printer will not work until more paper is inserted. Usually it switches the printer offline and when the new paper is supplied the printer must be switched back on line.

Print Style. Some printers have buttons which allow the choice of print styles and fonts. Select as appropriate.

Character pitch. On some printers there is a switch to select the pitch, that is, the number of characters per inch.

DIP and other switches might also be present, depending on the make of machine. These settings must be adjusted in accordance with the printer manual and will influence the default or basic operating mode of the printer. For example, the selection of a particular language character set will influence the inclusion of the $ or £ and # signs, availability of characters with accents, and the activation or deactivation of some of the controls mentioned above.

Buffers

When data is transmitted from a computer to a printer, the computer is usually unable to perform other tasks until the printing has been done. If the printer is fitted with sufficient memory chips, these can be used to absorb the data sent from the computer and thus free it for the user to continue with another task. Printer RAM (Random Access Memory) used for this purpose is known as the buffer. Obviously, the greater the buffer, the more data it can absorb. For the reasons given it is therefore an advantage to have a printer with a large buffer. 8K is about the minimum useful size.

Connecting the printer and testing

Make sure that all the protective packing has been removed from the printer and that it is set up in accordance with the maker's instructions.

Insert the paper and ribbon, ensuring that they both follow exactly the paths shown in any diagrams. Run the self test procedure as explained in the manual. The machine should then print out all the characters available without even being connected to a computer. You might need to turn the power switch off to end this process. Switching it on again will automatically reset it to the normal default state.

You must not connect the printer to the Portfolio or any other computer while either one of them is switched on. Before you connect the printer in any way, switch the Portfolio off by pressing [Fn]+[O] or typing Off[Enter] frcm the DOS screen and disconnect the printer from its power supply. If you are connecting a printer to a desktop PC, both printer and PC should be disconnected from the power. Remember that, in order to use a printer with the Portfolio, you also need an appropriate interface, usually the parallel interface. Refer to the instructions in the interface manual.

Printer control codes

A computer communicates with its printer by means of electronic signals. These usually conform to a standard known by the initials ASCII, which stands for American Standard Code for Information Interchange. Many of the characters in the ASCII standard are printable, including those for the normal alphanumeric set. Others can be used, as their name implies, for controlling equipment.

The functions a printer performs are controlled by means of special signals, sent from the computer, known as escape codes. These escape codes are included in the ASCII standard, and can be interpreted by a printer, but are not normally reproduced on paper with the printable data.

Esc is short for Escape. By now you will have realised that the Escape key is very useful for backing out of various menus and functions in the Portfolio's Applications software. So how do you use it for printing ? Please be patient, more on this later.

The printer usually interprets the Esc code as the preliminary to a command. The code sent after the Esc character is the real command which the printer obeys. Therefore, two or more characters may be sent to a printer to control a single function.

Printer compatibility

In this context, printer compatibility refers to the Escape codes which a printer recognises. Your printer should conform to one of the better known standards of compatibility.

For dot matrix printers with 9 pin heads it is usually that of the Epson FX80 printer. If the printer has a 24 pin head, the Epson LQ800 is the standard, though it conforms in many respects to the Epson FX80.

Many daisywheel printers are compatible with the Diablo standard, and similarly most laser printers can emulate the Hewlett Packard LaserJet. Some laser printers can also be used to print files configured for an Epson FX80 directly.

These standards have been widely accepted by manufacturers other than those named here. This is very important when running commercial software. If the software cannot properly control your printer, the matter is usually out of your hands and the software may be useless.

Compatibility, as indicated above, may be described as 'emulation'. So printers made by other manufacturers may emulate the Epson FX 80, the IBM Graphics printer, Hewlett Packard LaserJet and others. A point to watch with lesser known makes of printers is that sometimes the text emulation is satisfactory, but the graphics emulation is not.

Selected Printer Control Codes

Listed below are some of the control codes applicable to several popular printer types and their compatibles. A full listing and explanation cannot be given here, and readers should refer to the manufacturer's manual for the printer concerned. Examples which use escape codes embedded in documents are given later in the chapter.

Epson FX80 dot matrix Printer Codes

Function	*Printer Control Code*	*Keys to press on Portfolio when formatting within a document*
Character Commands		
Sets 12 c.p.i	Esc M	^[M
Sets 10 c.p.i.	Esc P	^[P
Sets proportional spacing	Esc p	^[p
Sets condensed mode	SI (Ctrl O)	^O
Cancels condensed mode	DC2 (Ctrl R)	^R
Turns on double width characters	Esc W1	^[W1
Turns off double width characters	Esc W0	^[W0
Sets emphasised mode	Esc E	^[E
Cancels emphasised mode	Esc F	^[F
Sets double strike mode	Esc G	^[G
Cancels double strike mode	Esc H	^[H
Set superscipt	Esc S 0	^[SO
Set subscript	Esc S 1	^[SI
Cancel sub or superscript	Esc T	^[T
Set or cancel underline	Esc -	^[-
Page Format Commands:		
Sets 8 lines per inch	Esc 0	^[0
Sets 6 lines per inch	Esc 2	^[2
Left margin set	Esc 1(n)	^[1n

Selected Diablo 630 Daisywheel Printer control codes

Daisywheel printers are not as versatile as dot matrix printers, and fewer effects are contolled by printer control codes.

Function	*Printer Control Code*	*Keys to press on Portfolio*
Character Commands:		
Bold on to end of line (Prints same character three times)	Esc O	^[O
Shadow on	Esc W	^[W
Switch bold or shadow off	Esc &	^[&
Sets underline on	Esc E	^[E
Switch underline off	Esc R	^[R
Superscript on	Esc D	^[D
Superscipt off	Esc U	^[U
Subscript on	Esc U	^[U
Subscript off	Esc D	^[D

Page Format Commands

Lines per page	Esc FF(n)	^[FFn

n = the decimal number given for the ASCII code. E.g. if this number is 65 you would type A on the keyboard.

Laser Printers

The Portfolio can be used with a laser printer, by entering the control codes with text, or by using the PostScript page description language. Laser printer control codes are rather more involved than those used for dot matrix and daisywheel printers.

Those who need to print many varied documents will probably find that it is generally more productive to transfer their files to a desktop PC with the capacity to use full scale word processor programs which will ease the task of producing well finished documents in printed form.

Using the Portfolio Printer Setup Menu

If you have just switched the Portfolio on, access the Setup menu by pressing [J|\J]+[S]. Then press [P] for the Printer Setup menu.

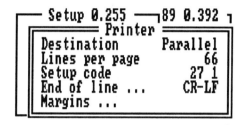

The Setup menu

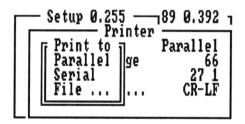

The Printer Setup menu

Printer Destination and Interface type

Press [D] from the printer setup menu.

The first selection on the Setup menu is for the destination to which text is sent; this includes setting the type of printer interface. There are three choices. The current selection is shown opposite the word Destination in the menu. When Destination is selected an option box is shown on the screen.

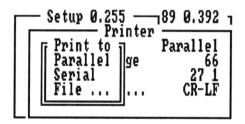

Destination selection box

Parallel

As already mentioned, a printer interface may be parallel or serial. Most printers are fitted with a parallel interface. This means that the data sent from the computer to the printer must be configured properly at the computer end for the printer to receive it. Press [P] to select the parallel interface option on the Portfolio. The optional parallel interface which can be fitted to the Portfolio will send the data to the printer along its cable when a print command is given from software or DOS.

Serial

If your printer is fitted with a serial interface. The data sent from the Portfolio must be sent in serial format. In this case press [S] to select Serial. The data will then be sent to the printer's serial interface via the optional serial interface which you need to fit to your Portfolio. The Serial interface must be connected by means of a serial cable which runs between the Portfolio and the printer.

File...

If you select File, the data will be saved as a formatted file which is suitable for printing directly from disk. By using a command such as COPY FILENAME.PRN LPT1: a formatted file can be sent directly from DOS to a printer and will be printed in formatted form, with all the margins set and form feeds included to ensure that the page length which you have set is observed by the printer.

Pressing [F] results in the Portfolio requesting that you input a filename. Any data that is printed from the Applications software after this will be sent to that file. Since this is done automatically, a second lot of data would overwrite the first. Therefore, it is necessary to select File and give a new name each time you want to save new data.

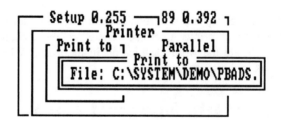

The file name box

You can save a formatted file to a memory card, for later printing from another computer. Formatted files can be accumulated in this way and then printed out all together in one session.

Lines per page

The page length is adjusted by setting a line number. This setting can be altered within certain limits, and the Portfolio offers a choice of 0 or 41 to 99. The Printer Setup menu shows the default setting. If you want to change this select [L] for Lines per page and you will then see the dialogue box on the screen. Normal tractor printer paper is 8.5 inches wide by 11 inches deep and accommodates 66 lines at 6 lines per inch. Not all this will be printed, because top and bottom margins are also included in the figure. When set to 66 a skip over the perforation at the end of the page will occur and printing will be started in the correct position on the new sheet.

If you configured the printer to produce 8 lines of print per inch, it would be necessary to set the Lines per page option to 88.

If you select 0, no form feeds will be inserted and the data will be printed without page breaks, as one continuous document.

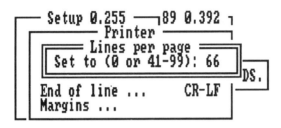

The Lines per page option box

Setup code

A global command can be entered to enable your printer to carry out a certain function throughout a document. For instance, you could enter a sequence here to instruct the printer to print at 8 lines per inch, or you could select a particular font.

When you choose Setup a dialogue box is shown on the screen and you should enter you instructions into it.

Method for entering setup code

Look up the Escape code you want to use. For example the Epson FX80 code which turns on enlarged printing is Esc W1. The code should be entered in the same form as it would be in a document. For Esc W1 you would enter ^[W1, which means pressing keys [Shift][^][[][W][1] [Enter].

Try doing this as an experiment, then take a look at the Setup code which has appeared in the box. It reads \027W1 . The Portfolio has converted the Escape code which you entered into its ASCII decimal equivalent and has added a backslash. In fact the character ^[which you entered was the control code equivalent of Escape, which is Control [, otherwise shown as ASCII decimal number 27.

If you now move to the Editor and type in a piece of text, when printed out on an Epson FX80 or compatible, it will appear in enlarged form.

Enlarged text printed on an FX100

Enlarged text printed on an Epson FX100 when the Printer Setup contains the Code Esc W1

Further Codes can be added. The Escape Code to turn on condensed printing is Esc SI. This is entered into the Portfolio in the form ^[^O. If you put this in the Setup code box, after the Esc W 1 which was placed there previously, you will see that the Portfolio will change it to \027\015. When the text is printed out from the Editor it will now be in enlarged condensed type.

Condensed enlarged text printed on an FX100

The same text printed on the same machine using Esc W1 with Esc SI

Note then, that when control codes, that is those ASCII characters preceded by ^, are entered into the Portfolio's Printer Setup code box, the machine converts them to the decimal equivalent and precedes that with a backslash. This does not happen when ASCII printable characters are used; they are shown in their normal alphanumeric forms.

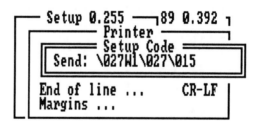

```
┌── Setup 0.255 ──┐89 0.392 ┐
│ ═══════ Printer ═══════════ │
│ ║═══════ Setup Code ═══════║ │
│ ║ Send: \027W1\027\015    ║ │
│ ║                         ║ │
│ │ End of line ...    CR-LF │ │
└─ Margins ...               ┘
```

The codes Esc W1 and Esc SI as they appear in the Printer Setup code box

Control codes can be entered with the text when you are using the Editor, and this offers greater flexibility for formatting. When you want to do this, you may choose to leave the Setup code blank. On the other hand, using a Setup code might be more convenient for printing worksheets, when you would be able to enter a code for condensed print which would allow you to print more data on a standard piece of paper.

If you try to clear the Printer Setup code box after entering a code, you might find that simply deleting the code will not work. Sometimes the Setup menu does not seem to want to forget! In this case, try entering Control ^, by pressing [Ctrl][^]. This doesn't mean anything and the box should clear when [Enter] is pressed.

End of line...

The printer must be told by the computer when to end a line of printing on paper. The computer achieves this by sending a special unprinted electronic signal. The usual end of line code is a line feed (LF is ASCII decimal code 10), but a carriage return (CR) may also be added. The exact combination of these which needs to be used depends on your printer and the way it is set up. Look at the manual for the printer and decide what it requires. Incidentally, it might be worth remembering that the carriage return is the code which is issued when you press [Enter] (often called Return).

Opposite End of line... in the Setup Menu you will see the default setting. If it shows CR-LF, both carriage return and line feed are set. Do not alter this setting unless your printer manual says you should. Some printers only require a line feed or a carriage return and if it receives both it is possible to get unwanted double spacing between the lines of type.

If you press [E] for end of line, you will see an option box on the screen which allows you to choose a carriage return (CR), a carriage return and line feed (CR-LF) or a carriage return and two line feeds (CR-LF-LF). Simply position the cursor on the option you want to select and press [Enter]. Pressing [Esc] lets you out without changing anything.

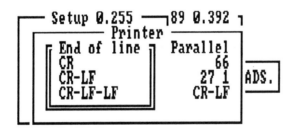

End of line option box

Margins . . .

The Portfolio Setup menu automatically sets left, top and bottom margins. You must adjust the right margin from the Editor or Worksheet menus. If you want to see the default values, or adjust the margins, from the Setup menu, choose [M] for margins.

When you press any of the initial letters for the Left, Top or Bottom margins, the dialogue box allows you to select a figure between 0 and 20 lines, or in the case of the left margin, character spaces. As far as top and bottom margins are concerned, the number of lines set will be counted as if they are printed lines in the whole page of any output sent to the printer from any of the applications software. This means that if you set the number of lines per page to 66 and the top and bottom margins to 5 each, the total number of lines of text printed on a page will be 56, assuming that you have enough text in your document to fill at least one page.

It can be an advantage to be able to set the margins to 0 and use a small character set when printing data from a worksheet.

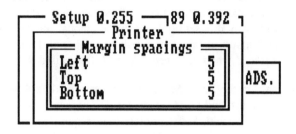

The Margins menu

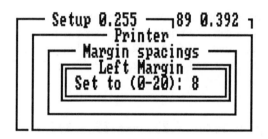

The Margin spacings entry box

Note that any left margin commands which you may include directly with your text will serve to additionally indent the text from the left, up to the maximum setting acceptable by the printer.

Using a printer with the Portfolio's Application Software

Printing from the Portfolio's Application programs can be very straightforward. The software will commit your data to print in whatever global format you use in the Setup menu. This may be good enough for many purposes, but inevitably there will come a time when you want a document to make a special impact. When this occurs, formatting the script from within can give you the desired result.

An appropriate page layout and meaningful emphasis on particular portions of the text can make a favourable impression on the reader and lead to better comprehension of the contents.

As indicated in the text of chapter 6, the Editor is a centre to which data from the other Applications programs can be transferred and assembled ready for transmission to the outside world. It is also true to say that it is easier to format text in the Editor than anywhere else. Therefore, you will probably use it more frequently than any of the other Applications programs for sending data to the printer.

Formatting Documents in the Editor

Many word processors have built in methods for controlling the appearance and layout of the text. With these programs, when you learn to use the word processor you also learn a standard set of commands for performing this kind of task. But the Portfolio's Editor is a fairly basic sort of word processor and only has a limited range of built in printer commands. Some of the printer's extra functions can usually be set by hardware switches, but if you want to get the best out of it, with the Portfolio, it will be necessary to have the patience to enter printer codes with your text, along the lines indicated below.

Once made, you can keep the settings for particular page layouts as blanks, or style sheets, for future use.

As already mentioned, the Printer section of the Portfolio's Setup menu allows top, bottom and left margins to be selected and also provides the facility to send a Setup code. The number of lines per page and end of line code can also be set from the Setup menu. The right margin is selected from the main Editor menu.

Some printers make only elementary provision for page formatting and, with these, you have no need to set any of the margins for the page, or the page length, *from within the document*. Other printers, like the NEC P2200, have more sophisticated formatting facilities and it may be necessary with these to set the printer's page format in such a way that the Portfolio's commands can operate within it. Certain other commands can be entered with your text, so that, depending on the printer used, it is possible to select different fonts: bold, italic, indent, superscript and so on.

Method of entering printer control codes with text

The sorts of codes which are used to control printers from computers have already been mentioned. They are listed with the ASCII character set included at the end of this book. Generally, but not exclusively, printers use the Esc character followed by another character. Each pair of such characters, sent from the computer, will activate a particular printer function.

When using the applications software, the Esc character cannot be entered by pressing the [Esc] key because it is used by the built in software to enable users to back out of the current task. But the caret (^) followed by the left square bracket ([) can be entered and is used instead of entering Escape directly. Escape code sequences can be placed in the text of a document as well as, or instead of, being entered in the Printer

Setup box. If you type [^][[]][W][1] in the Editor, an Epson FX80 printer receiving it will turn on double width printing, just like it did when you put the same code in the Printer Setup code box. The difference is that instead of the code affecting the whole document, it can be placed in a special position in the text, so that it only affects certain parts of it.

The following examples show how these control codes can be included with your text in the Editor. In each case the document was entered into and printed from the Portfolio. All the Escape codes used are listed in the manuals for the relevant printers.

Example 1. A letter

```
^[P^[E^[W1        Smilodon Cats
^[W0              Oscar's Hew, Queensville,
                      Herefordshire
                        England

^[M^[F^[x1^[k0
20th April 1990


Dear Sir,

        Thank you for your letter of April 1st.

I regret that we are unable to supply you with cats
suitable for security patrol duties.

The Russian Blue is not, as you mistakenly suggested, the
size of a Puma, but a breed of ^[-1Felis domesticus^[-0.

Many thanks for your enquiry.

                Yours sincerely,



                I. Feedem

The Manager,
Indian Security Services Inc.,
Little Bighorn,
U.S.A.
^[x0^[P
```

Smilodon Cats

Oscar's Hew, Queensville,
Herefordshire
England

20th April 1990

Dear Sir,
    Thank you for your letter of April 1st.

I regret that we are unable to supply you with cats
suitable for security patrol duties.

The Russian Blue is not, as you mistakenly suggested,
the size of a puma, but is a breed of Felis
domesticus.

Many thanks for your enquiry,

                    Yours sincerely,

                    I. Feedem

The Manager,
Indian Security Services :nc.,
Little Bighorn,
U.S.A.

Example 1 when printed

Notes on formatting

Printer used: Epson FX100+ fitted with the 8190 Word Processing Card.

The Epson FX100 is a dot matrix printer which does not have any sophisticated page formatting abilities. Therefore, the spacing of characters and positioning of headings must be worked out by the user. Initially, this is best done on a trial and error basis, but with experience it is possible to calculate the positions where they should be placed.

The machine I use has a built in font which does not include the IBM extended character set.

If the printer is switched off at the end of the letter, it reverts to its default settings, which include the Elite 10 c.p.i. mode. The purpose of using Esc P at the beginning of the letter is to ensure that the 10 c.p.i mode is set, in case the printer has previously been used for some other character setting and not reset.

Characters Entered	Codes Used	Effect on final print
^[E	Esc E	Turns on emphasised print
^[W1	Esc W1	Turns on double width printing
^[M	Esc M	Elite mode on (12 c.p.i.)
^[F	Esc F	Turns emphasised print off
^[W0	Esc W0	Turns off double width print
^[x1	Esc x1	Turns on letter quality (LQ) printing
^[-1	Esc -1	Turns underlining on
^[-0	Esc -0	Turns underlining off
^[x0	Esc x0	Turns off letter quality printing
^[k0	Esc k0	Selects Roman LQ characters
^[P	Esc P	Turns off Elite and turns on Pica (10 c.p.i.)

Example 2. An extract from some scientific notes

```
^[l
^C
^[Q<
^[a^A^[k^F^[-1Raillietina cesticillus^[-0
^[a@
^[k^0
```

Ultrastructure of the cyst wall.

Use a plan slide of a cysticercoid to show the layout of the tissues. Point out the relationships between the tegument of the scolex and various other elements within the cyst wall.

```
^[l^E
```

i) ^[EHyaline coat^[F with smooth outer surface. 1.4 μm – no microtriches.

ii)^[E Globular layer.^[F Globules appear to originate in
the deeper parts of the cyst wall, travel up 'cytoplasmic
intrusions' and accumulate in the globular layer, eventually to pass out as proteinaceous material. The secretory substance may be connected with an antibody-antigen
reaction, but there is no firm evidence for this.

iii)^[E Intermediate zone.^[F Layers of fibrils 0.5 - 2.0
μm deep. Maybe collagenous in nature, but tests with
collagenase have not been successful. Possibility of a
related protein.

Notes on formatting

Printer used: NEC P2200

The NEC P2200 has sophisticated page formatting commands, which enable the user
to justify text and utilise varied margin settings. When doing this, regard must be paid
to the margin settings of both the printer and the Portfolio.

This printer also has a number of letter quality fonts, as well as the usual draft
facilities.

Characters entered	*Codes used*	*Effect on final print*
^[l^C	Esc l Ctrl C	Sets left margin to n spaces. Ctrl C has an ASCII code of 03.
^[Q<	Esc Q <	Sets right margin to n spaces. < has an ASCII value of 60.
^[a^A	Esc a Ctrl A	Justification. Ctrl A has an ASCII value of 1, and 1 is the code for centre justification.
^k[^F	Esc k Ctrl F	Select letter quality characters. On the P2200 6 selects Super Focus 1O font. Ctrl F has an ASCII value of 6.
^[a@	Esc a @	Justification. @ causes the value to default to 0.
^[k^0	Esc k Ctrl 0	Value 15 selects font ITC Souvenir. Ctrl 0 has an ASCII value of 15.
^[-1	Esc -1	Turns on italics
^[-0	Esc -0	Turns off italics
^[E	Esc E	Turns on emphasised printing
^[F	Esc F	Turns off emphasised printing

<u>Raillietina cesticillus</u>

Ultrastructure of the cyst wall

Use a plan slide of a cysticercoid to show the layout
of the tissues. Point out the relationships between
the tegument of the scolex and various other elements
within the cyst wall.

i)   Hyaline coat with smooth outer surface. 1.4
μm — no microtriches.

ii)   Globular layer. Globules appear to
originate in the deeper parts of the cyst wall, travel
up the 'cytoplasmic intrusions' and accumulate in the
globular layer, eventually to pass out as
proteinaceous material. The secretory substance may be
connected with an antibody—antigen reaction, but there
is no firm evidence for this.

iii) Intermediate zone. Layers of fibrils 0.5 —
2.0 μm deep. May be collagenous in nature, but tests
with collagenase have not been successful. Possibility
of a related protein.

Example 2 when printed

Example 3. A heading for a book list.

```
^[al^[k^F
^\E^A List 36 - September 1990

^[^OSubject Classification and Page Numbers

General Computing..............20
Information Technology..........31
Robotics & Electronics..........33

^[!^BScience Books are on a separate list
```

Notes on formatting

Printer used: NEC P2200; The whole text is centre justified.

Characters entered	Codes used	Effect on final print
^[a1	Esc a1	Justification. 1 is the code for centre justification.
^[k^F	Esc k Ctrl F	Selects LQ font Super Focus 10. ^F has an ASCII value of 6 and this is the figure which must be used with Esc k.
^\E^A	FS E Ctrl A	Selects double width characters.
^[^O	Esc SI	Selects condensed printing. This has been combined here with double width printing.
^[!^B	Esc! Ctrl B	A font style code which also cancels both double width and condensed printing. Value 2 selects proportional printing.

```
List  36  -  September  199Ø

Subject Classification and Page Numbers


    General Computing................2Ø
    Information Technology..........31
    Robotics & Electronics..........33


        Science Books are on a separate list
```

Example 3 when printed

Note that many of the basic control codes which are used by the NEC P2200 are the same as those used by the Epson FX100.

Sometimes an escape code sequence requires the input of a number. For instance ^[k(n), where (n) is the number. You may be able to enter this simply as the number, but if this does not work try putting in a letter or control code which represents the ASCII decimal code for the number.

Using a printer with the Address Book, Diary and Worksheet

It is possible to print files from these three Applications in the file format used by the software. To do this you just need to press []/[] to get the relevant main Application menu and then use [F][P], in the case of the Worksheet filling in any range which you want to print. The current file will then be output via a parallel or serial interface to the printer, and printed according to the default settings on that printer and any control codes which you have placed in the Printer Setup code box.

This will result in the files being printed in the following formats:

Address Book

```
WlN 4AL

Ministry of Agriculture, Fisheries and Food, (01) 233 3000
Whitehall Place,
London, SW1A 2HH

Science and Engineering Research Council, (0793) 26222
Polaris House,
North Star Av.,
Swindon,
Wilts,
SN2 1ET

Scottish Home and Health Department, (031) 856 8501
St. Andrew's House,
Edinburgh,
EH1 3DE

Welsh Office, (0222) 753271
Cathays Park,
Cardiff,
CF4 5PL
```

The format of part of an address file

Diary

```
   21/01/90 11.30 Sat on dog. Poor dog
 @ 12:30 Take dog to vets
   20/02/90
 @ 11:17 Coffee with John Cash at Bloom's
   27/02/90
m@ 11:51 Pay mortgage monthly
   1/03/90
y@ 11:51 Pay BSP sub
```

The format of a Diary file

Worksheet

The hard copy format of a worksheet cannot be derived from a WKS file by using the TYPE or COPY commands. See *Printing the Worksheet* on the next page.

Printing from DOS

The files produced by the Address Book, Diary and Editor are all in plain ASCII code. Printing them from DOS is simply a matter of typing the name of the file with a suitable command. For example, any of the following commands would send a file called DIARY.DRY from the current directory to the printer connected via the parallel interface.

```
Copy DIARY.DRY LPT1:
Type DIARY.DRY > LPT1:
```

Or you could use a PRN instead, as follows.

```
Copy DIARY.DRY PRN
Type DIARY.DRY PRN
```

If you save a formatted document from the Editor by using the print to file option in the Printer Setup destination box, it can be sent to a printer from DOS in the same way, but the file ending will be .PRN. Therefore, a formatted text file called LETTER.TXT will be printed to disk in formatted form as LETTER.PRN.

Also note that if you have entered printer controls into the text while it is in the Editor, the Portfolio will convert these to printable characters when the file is saved. These may have varying effects on your printer, but on the whole, should still be understood as escape codes.

Printing the Worksheet from DOS

Worksheet files are not saved as ordinary ASCII files. If you look at one on the screen by using:

```
TYPE FILENAME.WKS
```

you will see that it is full of control codes. By using the print to file setting, these can be saved as .PRN files and printed later from DOS, in legible form, by using one of the methods mentioned above. .PRN files can also be loaded into the Editor.

Don't forget the Clipboard

No printing can be done directly from the Clipboard, but it is an indispensable aid to copying items from the various Applications, including the Worksheet, to the Editor. Once in the Editor, the information can be formatted and combined with other data prior to printing.

11

Extra Software for the Portfolio

Is it necessary?

For many people, the built in applications software supplied with the Portfolio will perform most of the routine jobs to be done, but one of the attractions of this little machine, is that it has a high degree of compatibility with IBM-type desktop PCs. An advantage of compatibility is that data, such as that in Lotus 1-2-3 worksheets can be directly transferred to and from PCs. But in the minds of many there will be a query about the possibility of using full-blown PC software as well.

Although it should indeed be possible to run many public domain and commercial programs designed for IBM type PCs on the Portfolio, in practice there may be some difficulties.

The Random Access Memory of the Portfolio can be expanded to 640K Bytes, though it is sold with only 128K (less 4K for video RAM) in the main case. Expansion RAM is available as an add on peripheral, but for the time being many users are likely to be restricted to whatever compromise they can reach between their demands on the RAM disk partition and that memory which remains to fulfil a desire to run external software. With the use of memory cards, from which external software can be run, the RAM disk could be configured at its minimum size of 8K, leaving a substantial amount of the original 128K available for other purposes.

Public Domain Programs

A glance through any public domain software list will show that there are many programs, especially small utilities, which can be downloaded from desktop PC disks to memory cards, that should work within the limitations imposed by the Portfolio's available RAM. Whether you, the user, consider them to be of practical use with the available screen size is another question.

The two public domain programs mentioned below, which I think are useful, illustrate these points. For both, it is necessary to set the External Display option of the Setup menu to Static PC.

D.T.A. (Directory Tree Attributes)

This is a rather nice directory utility. It offers the following options, which are used in the form /X after entering DTA on the keyboard.

D - Directories	T - Subdirectory tree
V - Version of DTA	W - Wide mode
P - Page the list	U - Universal (shows files and directories)
F - Full mode	C - Change attributes
M - Modified today	N - Narrow (Helpful on the Portfolio)
? - Help	
A,a - set or clear Archive	R,r - set or clear Read only
H,h - set or clear Hidden	S,s - set or clear System

To use it, one simply enters DTA, followed by the path, file name and /initial letter of any of the above options. The syntax is therefore:

```
DTA <d:> <path> <filename> </options>
```

DTA/F/N shows all the details of the files on the default drive in narrow screen format.

At least two /options can be used together and this means that the width of the directory display can be reduced to something in the region of 40 columns. To a large extent this then avoids the need to use [Alt]+[cursor] keys to move round the Static PC screen on the Portfolio.

Individual file sizes below 1K are rounded up and this can lead to minor errors in showing the total space occupied by files in a directory.

Obviously, for free, this one is worth considering as an addition to the Portfolio owner's collection.

N.B.C. (Number Base Converter)

This program, as its name indicates, converts any number from one base to another, though it cannot use hexadecimal notation. You choose the numbers and the bases.

When NBC is executed on the Portfolio, it behaves in the same way as it does on a desktop PC.

The program first shows its title, then requests input for the first number. When this has been done, the question 'From which base?' is asked. If you enter, say 10, it moves to the next question 'To base ?'. Finally, after entry of this figure, the answer is given and the program will then return to its first question. NBC can be stopped by pressing [Ctrl]+[C].

The request for input made by NBC appears in the middle of the 80 x 25 PC screen. On the Portfolio, these lines do not appear within the 40 x 8 screen and one must therefore use [Alt]+[cursor] to bring the screen window into a position where the requests, entries and answers can be read. Once this has been done, this software can be used as well as it could be on a PC.

Other Public Domain Programs

I have personally tried to execute a number of other small public domain programs on the Portfolio and have been successful with those listed below.

CAT.COM A novel program which lists files in a directory, according to the file extension. Therefore, it classifies and lists files by categories. It is necessary to move around the Static PC screen to read all the data.

D.COM Shows directory files in alphabetical order. It pauses when the first PC screen has been filled with file names, but you still need to move around the Portfolio's screen with [Alt]+[cursor].

LC.COM Counts the lines in an ASCII text file. You type LC <filename> [Enter] and it returns the figure for the number of lines in the file specified. This one could be quite useful as a labour saver. Although the Editor has a Goto command in its Search menu, this does not allow you to count the full number of lines in a file.

WHEREIS.COM This will search all DOS directories for specified files and then list the files with appropriate directories and subdirectories. It works in the current volume, but may need to be transferred for use on other volumes. Wildcards can be used in the file names. To do this you would type WHEREIS JACK.* [Enter] or WHEREIS *.LET [Enter].

Of course, this list is not exhaustive and represents only a proportion of the small number of PD software programs which I have tested. Other possibilities for use on the Portfolio might fall into the categories of small printer utilities and other text or mathematical labour-savers.

It is probably worth while collecting proven programs of this sort on PC disks, so that they can be copied to Portfolio memory cards for use as required. I intend to build up a list of public domain software suitable for use on the Portfolio and readers are invited to contact me at P.O. Box 790, London N21 1LB, for further information.

Commercial Programs Marketed by DIP and Atari

DIP, the company which designed the Portfolio, has also written a good deal of extra software for it. This can be obtained by writing to DIP, or through the normal Atari dealer network.

So far, the following general programs are available on memory cards:

Utilities Card

General utilities

The utility card programs provide commands which enhance the facilities of the Portfolio. Some of them can be used from the DOS prompt, but they are especially valuable to the writers of batch files.

ANSI.SYS Not strictly a utility, but a device driver which provides enhanced display handling for certain applications, together with an ability to redefine the keyboard.

CMDEDIT Installs a terminate and stay resident program which replaces the standard DOS line editor, available through Fn1 and Fn2, and a facility which stores DOS commands of three or more characters so that they can be viewed and reused with fewer keypresses.

SPOOL Installs background printing, so that anything printed to PRN will be placed in a buffer, which can be set to between 1 and 32767 bytes, and printed in background. This allows one to continue using the computer for some other task.

Enhancements for batch files

ASK Shows the prompt and waits for the user to press a key. The key to be pressed can be specified on a key list.

ATTRIB This program displays and changes the attributes of files. Wildcards can be used. Attributes, though not the rest of the information, would be listed in the same sort of way as in D.T.A.

BEEP Sounds a tone and allows the duration and pitch of the sound to be specified.

DIF Compares text files and displays any differences, located by line number, between them.

DSKCHK Checks for faults on the 'disk'. Finds and attempts to correct errors such as lost or corrupted clusters.

FIND Searches files for a specified text string and shows the names of the files in which the string is located.

FREEDSK Displays the amount of free space on the disk in the drive specified. Also sets ERRORLEVEL.

FREEMEM Shows the amount of free memory in the largest block and sets ERRORLEVEL. Could be useful for checking to see if enough memory is available to execute a particular program.

KSIM Can be used from a batch file to simulate keypresses. It therefore allows the program writer to automate a process which would normally require keyboard input.

KSIMCOMP This program compiles object files from ASCII text sources which specify keypresses, so that they can be used by KSIM.

MODE Allows SETUP options to be assigned from a batch file or the DOS command line. The sequence of keypresses required is the same as that used with the SETUP menu.

PASSWORD Controls access to the Portfolio and thus provides some degree of security for the user, who can define a password to be used before access is granted.

REBOOT This program can be used to cold or warm boot the Portfolio.

SORT Performs an alphanumeric sort of each file specified. Each line of text file can be sorted in ascending or descending order.

TOD When used displays the day, date and time and sets ERRORLEVEL to the language currently in use.

UPDATE.COM Invaluable for owners of early Portfolios, this program installs any relevant DOS software update. Among other things it should correct the loss of data nuisance. The UPDATE.COM statement should be included in the AUTOEXEC.BAT file so that it is executed at each reboot.

XCOPY Works like the COPY command, but is more suitable for making and restoring backups.

XDIR Like the DIR command, but shows the path, filename, size, date and time, the number of files found and total size of all files.

Pocket Finance Card

This card contains specially written software which acts as a powerful financial calculator and provides facilities for producing graphs.

It allows compound interest, loans and savings with tax relief and loan amortisation to be calculated. The facilities also allow calculations of loans or savings between specified dates, APR, leasing, NPV, IRR and simple payback, as well as percentage markup, mark down, commission and VAT. Different types of depreciation can be examined.

The Finance card also provides for breakeven analysis, statistics and forecasting with linear regression fitting.

File Manager

This is a great little utility which makes it very easy to operate the applications software and DOS commands from a single screen.

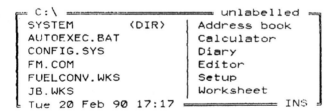

```
C:\  ═════════════════════════ unlabelled ═
  SYSTEM          (DIR)  │  Address book
  AUTOEXEC.BAT           │  Calculator
  CONFIG.SYS             │  Diary
  FM.COM                 │  Editor
  FUELCONV.WKS           │  Setup
  JB.WKS                 │  Worksheet
  Tue 20 Feb 90 17:17 ═══════════════ INS
```

The File Manager screen

An application is chosen by locating the cursor on its name and then pressing [Enter]. If you want an application to use a particular data file, the cursor is positioned on the name of the data file and [Enter] pressed.

The file manager also allows .BAT, .COM, .EXE and .RUN files to be used by similar means. The cursor is positioned on the file name and when [Enter] is pressed the file is executed in the same way as if its name had been typed at the DOS prompt.

If the file to be executed is like some batch files, in requiring an argument or text statement to be entered as well, pressing [Fn][3] will cause a dialogue box containing the program's name to be shown on the screen. The command argument is then typed into the box and when [Enter] is pressed the program runs.

DOS commands can be used, but simpler alternatives are provided. These include a command to allow files to be tagged so that they can be processed together. For example, if you wanted to delete a set of dissimilar files, you would first pick out the files from the list and individually tag them, then the delete command would be used and all the files would be deleted together.

```
 . C ╒═══ Other ═══╕ ┌─── unlabelled ─┐
 SY │ New drive    │ │ Address book   │
 AU │ Make Directory│ │ Calculator     │
 CO │ Check disk   │ │ Diary          │
 FM │ Format A:    │ │ Editor         │
 FU │ Label        │ │ Setup          │
 JB │ Time/date    │ │ Worksheet      │
 └───┴──────────────┘ └────────────────┘
```

The File Manager's DOS menu

The figures included here show more completely the menu commands available with the File Manager.

APP for the PC

APP, the PC Applications software, does not run on the Portfolio, but allows you to use its built in software on your PC. By using APP, files which have been transferred from the Portfolio can be displayed with the same software on a desktop PC. The APP software allows many choices of screen size, so that the Portfolio's screen can be simulated, or the full size of a PC VDU employed.

Commercial Programs Marketed by third parties

At the time of writing there is a list of 36 companies and individuals who are developing software for the Portfolio. Some will be general programs which may be used in the same way as those on other computers, but a significant number of developments will enable the Portfolio to be employed as a dedicated machine. In other words, the user will see the application as an integral part of his business or professional procedure. The software and the Portfolio, together, will thus be regarded as an essential item in an information processing scenario. This sort of approach is already being used in medical pharmaceuticals, civil engineering and leasing.

The other areas in which applications are being developed mostly follow a similar vein. For instance various financial packages will deal with bond yields, accountancy and insurance calculations. Some will be organising communications like PC links, computerised lighting control and possibly robotics. A vehicle management tool is being developed as well as one for specialised data validation in connection with local authorities.

The games programs so far available mean that you can play chess, Othello or Quarto on your Portfolio.

Sideways printing utilities

There are a number of commercial and public domain utilities which allow a computer user to print a spreadsheet, or other document, which is wider than the 8.5 inches available on normal tractor paper. These utilities rotate the printout by 90 degrees so allowing continuous output along the width of the spreadsheet which is aligned with the length of the printer paper.

Sideways is the name of a commercial program, marketed by Funk Software, which will do this. It has a menuing system which makes it especially suitable for Lotus users, though it does require 128K of memory. I do not know whether it can be used on a Portfolio, but it is certainly an asset to be considered by PC operators who may be processing spreadsheets uploaded from the Portfolio's Worksheet.

Onside can be obtained from public domain sources and this too will allow sideways printing of ASCII files on an Epson or IBM Graphics 9 pin printer. It offers several fonts and requires 256K RAM.

Appendix A

ASCII Character codes

Codes Decimal 0 - 31 Control Characters

The Portfolio usually uses these characters as control codes, and they are seen on the screen as a letter, prefixed by a caret (^X). Sometimes the Control characters are named by their function. For example **ff** is a form feed and **lf** is a line feed. There is also a printable character set which corresponds to this range of ASCII characters and, usually, some of these characters are shown when you display one of the .DAT files, such as UNDELETE.DAT, on the screen by using the TYPE command.

Character	Abbreviation	Decimal code
CTRL @	nul	0
CTRL A	soh	1
CTRL B	stx	2
CTRL C	etx	3
CTRL D	eot	4
CTRL E	enq	5
CTRL F	ack	6
CTRL G	bel	7
CTRL H	bs	8
CTRL I	ht	9
CTRL J	lf	10
CTRL K	vt	11
CTRL L	ff	12
CTRL M	cr	13
CTRL N	so	14
CTRL O	si	15
CTRL P	dle	16
CTRL Q	dc1	17
CTRL R	dc2	18
CTRL S	dc3	19

CTRL T	dc4	20
CTRL U	nak	21
CTRL V	syn	22
CTRL W	etb	23
CTRL X	can	24
CTRL Y	em	25
CTRL Z	sub	26
CTRL [	esc	27
CTRL \	fs	28
CTRL]	gs	29
CTRL ^	rs	30
CTRL_	us	31

Decimal Codes 32 - 127; Standard Characters

The ordinary alphanumeric characters are included in this range.

Character	Decimal Code	Character	Decimal Code
SPACE	32	=	61
!	33	>	62
"	34	?	63
#	35	@	64
$	36	A	65
%	37	B	66
&	38	C	67
'	39	D	68
(	40	E	69
)	41	F	70
*	42	G	71
+	43	H	72
,	44	I	73
-	45	J	74
.	46	K	75
/	47	L	76
0	48	M	77
1	49	N	78
2	50	O	79
3	51	P	80
4	52	Q	81
5	53	R	82
6	54	S	83
7	55	T	84
8	56	U	85
9	57	V	86
:	58	W	87
;	59	X	88
<	60	Y	89

Character	Decimal Code	Character	Decimal Code
Z	90	m	109
[	91	n	110
\	92	o	111
]	93	p	112
^	94	q	113
_	95	r	114
`	96	s	*115*
a	97	t	116
b	98	u	117
c	99	v	118
d	100	w	119
e	101	x	120
f	102	y	121
g	103	z	122
h	104	{	123
i	105	|	124
j	106	}	125
k	107	~	126
l	108	Δ	127

Decimal Codes 128 - 255: IBM Extended Character Set

All the graphics, foreign language, mathematical and Greek characters are included here.

Character	Decimal Code	Character	Decimal Code
Ç	128	æ	145
ü	129	Æ	146
é	130	ô	147
â	131	ö	148
ä	132	ò	149
à	133	û	150
å	134	ù	151
ç	135	ÿ	152
ê	136	Ö	153
ë	137	Ü	154
è	138	¢	155
ï	139	£	156
î	140	¥	157
ì	141	Pt	158
Ä	142	ƒ	159
À	143	á	160
É	144	í	161

Character	Decimal Code	Character	Decimal Code
ó	162	┯	209
ú	163	╥	210
ñ	164		211
Ñ	165	╘	212
ª	166	F	213
º	167	╓	214
¿	168	╫	215
⌐	169	╪	216
¬	170	┘	217
½	171	┌	218
¼	172	█	219
¡	173	▄	220
«	174	▌	221
»	175	▐	222
░	176	▀	223
▒	177	α	224
▓	178	ß	225
│	179	Γ	226
┤	180	π	227
╡	181	Σ	228
╢	182	σ	229
╖	183	μ	230
╕	184	τ	231
╣	185	Φ	232
║	186	Θ	233
╗	187	Ω	234
╝	188	δ	235
╜	189	∞	236
╛	190	ø	237
┐	191	ε	238
└	192	∩	239
┴	193	≡	240
┬	194	±	241
├	195	≥	242
─	196	≤	243
┼	197	⌠	244
╞	198	⌡	245
╟	199	÷	246
╚	200	≈	247
╔	201	°	248
╩	202	∙	249
╦	203	·	250
╠	204	√	251
═	205	ⁿ	252
╬	206	²	253
╧	207	■	254
╨	208		255

Appendix B

Error Messages

An error message is usually given when the Portfolio cannot proceed with a particular task. When this happens, the standard procedure is for the user to backout of the siuation by using [Esc] and to rectify the situation by correcting the error or following an alternative route through the procedure. Occasionally some stronger action is required like rebooting with [Ctrl]+[Alt]+[Del], or in extremity, removing the batteries and pressing the RESET switch - but beware, you will lose all your data if you do this.

Access denied
The user has attempted to delete or write to a file which is read only. This can only happen if you have changed the file's attributes, or transferred a read only file from another computer.

Bad command or **program not found**
Either the DOS command, or, for example, the batch file name does not exist. The commonest reason for this is that you have made an error in typing the command. Alternatively, a batch file might be in another directory or drive.

Bad filename
You may have included too many characters in the file name; only 8 are allowed, plus three in the extension.

Bad number
The system expected a number and you haven't given it one! Or you may have given a number outside the expected range. When entering numbers in the Calculator or Worksheet, they must be in the range of plus or minus 9.9999 to the power 99.

Basic not available
There is no BASIC interpreter in the Portfolio. The error occurs only if you try to run BASIC programs which have been imported from elsewhere.

Bad or missing (DEVICE)
The message occurs when you have attempted to include a non-existent device driver in the CONFIG.SYS file. Instead of (DEVICE), the message will give the name of the non-existent driver concerned. Either include the driver file in the current path, or remove the statement from your CONFIG.SYS file.

Cannot create file
An attempt was made to create a file with invalid characters, or the file name was missing. Possibly due to a typing error.

Cannot move - target day is occupied
You have tried to MOVE Diary date header text to a date which already contains header text.

Checksum error
The checksum is an error checking mechanism. This message means that an error was found during the use of the Setup File Transfer facility. Check that all the connections between cables and interfaces are in order.

Communications error
This error can occur during the initialization of the serial communications port, or when File Transfer in being used. Check that all cable and interface connections are made properly.

Configuration too large for memory
This message will appear if the commands in the CONFIG.SYS file specify parameters which need more memory than is available.

Corrupt file
An attempt has been made to load a Lotus 1-2-3 file, which does not conform to the Release 1a file format, into the Worksheet. Sometimes Lotus look-alike programs can cause this problem.

Data error reading/writing drive <d>
Abort, Retry, Ignore?
An attempt has been made to read or write to a memory card which is not properly formatted, or which has been corrupted. The card must be formatted with the FORMAT command before use. Pressing [A] will return you to DOS, [R] will cause it to have another try. [I] won't get you anywhere if the system has rejected the card.

Date repeat skipped as target day occupied
When the Diary loads a data file it automatically processes repeating date entries. If the target date is already occupied, the date repeat is moved into the future until a free date is found.

Device read error
The memory card was moved when the Portfolio was trying to read data from it, or

an attempt was made to load a file from a sub-directory which didn't exist. Make sure that the path name is correct and that the card is inserted properly.

Device write failure
The system has not been able to write to a disk or memory card. The relevant card or drive may be full. Make sure that the path name is correct and that the memory card is inserted correctly.

Directory exists or cannot be created
You have tried use the MD command to create a sub-directory which already exists, or the name specified may already belong to a file.

Directory not found or not empty
If you use RD to remove a directory which cannot be found (perhaps because it is still current), or which still has files in it, this message will be shown. Remove the files and ensure that you are one level closer to root when you use the RD command.

Disk full
This one is self evident. Try a new memory card, or remove some of the files from the RAM drive and then have another go.

Disk is write protected
The memory card switch is in the write protect (on) position. This is intended to ensure that data, which you do not want to accidentally erase, is protected. Make sure you know what is on the card and then set the write protect switch to off, so that a write or delete operation can take place.

Divide by zero
This is due to an internal error in the Portfolio. It may occur when a corrupted external program is executed, but has happened on my Portfolio when only internal software has been in operation. You can try to use [Ctrl][Alt][Del] to warm boot the Portfolio. When this has been done you can try to run the program again. If [Ctrl][Alt][Del] does not work, you may have to do a cold reboot, which means removing the batteries and starting from scratch. If you do this, the data on your RAM drive will be lost and you will have to rely on the files which you backed up to the desktop PC or memory cards to recover the lost data.

Drive in search path not found
The drive specified in the DOS command is not available.

Enter new drive
The current drive cannot be used, so enter a new drive name.

Environment full
The memory assigned for use by PROMPT, PATH and SET is full. Some of the existing settings must be removed before any more can be inserted.

ERROR: Card access

The memory card was removed at the time that DOS was trying to access it. The remedy is not to do it!

ERROR: Low battery

Battery power has diminished to an unacceptable level. Switch the Portfolio to standby immediately and replace the batteries as soon as possible with some which have a full charge.

Exec error

An attempt has been made run an .EXE file which is corrupted, or with insufficient memory available. If the file has been corrupted during transfer to the Portfolio, you could try transferring it from the original source again.

Failed to run program

This message is similar to that above, but applies to an add-in Editor program.

File not found

The application could not find the file which you specified. Perhaps you made a typing error or gave the wrong path?

FOR cannot be nested

The DOS command FOR cannot be used as part of another FOR command. This mistake seems most likely to occur during batch file construction.

Format error

The memory card has not been properly formatted. Try reinserting the card and formatting it again. If this doesn't work the card may be faulty.

Formula too long

The formula typed into a Worksheet cell was too long. Split the formula into smaller parts and enter these into several cells.

General error <n> reading (writing) drive <d>
Abort, Retry, Ignore

The memory card may not have been formatted, or it might have been corrupted by leaving it near a magnet or telephone ringer. In either case you have probably lost the data on it and it will have to be reformatted.

Halt batch job (y/n)?

Using [Ctrl]+[C] or [Fn]+[B] to stop a batch program will produce this message. If you really do want to halt the batch file press [Y][Enter], if not press [N][Enter].

Illegal cell reference

The Worksheet cell reference which you typed does not exist. You might have made a typing error or attempted to use a reference beyond the range of the available cells.

Illegal character
The Calculator will not accept any character which is not a legal arithmetical operator or a number and shows this message when you break these rules.

Illegal date
The date format used for entries in DOS or the Diary must conform to the current country code. Chapter 2 explains this.

Illegal time
This message is similar to that above. You must conform to the proper format of hh:mm:ss:hundredths when entering the time in DOS or the Diary. You may omit the seconds and hundredths.

Insert disk with batch file
A batch file was executed from a memory card. The memory card has been removed, or the batch file has deleted itself. If you removed the memory card, reinsert it, or press [Ctrl[C] to stop the program.

Internal disk error
The Portfolio encountered an error when trying to format the RAM disk C: Try a cold reset by removing the batteries and pressing the reset switch, which is located inside the hole, marked RESET, in the base of the case.

Invalid characters in label
When the DOS LABEL command was used spaces or illegal characters were entered.

Invalid country code
A country code not known to the system was included in the CONFIG.SYS file.

Invalid directory
The directory name given in the CD or DIR command is not known to the system. Probably you made a typing error. Check the name and try again.

Invalid drive
The drive specified does not exist, or, possibly, a device driver specified in the CONFIG.SYS file has not loaded correctly.

Invalid parameter
A parameter included with a DOS command is not known to the system. Check the DOS command and the parameters which may be used with it. This message will also appear if a Worksheet function is given the wrong parameter.

Label not found
The GOTO command in a batch file did not have a matching label. Check the batch file concerned to see that the label is included and correctly typed.

Max size allowed is <n>k
An attempt has been made to exceed the maximum size allowed for the Portfolio's RAM drive. Use FDISK with a smaller number.

Memory full
The Portfolio has insufficient RAM to continue. This may be caused by attempting to run an external program which requires more memory than is available, or by attempting to load a data file, which is too large, into an application. You cannot run the external program with insufficient memory, but, if the problem is caused by a data file, you can split the file into two and use either part.

Some memory can be regained by deleting the files CLIPBORD.DAT and UNDELETE.DAT from C:\SYSTEM.

Minimum drive size <n>k
The figure you gave with FDISK was unacceptably low. Use a higher figure to create the RAM drive.

Mismatched brackets
The expression entered into the Calculator or Worksheet has a bracket missing. Check the statement and make sure that open and close brackets are present in equal numbers.

Missing operator +-*/^!
In the Calculator, one of these operators is absent from the indicated part of the calculation.

Must specify on or off
An attempt was made to use the DOS VERIFY and BREAK commands with a parameter other than the permitted on or off .

Must specify source and target files
The DOS COPY command requires both source and destination file names to be specified. They must not be the same names.

No path
Currently, there is no search path. The PATH or SET commands should be used with appropriate parameters to set a path.

Not ready error reading(writing)
Drive<d>
Abort, Retry, Ignore
If you try to gain access to a drive which does not contain a memory card, or if the Portfolio's battery power fell to an unacceptably low level during the operation, this message will be shown.

Out of range
If you give a number which is greater or smaller than it can accept, this message will appear. Entry of a number greater than 255 in response to the Editor's Right margin setting will cause the Portfolio to object in this way.

Ram check failure
During the startup procedure, a RAM error has been detected. Try doing a cold boot by removing the batteries and pressing the RESET switch in the bottom of the case. This will cause the machine to go through its startup procedure again.

Root directory full
A self evident message. If you want to deposit more files in this directory, you must delete some of those already there.

Second drive not installed
Drive B: is the send memory card drive. If you try to format it when it is no installed, the Portfolio will show this message.

Some alarms are set in the past and so will not go off
This one is shown when you attempt to save a Diary file to C:\SYS-TEM\DIARY.DRY which has alarms set before the current date. You may already know this, but it is also possible that the Portfolio's date is set incorrectly.

Stack full
The calculation attempted is too complicated for the Portfolio. Break the procedure down into smaller parts and try again.

String not found
The text which you are searching for does not exist in the direction of the search. Try searching in the other direction, and under the current cursor position.

Syntax error
Probably the most familiar error message in personal computing! It means that the command given is not in the form required by the system. On the Portfolio, this could be a wrongly formed command to DOS or a calculation in the Worksheet or Calculator.

** SYSTEM ERROR **
Note what you last did;
ESC will attempt recovery.
Quit and save if possible.
This is an applications software error message. Press Esc to remove the message and then try to save the file which you were working on. Then go into DOS and restart the application. It is possible that the cause of the error message is in the file which you were working on, for example you might have inadvertently typed a control code into the Worksheet. If this is the case, it might be necessary to remove the offending character from the file.

Target file exists
The file name which you attempted to use with the REN command already exists. Use another name.

Target is over the edge

If the Worksheet COPY command is used to copy a block of cells to a range which overlap the edge(s) of the grid, this message will be given. The remedy is to copy to another location, or to copy a smaller block of cells which will fit into the available area.

Too many cols or rows

This message is shown if an attempt is made to insert more rows or columns into the Worksheet than it has empty. Reduce the number of rows or columns which you are trying to insert and then proceed.

Unrecognised command in CONFIG.SYS

The CONFIG.SYS file contains a command not understood by DOS. You must examine the CONFIG.SYS file and check that all the commands in it are legal.

WARNING! Alarms won't ring - must be in C:\SYSTEM\DIARY.DRY

This warns you that any alarms set in the current file will not sound. The alarms must be in DIARY.DRY in the sub-directory SYSTEM

WARNING! Monthly repeat has been moved due to earlier end of month

The day specified for the repeat does not exist in the relevant month, so the repeat has been moved closer to the beginning of the month. e.g. A monthly repeat set on January 31st will show this error because February only has 28 days. The Diary automatically sets the repeat for February 28th.

WARNING! Some data cannot be loaded

This is a Worksheet error message which is shown when an attempt is made to load a file containing Lotus 1-2-3 Release 2 functions.

Write protect error writing drive <d> Abort, Retry, Ignore

If the Portfolio attempts to write to a memory card when its write protect switch is on this message will be given. Turn the card's write protect switch off.

Wrong number of params

Displayed when a DOS or Worksheet command is given with the wrong number of parameters. Check the form of the command you are trying to use and correct it.

INDEX

BEST SELLERS AND NEW TITLES FROM SIGMA PRESS

Manage Your Business - Computerise your Accounts: Malcolm Briggs

After word processing, most PC users need an accounting package. Although this book uses the Sage Sterling package as an illustration, the principles are sufficiently general for any other package to be used. It explains the principles of small business accountancy and how to transfer smoothly from a manual system. Contents include: simple accounting; setting up a computerised system; nominal ledger; sales (or debtors) ledger; stock control and order processing; benefits of integration.

Spring 1990 ISBN: 1-85058-147-9 250 pages £12.95

Inside dBASE IV: Mike Lewis

One of the first books on dBase IV - the long-awaited successor to dBase III from Ashton-Tate. It is comprehensive whilst being more readable than the official manual. The contents include: designing the database; using the Control Centre; creating a working application; using the application generator; enhancing the application - indexing, sorting, multiple databases, views, query by example; programming with dBase IV; macros; programming the user interface; building large applications; advanced features - networks, SQL, links, tools.

Summer 1989 ISBN: 1-85058-133-9 280 pages £12.95

Packet Switched Networks- Theory and Practice: Richard Barnett and Sally Maynard-Smith;

This highly praised book has two main aims. The first is to provide the basic theory of packet switched networks and their protocols. The second is to provide sufficient information to allow the reader to implement a packet switched network in a real situation. Contents: Packet switched network basics and components; Network Protocols; International standards; Open Systems Interconnection (OSI); Security; Private Networks; Equipment for packet switched networks; Network management; Future Developments.

Summer 1988 ISBN: 1-85058-095-2 274 pages £19.95 (hardback only)

Timeworks Publisher Companion – DTP on a PC: Ray Morrissey

This is a 'hands on' approach to using the popular, low- cost Timeworks package. The package has been widely acclaimed as having many features only found on Ventura, Pagemaker and other high-cost packages. With Timeworks and a low-cost PC, you really can get started in desk-top publishing. Contents: Word Processing and DTP; Introduction to typography; Installing Timeworks; Designing the layout - using the 'toolbox'; Text and graphics manipulation; Preparing single page and multi-page documents; Choosing printers; Advanced applications.

Summer 1989 ISBN: 1-85058-149-5 250 pages £12.95

Ventura Adventure - moving up to Version 2: Philip Crookes

This explains what the manual never told you - and it also shows the differences between version 1.1, 1.2 and the new, greatly enhanced version 2.0. See how to deal with the ordinary and extraordinary problems of desktop publishing, and how you can use Xerox's Ventura Publisher packages even on such a low-cost machine as the Amstrad PC1512. After an introduction to DTP and Ventura, you'll see how to: read in text from word processors, spreadsheets, and databases; how to edit and typeset on the screen; exploiting the full character set; creating graphics not just from Ventura, but also from GEM, from spreadsheets and from CAD programs; placing pictures in the text; letting the computer do the work of indexing, preparing contents pages, building tables

Winter 1988 1-85058-123-1 216 pages £12.95

Amiga in Depth - the complete owner's guide: Patrick Hall

Patrick Hall has the knack of explaining difficult concepts in an easy, relaxed manner. This is essential for Amiga owners struggling to do more than scrape the surface of this powerful machine's capabilities. Unlike other Amiga books, this is comprehensive and complete in one volume.

Spring 1990 ISBN: 1 85058 178 9 250 pages £12.95

Novell Networks Companion: Phil Croucher

Novell provide networking software for all industry standard hardware. Their "Netware" products are industry leaders and dominate the market from standalone PCs and Apple, Macintosh to UNIX workstations. The interface to Netware is such that the user is provided with the same facilities regardless of the hardware servers or workstations being used.

Phil Croucher, in his second book for Sigma, writes this companion that will be useful for first-time users of Novell "Netware", for those considering the purchase of Novell products, and for regular users who need reference information without ploughing through copious manuals.

Spring 1990 ISBN: 1 85058 168 1 250 pages £12.95

Programmer's Technical Reference: MS-DOS and the IBM PC (to version 4.01): DaveWilliams

This book is intended for advanced PC users, programmers, system builders and others wishing to exploit the full power of MS-DOS.

Packed with tables of reference data, the Technical Reference has been developed and tested over a period of many years prior to publication. The Technical Reference includes copious detail on every aspect of the PC and its operating systems. Writing in a friendly style appreciated by other programmers, Dave Williams examines all technical features in depth.

Numerous appendices are included for reference.

Spring 1990 ISBN: 1 85058 199 1 350 pages £14.95

The Comms Book - edited by Dennis Jarrett

Communications is now the most rapidly expanding area of computing but it is sometimes difficult for the newcomer to understand the terminology, or experienced users to keep up with the trends. The COMMS BOOK is a comprehensive and practical answer. Written by many of the well-known names in the computer industry, it offers a wide-ranging survey of the background and applications to computer communications.

Summer 1989 ISBN: 1 85058 179 7 300 pages £12.95

Managing the High-Tech Sales Force: John Lynch

The highest paid people in today's workforce are Sales Managers operating in the computer, telecommunications and other High Technology markets. This book is aimed at established managers who are aiming for excellence, and at the sales force wishing to enter management.

Winter 1989 ISBN: 1-85058 - 125 - 8 250 pages £12.95

Computers in General Practice:: R Peckitt, Practising GP

This aims to be the definitive book for GPs and all other medical workers intending to use computers. The coverage is comprehensive - including hardware and software selection, computing concepts, ethical aspects, training and much more. The book is illustrated with case histories of successful implementations in simple non-technical language.

Winter 1989 1-85058-144-4 250 pages £12.95

Communications and Networks - a handbook for the first time user: Phil Croucher

Many PC users want to transfer files from other computers, or to network their hardware so that expensive resources such as laser printers are shared between computers. Phil Croucher provides low cost solutions, in practical terms for the beginner, in an easy conversational style. The first part covers computer communications and includes: Principles; Protocols; Communication packages (including Kermit); Hardware (modems, fax cards, telex cards) ; Troubleshooting. The second part describes networking: Advantages; Networking versus multi-user; Hardware and software; Packet switched systems; Security.

Spring 1989 1-85058-136-3 180 pages £11.95

Inside LotusRelease 3 - developing applications: Howard James

This is a book for the spreadsheet 'Power User' and for all those who need to develop spreadsheets beyond the basics. It emphasises the use of Lotus 1-2-3 and includes features of the latest version - Release 3. Contents include: Effective memory usage; Data processing in a spreadsheet; Interactive spreadsheets - why macros are needed; Assembling macros; Macro examples; Deeper than macros - add-ins and add-ons; The Developer's Tool Kit; Linking into networks; Exporting and importing; 3D spreadsheets; Spreadsheets as data processors.

Spring 1990 1-85058-138-X 280 pages £12.95

Moving Up To WordStar 5.5: Tony Hollins

This book, written in a friendly practical style, covers the latest releases of WordStar - enabling users of version 4 and earlier to move up to the newest versions. It covers: installation; upgrading; file management; mailmerge; DTP applications; short cuts; communications

Spring 1990 ISBN: 1 85058 184 3 £12.95: 250 pages

Hypertext and HyperCard - Theory and Applications: Nigel Woodhead

This book presents an overview of the theory, core Hypertext features, available applications and specific case studies. It will be of interest to those who need an introduction to the area and to those needing to see Hypertext in the context of database models, object-oriented and frame-based programming. Contents include: History of Hypertext; early models; innovations and methodological issues; Potential of Hypertext: identifying application areas; Case studies: the Stackware culture; financial and library management; real-time databases; Available packages. Companion tables of relative costs and features; bibliography and source addresses.

Spring 1990 ISBN: 1 85058 183 5 £12.95 250 pages

The Shareware Handbook: Odd de Presno

Thousands of public domain and shareware programs are available for the cost of a telephone call from a bulletin board, or for a few pounds by mail. But how to select the best from the crowd? Published comparative evaluations of shareware is rare - and that's where this book comes in. It presents a selection of the best public domain and shareware products available. It guides the reader to choose the best and to judge whether it suits his or her needs. It highlights strengths, weaknesses and indicates applications.

Summer 1989 ISBN: 1 85058 157 6 220 pages £11.95

Small Real-Time System Design: Malcolm Adamson

This unusual book is aimed at professional software engineers with an interest in microcontroller applications, and at students of electronics or computer science. It concentrates on "very small" systems that do not normally support real-time operating systems or high level languages. Such systems are far from esoteric, and are to be found in most car dashboards, washing machines and printers. They use such single-chip controllers as the Intel 8031 to perform complex multi-tasking without the sophisticated executive programs.

Spring 1990 ISBN: 1-85058-176-2 250 pages £18.95 (hardback only)

Clipper dBase Programming: Michael Towle

Clipper is a widely-used dBase compiler from Nantucket, enabling programmers to generate dBase code easily and rapidly. This book covers all major releases of Clipper and presents it in a way that dBase users will understand. A further attraction is that the book is comprehensive, drawing together all relevant information on Clipper in one volume. It assumes some knowledge of dBase and some familiarity with BASIC or C. After a background to Clipper usage, the author shows how to design complete applications and - for more advanced users - how to add functions written in C or assembler, to include interrupts and how to generate graphs. Limitations and known bugs with advice on how to get round them.

Spring 1990 ISBN: 1 85058 173 8 300 pages £12.95

Applied Expert Systems: Sunil Vadera

This practical book is aimed at those people planning to develop an expert system, but are unsure of the techniques available. It is divided into three parts: Tools and techniques: knowledge representation schemes; expert system shells; specialised AI languages; Practical applications: finance; marketing; education; training; industrial; medical; ecology; User experiences: matching tools to the application; user guide-lines; future developments.

This book is edited by Sunil Vadera, from Salford University, and includes contributions from many leading academics and industrial workers in the expert system field.

Winter 1989 ISBN: 1-85058-127-4 250 pages £18.95 (HB)

Mastering Protext: Jeremy Williams

The book specifically covers versions 4.2 and 4.3, the most recent and enhanced versions of this popular and powerful word processing package. Protext is available for a wide range of computers, including the IBM PC, Atari ST, Amiga and Amstrad PCW. For PCW owners, who invariably start with LocoScript, there are great attractions in using the more powerful and standardised Protext which enables them to move easily to other machines.

Spring 1990 ISBN: 1 85058 182 7 250 pages £11.95

Foxbase and Clipper Tools of the Trade: David M Bell

Over several years, the author has developed software and databases using dBase III and similar languages. Great use has been made of Foxbase Plus and Clipper, and the wealth of tools associated with these products. Many of these powerful tools are little known in the UK, but they can help to make software development more productive and pleasurable.

The book is aimed at those who already know dBase and are considering Clipper or Foxbase. Also, regular users of these products will find the book to be an invaluable reference.

Spring 1990 ISBN: 1-85058-205-X 280 pages £12.95

Inside The Z88: Dave Oborne

The Z88 portable computer from Cambridge Computers retains a solid following despite the near-absence of in-depth books. This new book is not a re-write of the manual, but instead an exploration of how to get the best from the machine. For example, the word processor contains many functions and facilities to ease the programs use. Numerous examples and actual screen dumps illustrate the techniques used.

Spring 1990 ISBN: 1-85058-204-1 250 pages £12.95

A complete catalogue of all of our books is available. Order our books from your usual bookseller or, in case of difficulty, contact us direct:

Sigma Press, 1 South Oak Lane, Wilmslow, Cheshire, SK9 6AR. Phone 0625-531035; 24 hour tele-ordering and message service. Fax 0625-536800. Access and Visa orders are welcome.